LATE BABYLONIAN LETTERS.

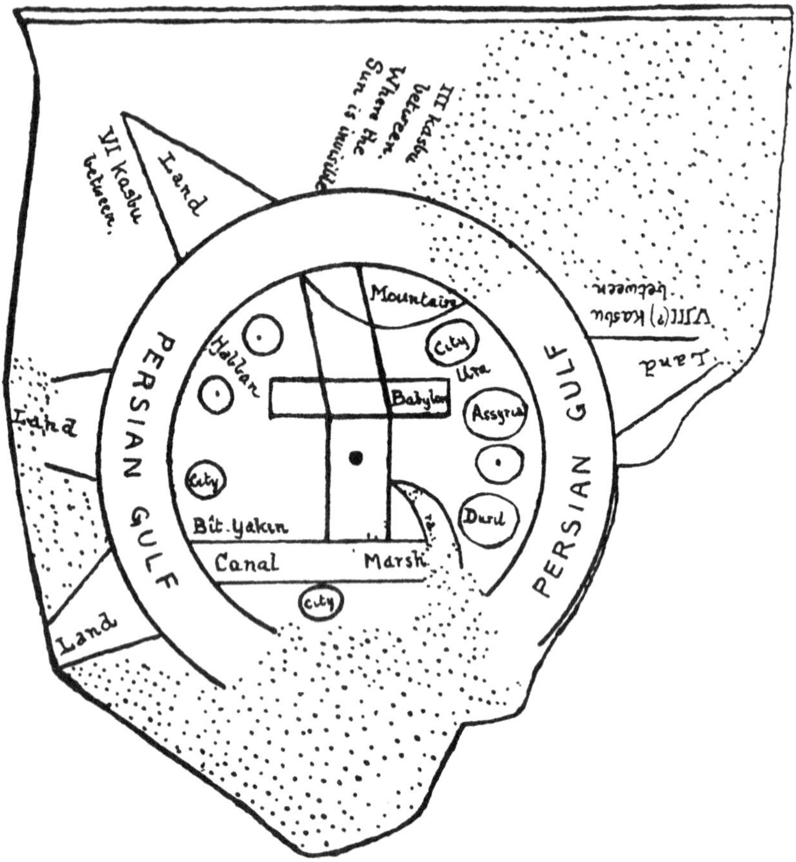

Part of Clay Tablet (B.M. No. 92,687) inscribed with a Babylonian map of the world, *circâ* B.C. 500 (?).

LATE BABYLONIAN LETTERS,

TRANSLITERATIONS AND TRANSLATIONS OF A SERIES OF LETTERS WRITTEN IN BABYLONIAN CUNEIFORM, CHIEFLY DURING THE REIGNS OF NABONIDUS, CYRUS, CAMBYSES, AND DARIUS

BY

R CAMPBELL THOMPSON, M A.

WIPF & STOCK • Eugene, Oregon

Wipf and Stock Publishers
199 W 8th Ave, Suite 3
Eugene, OR 97401

The Tyranny of Time
When 24 Hours Is Not Enough
By Banks, Robert
Copyright © by Banks, Robert All rights reserved.
Softcover ISBN-13: 978-1-57910-029-2
Hardcover ISBN-13: 978-1-6667-4960-1
eBook ISBN-13: 978-1-7252-0783-7
Publication date 3/4/1997

This edition is a scanned facsimile of the original edition published in 1985.

Preface.

It is hoped that the present volume will provide Assyriologists with additional material to study the large selection of late Babylonian cuneiform letters published in Part XXII of *Cuneiform Texts from Babylonian Tablets, etc.* These letters form a class that has been almost entirely unstudied, and, in consequence, many of the renderings of words and phrases herein now given are put forward with considerable hesitation. It is fortunate that we possess so many tablets of this type, for it is from these that we can draw such evidence as is possible for the peculiar forms of the colloquial language spoken by the Babylonian people during the later Empire.

The main collections of cuneiform letters, which are now extant, fall naturally into four classes or periods:—

(1) The letters of Ḫammurabi and his period, which give the details of Babylonian government and social conditions about 2000 B.C.

(2) The Tel-el-Amarna letters, which give the relations between Mesopotamia, Egypt, and the Syrian Coast, about 1500 B.C.

(3) The letters from Aššurbanipal's Library, dealing with every kind of subject, which were written during the period of the Late Assyrian Empire.

(4) The late Babylonian letters, with which this volume is concerned, which cover the period from Nabonidus to Darius.

It is consequently possible to trace fairly completely the changes in the colloquial language, as far as it is used in the ancient correspondence, over a period of fifteen hundred years.

The whole trend of the material afforded by these letters goes to show that very little really has changed in Southern Mesopotamia during the last two or three thousand years, the products being materially the same, and the people closely allied by race and descent. The religion and language have changed, but the manners and customs of life are much the same as they have always been.

I am indebted to Mr. L. W. King, M.A., F.S.A., of the British Museum, for many kind suggestions made during the preparation of this volume.

R. CAMPBELL THOMPSON.

LONDON, October, 1906.

Introduction.

Introduction.

THE letters translated in this book are all written in the late Babylonian script, and practically all of them may be assigned to the period which followed after the fall of the Assyrian Empire, when the Northern Kingdom ceased to exist, and the seat of government shifted southwards to Babylon. More definitely, the few letters which are dated refer us to the years 555-485 B C., for we find Nabonidus, Cyrus, Cambyses, and Darius all mentioned therein. But, even if we had not these names by which they might be dated, the general appearance, style, and language are amply sufficient to assign them to that period known as the Late Babylonian.

The conditions of life in Babylonia at this time may be briefly summed up as follows Assyria, the great power to the north, was finally overthrown about 609 B.C., and for sixty or seventy years, until the Persian Conquest, the southern land had rest. But even the capture of Babylon by Cyrus, about 538 B.C, with its subsequent domination by the Persians, seems to have made very little difference in the character or habits of the Babylonian people at this epoch. They have always been considered an unwarlike but commercial people, and such evidence as these letters show goes to confirm this, for the greater part consists of mercantile and business correspondence. Under these circumstances, it is hardly to be wondered at that the ordinary word for "army" or "troops" among the Assyrians degenerates into merely "workmen," in many cases of a low class, in these texts, and it is not improbable that we may see in this condition of society a potent factor in the defeat and subjugation of the Babylonians at the hands of the more virile Persians.

The land of Babylonia is fertile and well watered by the two large rivers, the Tigris and the Euphrates, and the ground in the vicinity of these streams was irrigated by canals, a system which was in use as far back as the period of Ḫammurabi. The greater part of the produce consists of cattle, sheep, and goats, dates, cereals, vegetables, and fruits. It is a curious thing that the camel is not mentioned in these letters, nor in any of the enormous collection of contract-tablets published by Strassmaier, and it is rarely spoken of in the Assyrian texts proper save in lists of captured booty or tribute. Its name, ^{imeru} A-AB-BA, "Beast of the Sea," would imply that it first came into Mesopotamia by way of the Persian Gulf. At any rate, we must consider that this silence about such a valuable animal is remarkable.

The animals actually mentioned in the letters are

the horse,[1] ass,[2] the ox,[3] the sheep,[4] and the goat[5]; birds[6] and fish,[7] without their species being described.

Of other produce, we find vegetables such as corn[8] (flour[9] and straw[10]), sesame,[11] dates,[12] grapes[13] (and wine),[14] garlic,[15] cucumbers,[16] cassia,[17] and possibly pepper;[18] of other eatables, salt,[19] *šamnu*[20] (some kind of fat or oil, the equivalent of the modern *semne*), and perhaps spiced bread.[21] Of other materials, gold,[22] silver,[23] iron,[24] wool[25] (blue cloth[26] and coloured stuffs[27]), burnt brick,[28] fleeces,[29] bitumen,[30] pitch,[31] and *magan*-wood[32] are mentioned.

It is not easy to see, from any internal evidence that these letters may give, whether there was a regular system of post. Indeed, from the frequency with which we find the writer asking the recipient of the letter to set his messenger speedily on his return journey, it would appear that even if such a system existed, it was not too often made use of. At any rate, there is no evidence at present to show that there existed in Babylonia a regular post like the ἄγγαροι which the Persians instituted. If we may

[1] No. 60 [2] No 58, etc. [3] Nos 36, 46 [4] Nos. 24, 49, 131, etc. [5] No. 63 [6] Nos 7, 12, 14 [7] No. 92 [8] Nos. 7, 19, etc [9] Nos 11, 17, etc [10] No 5. [11] No 37 [12] Nos 11, 31, 40, etc [13] No. 37 [14] No 38. [15] Nos. 8, 80 [16] No 20. [17] Nos. 40, 123 [18] Nos. 2, 130, etc. [19] No. 2 [20] No 143 [21] No 14 [22] No. 52. [23] No 40, etc [24] Nos. 2, 3. [25] Nos. 16, 17, 49, etc. [26] No. 13. [27] No. 57. [28] Nos 18, 32, 118, 137. [29] No. 25 [30] No 84. [31] No. 84. [32] No. 158.

judge from the one envelope of this period that the British Museum possesses (No. 142A), all letters were encased in an outer covering of clay, similar to that of the contract-tablets, with the following inscription :—

> "Letter of So-and-so to
>
> SEAL
>
> So-and-so."

The ordinary way of beginning a letter at this period was as follows :—"Letter of So-and-so unto So-and-so, my brother; may Nabû and Marduk bless my brother," or "May Bêl and Nabû grant peace unto my brother." Sometimes the greeting took the form of "Letter of So-and-so unto So-and-so, my lord; daily I pray unto Bêl and Nabû for the life of my lord." In the one case extant of one lady writing to another the beginning runs, "Letter from the lady Kudnanu unto the lady Inṣabtum ('Ear-ring'), my sister, may Bêl and Nabû grant peace and life unto my sister" (No. 226). The terms "brother," "father," "sister," are, of course, merely spoken with friendly intent, just as they would be in the East at the present day, and have no reference to any family relationship.

The ordinary method of transport was either by rafts or boats down the river, just as it is now, or by caravans of donkeys, mules, or horses.

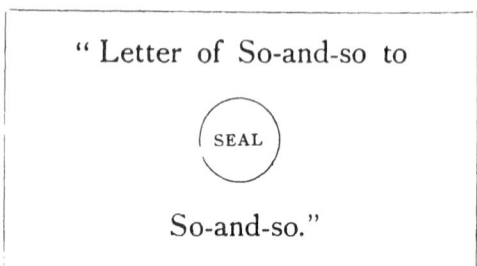

Water-transport is constantly mentioned in the letters; for instance, we find Uballiṭsu-Marduk (No. 5) writing to the Warden of the temple and two other officials, saying, " . . . So, if "it be according to your will (for ye be three "gentlefolk), go and send a ship. There is no straw; "if ye will pay the dues, send (some)." In No. 74 a certain Liblutu is described as being in charge of the "wine(?)-boats." Daîan-bêl-usur (No. 81) writes to Iddina-Marduk to say that fresh garlic has been gathered, but that Nabû-šuma-ukin is to deliver to Iddina-Marduk all the 'cut' garlic that he has; but if this garlic should not be enough, then Daîan-bêl-uṣur himself undertakes to make up the deficiency, if a boat is sent up to him. In No. 158 Nabû-ludda writes to a priest of the Temple at Sippar, to say that he is sending Dumuk into his presence that he may bring up in a boat all the *magan*-wood, which he had previously shown him, and he begs that his messenger may be set on his way speedily, for he has much work for him to do. In No. 174 five boats or rafts for transporting burnt brick are mentioned.

Several of the tablets relate to questions of transport by beasts. In No. 190 Suḳâ writes to Nabû-zira-ibni to say that he is setting out without an ass, but he asks that one may be given to Šamaš-eṭir, so that the loads in his charge may be brought. In another (No. 58) Bêl-iddin writes to the Priest of

Sippar, saying that an official has demanded an ass from him, assuring him that the money for it is already on the way, but the writer thought that it was inconvenient for him to send one then, and so he sends Sukâ to see if he can obtain one with its harness from the priest

The majority of these letters is connected with the business of the great temple of the Sun-god at Sippar. From the number which are extant, it is easy to see how much correspondence was carried on by the priests, who, besides their sacerdotal functions proper, had at least an indirect control over the landed property belonging to the temple, from which they drew their revenues, and also over the arrangements for the temple-dues, which were often paid in kind[1] We find, for instance, a mention made of the "Field of Šamaš" in No 19, in which the writer states that so many *gur* of corn have been delivered to the temple, and, further, as far as can be at present made out, goes on to upbraid the recipient of the letter for carelessness in looking after the field which has been entrusted to his charge, when the young corn is already sprouting In another letter (No 11), Aḫi-iddin-Marduk quotes a previous note which he is now answering. "Thou didst say to me, 'Let my "lord despatch two hundred measures of corn—let "'not my lord withhold the corn' How should

[1] In No 153, one ox and two sheep are mentioned as the tithe

"I withhold corn from Šamaš?" Another letter (No 121), again quoting a previous one, after saying, "Of that which ye did send, saying, 'Send the "'gardeners of Šamaš and the seed-corn for Šamaš,'" promises that the corn shall be sent. One of the officials of the temple of Nergal in No 8 complains of a deficiency in the garlic and vegetables belonging to that god. Another writer (No 42), as far as can be made out, sends a note that certain of the dues belonging to Ninib have been given to Šamaš instead, by the direction of two high officials.

In No 126 we have apparently a case of misappropriation. "Bunene-ibni, the son of Marduk-"na'id, the servant of the palace, who standeth at the "door, hath opened the tithe for Šamaš. Wherefore, "do thou speedily despatch (another?) tithe on its "way . . . Let not Bunene-ibni take holiday "with you; (it is) for this (forsooth) that a whole "year's wages in food have been paid him!"

The collection of the temple-tithe seems sometimes to have been a source of trouble, as is not unlikely. Etir-Marduk (No. 21) writes to certain people, saying, "I call Bêl and Nabû to witness that from to-day "(when I write this letter to you) until your . . . "shall arrive, ye shall not open a single cellar, or "change a single . . . , nor shall ye be given "a single order for the temple. Send me two-thirds "of a mana of silver, and the former tithe"

Of other business connected with the temple we

find considerable evidence, and among other things noticeable are the orders for robes to be worn in connection with the worship of the patron deities; for instance, Etir-Marduk, who is evidently an important personage in the Sippar temple, writes to three men (No. 13), saying that he has been informed that, although there is much work to be done on the stoles for Šamaš and Bunene, and their vestments for the months of Adar and Nisan, there is no blue cloth for the purpose; the cloth must therefore be sent speedily, that the work may not come to an end. Šamaš-eriba (No. 208) writes to the Priest of Sippar, invoking peace upon the temple, city, and house of his lord, and saying that he will send whatever his lord desires, but that he prays him not to be slack in arranging for the purple cloth for Anunitum. Bêl-ibni (No. 69) writes to hasten the addressee of the letter in the fulling of some woollen stuffs for Šamaš

Another of the duties of the priesthood appears, as was to be expected, to have been to settle whether the lunar month contained twenty-nine or thirty days. In No 167 Nabû-šuma-iškun writes to the Priest of Sippar, saying, "Speedily let me hear word from my lord as to whether the day is *kunnu* or *turru*," the ordinary expressions used in describing the length of the month.[1]

[1] On this, see my *Reports of the Magicians and Astrologers*, Introduction.

Several of the letters, especially those from the Judges, throw some light on the legal methods of the Babylonians. In No. 228 the Judges write to the Priest of Sippar about a case between Šamaš-šuma-ešir and Šamaš-uballiṭ, asking that the latter should be sent to them that they may deliver judgment. Similarly, in No. 229, about a case in which a lady, by name Kalatu (?), is concerned, the Judges ask the Priest of Sippar to send them the two men who are the opposing parties. In No. 210 Šamaš-šarri-uṣur, who expresses surprise at an accusation, demands that the matter shall be laid before the courts that it may be finally settled. No. 56 is a complaint against the fishermen of Mušezib-Marduk, who have broken into the house of Musezib-Bêl, the servant of Bêl-iddin (who is the writer of the letter), and have stolen certain articles of clothing. The writer threatens to bring the case into court, and demands that the stolen goods shall be found No. 87 is another letter threatening imprisonment. "Behold, "the first letters which I sent to Kasusu were "entrusted to Lugalmarada-ibni, an officer; read "this in his presence, if thou seest him. Prison is "ready for him for what he hath done; [if] thou "canst not [see] the reason why prison is ready (for "him), ask and send."

A long letter (No. 105), from Libluṭu to Rimut, demands the payment of eight shekels of silver to Aggiya, apparently a corn-dealer. The writer declares that he stands as guarantee to Aggiya for such a sum, and he fears that if it is not forthcoming Aggiya will withhold his corn, and he ends his demand by saying indignantly, "Am I here to buy corn for thee?" His next complaint is that he is being pestered by Nabû-zira-ešir for corn, and consequently he demands ten shekels more "By Bêl and Nabû, if thou dost "not send the money quickly according to our agree- "ment, I will summon thee at the tribunal of the King "of Babylon, and as for the corn for the journey for "Nabû-zira-ešir, I have already bought it for thee. "I call Bêl and Nabû to witness that I have not set "eyes on a single shekel of your money in Babylon"

The slaying of a man in a brawl is apparently the reason for Marduk-nasir writing to three officials in Babylon (No 114). "Ye stand as my protection "towards the gentlefolk of Babylon . . . I have "heard that in a riot So-and-so was wounded by "a noble, and his wound suppurated As he did not "understand how to treat it, it enlarged and spread, "and finally he died from it. Bêl-balatsu-iḳbi told "me(?). Be not neglectful, [act] quickly, for if "[something be not done] quickly, no one will restrain "their anger."

One tablet (No. 183) throws an interesting light on the condition of slaves in Babylonia. Nergal-Mušallim writes to Iddina-apli, saying, "After that female slave "of mine had run away over yonder to Banunu "and Khaddâ, they wrote to me and said, 'Send

" a messenger to fetch her.' Now, I myself have " business in the city ; am I to go or not? See, " I send Nabû-mulidi-imbi unto my lord, that my " lord may fetch her and deliver her by his hand. " Thou art as our father in this matter. Unto my " lord I write "

Another letter (No 155) is from Nabû-zira-ibni, who champions his friend Bêl-epuš. " Bêl-epuš, who " is over yonder with you, is my brother, (and) " someone hath maliciously slandered him. If my " brothers see fit, let that person hold his peace. " For he and I have been brothers from first to last. " If I be unduly importuning my brothers (the " recipients of the letter), then let my brothers do " this as an act of kindness towards me. Let me " see an answer from my brothers."

Of various forms of excuses or complaints there are several instances. Sukâ (in No. 191) writes to a customer, saying, " In the matter of the flour about " which thou didst instruct me ; when I obtained the " flour it was set aside stored up, as I fell sick. " I cannot find all that was sent. I have been sick " from the day of the Festival It is for this reason " that I have not sent the flour to my lord, and thou " hast not heard news of me. Now, by the favour of " the gods, the sickness hath left me, behold, daily " I pray to Bêl and Ninib on my lord's behalf." In another (No. 4) Ebabbara-šadunu protests against the unreasonable anger of his patron. " Concerning the "iron about which my lord hath sent, by Bêl and "Nabû, after my lord's messenger had brought me "instructions, I neither ate food nor drank water "until I had obtained . talents' weight of iron "for the money, and sent it to my lord. I have in no "wise cheated my lord, what is the reason that thou "art angry, and the face of my lord is unkindly turned "against me?" Iddina-Bêl, writing to Ubar (No. 7), complains that he has avoided payment for certain services. "Thou hast not given men, nor hast thou "paid their wages for the King's house. I call Bêl "and Nabû to witness whether, since I gave thee the "present of the food, I have ever received of thee "corn and wages for the men, (who number) twenty-"eight from thy house" Another complains to the Priest of the Sun-god in Sippar (No 12) "I have "also sent unto the scribes, saying · 'Touching the "'matter of the Šamaš-tithe, let no corn come near "'you. Let me see a letter from you, telling me how "'ye have arranged.' Although I have written two "or three letters to them, they will not obey, nor have "they arranged" In No 36 Eriba-Marduk answers what has evidently been a charge of mismanagement against him. "In the matter of the money for the "labourers on the harvest, about which my lord (the "Governor) hath sent, by Šamaš and Marduk, from "the time when the Priest of Sippar saw my lord "until now, they have not been in any way sick "or quarrelsome, and also in the matter of the

"Babylonian caravan, about which my lord hath sent, "there have been no quarrels with me."

No 54 is a more gently-worded petition from Bêl-uballiṭ to the Priest of the Temple of Sippar: "Is it "not true that up to this present time my lord hath "not given the slave the dates as he promised? Is "it not a year that thou hast delayed? Now let my "lord give the dates unto the slave—let him deliver "them in plenty." In No 150 the wording is more abrupt "Nergal-šuma-epuš, the scribe who is with "thee—why hast thou withheld his food? If he is to "do his work, (give him) his food; see that thou "omit it not . (For) why should he complain, "'I have my work here, yet he withholdeth my food.' "I will speak to the King's son on his behalf; the "King will arrange for his food" But in this case it is a royal chamberlain that thus addresses the Priest

In No. 215 Širki blames Nabû-šar-anni, a corn-merchant, for not attending to his order "Although "I have written to thee two or three times, thou wilt "not send the corn, yet the harvest is ready. Now "I am sending Daîan-iddin unto thee, deliver to "him all the corn that he desireth of thee" On the other hand, it is not infrequent to find dealers complaining that the price paid for their labour or goods is insufficient. Kalbâ, a brewer or cooper (No. 96), writes thus to Iddina-apli. "After I have "made forty-one casks of one-year-old beer, (and) "twelve casks of old beer in four months in the cellar "adjoining (that of) Rimut-Ba'u, one mana of silver is "too little" Or again, in No 182, Nergal-aḫi-iddina demands a further payment from Iddina-Marduk· "In the matter of the money which my father hath "sent, the money which hath been paid for the dates "is too little. Let my father speedily send two manas "of silver in addition, or I shall gain nothing on the "transaction" Or it may be that the materials sent for working up are too scanty, Bêl-uballiṭ, who is apparently a goldsmith or metal-worker, in No 52 writes to the Priest of the Sun-god, saying, "The "gold which thou didst send is too little. Lo, I am "doing the work on the chalice (?)[1] Lo, I am sending "Kalbâ unto thee to settle the matter of the gold in "this case, and do thou send a mana's weight of "'red' gold"

Another point which these letters indicate is that workmen are frequently paid in kind, generally in food. At any rate, this is the natural inference from the frequent "orders to pay" to merchants, who are directed to deliver over to the bearer of the note enough dates or corn to last him for a stated period The following examples show the forms used — (No. 31) "Letter from Ina-Esagila-lilbur to Bêl-iddin "and Nabû-aḫi-ukin, my brothers May Bêl and "Nabû grant peace and life to my brothers. Send

[1] The word used is mutilated, and only the character *nam-* remains. It should probably be restored *namzitu*.

"a hundred *gur* of dates to Sukâ, the PA-officer of the ". . . -men, and for each of those hundred *gur* of "dates thou shalt be paid at the (usual) monthly value. "Speedily set them on their way" Or even a shorter form is more common After the usual greeting, the writer briefly says, "Send twelve *gur* of corn to Ardia. "Speedily set it on its way" (No 33), or "Send three "*gur* of dates [as the food of] the *rikku*-officials for the "months of Tammuz and Ab, by the hand of Nadin" (No 50), or "Give ninety-one *gur*, twenty *ka* of dates "as payment for the . . -work for Mušallim-"Marduk to Šitkul, the son of Šamaš-aḫi-iddin; "twelve *gur* of dates as the food for Šitkul for the "fifteenth year, and six *gur* as the food for Bunene-"šarri-usur, the weaver" (No. 51) Another (No. 219) is an order for flour for the labourers engaged in digging out a canal No 57 is a request for pay for workmen. "I have no weaver of coloured stuffs or basket-weaver "here with me, nor for five days have I had a carpenter. "Eighteen days (only) they paid the workmen for the ". . (Now?) it is the eighteenth day, (someone) "must pay the workmen for twenty days' work, and "deliver to them their sustenance, (or) there will be "no workmen here and no one will engage with me. "Let me hear my lord's instructions, for if there be "none the work will cease."[1]

It was also customary to pay a lump sum of money

[1] This is probably a better rendering than that on p 55

down in lieu of actual food This is shown by No. 60 "Arad-Gula, whom I sent unto [thee?], I delivered "over to him ten shekels of silver for his sustenance. "I have made him eat (i.e. provide) his own "vegetables (?)" There are several other orders for the delivery of food to workmen, which need not be quoted here In one case the failure to comply with such an order caused a man named Labâši to write to Adad-riṣû (No 104), saying "I sent thee a letter "saying, 'Give forty *gur* of . . dates to So-and-so.' "Why hast thou omitted to do this?"

A rather pathetic note bearing on this subject (No. 115) relates that a workman has said that he has gone blind, and the writer of the letter notes that his pay shall therefore be stopped and the work done by another.

There are several interesting incidents related in many of these letters, which go far to show how closely akin the former inhabitants of Mesopotamia were to their descendants of the present day. In No. 160 the writer explains at length a case demanding judicial intervention from the *šatam*-officer, to whom he writes. "The King hath put Nabû-šarri-usur, the "son of Šuma-usur, in charge of his workmen, but "they are not pleased at it, and will not do the "King's work. So the King spake to me, saying, "'Send to the *šatam* that he may send them to thee.' "Wherefore do I write unto my lord, that he may "speedily send Ba'u-na'id, the son of Šamaš-iddin,

" . -etir, the son of Rimut, Rimut, the son of " Ŝa-pî-Bêl, Nabû-na'id, the son of Nabû-iddin, under " guard for thy judgment. When the King hath " confirmed this, he will give orders thereto. Mean- " while all the stonemasons have been uttering " discontent, saying, 'He oppresseth us; none giveth " us our pay for Siwan or Tammuz.' Let my lord " command that they pay them, for they are growing " very threatening."

A still more interesting one is that written by Rimut-Nabû to Bêl-ibni and Ŝuma-iddin (No 202) " Now for three or four years I have not seen your " sister; the day I saw her last, she sat down on my " stool.[1] These last two years, however, Nabû-kisir " hath said, 'She is my slave.' The woman Ḫiptâ " did not inform me of this, (and) ye are afraid of " the *ŝaku*-official—ye will not speak to the King, " nor take up my cause against[2] the man who hath " wronged me. (But) there is no doubt that ye " are not unconsenting to all this. It is not fitting " Nabû-kisir is (still) dwelling (here), but if he were " to leave, then would she kiss me and Pirku. How " would it be if ye yourselves gave her to me? Will " ye not fulfil (?) this—the ruin of my home? I would " send a female slave as a present to the lady Kabitti."

But the most interesting of all these letters are those written by husbands to their wives, or by

[1] Or, less probably, " was dwelling in my abode "

[2] Or "take out of my hands."

women to their husbands. Travellers on a journey writing home, sojourners in far cities asking for news of their families or giving domestic counsel, or women sending family greetings to distant kinsfolk, are all represented in this class of tablets. A man named Nabû-zira-ibašši writes to his wife, the lady Sikkû ("the Mouse"), saying that he has ordered supplies for his house (No 151) "By the grace of the gods "I am well, as also is Bêl-iddin See, I am sending "a letter to Iddina-Marduk, the son of Ikiša-apli, that "he may give thee ten *gur* of wheat. Be not remiss "in the housework, but be careful; pray the gods on "my behalf, and speedily let me have news of thee "by the hand of some traveller" Surely a model of a domestic letter without a superfluous word in it

Another comes from a traveller in a far country to the lady Kudašu, also presumably of his family (No. 6) "As for me, I am well, by the grace of the gods, as "also are those that are with me, but thou hast not "asked of the hardships (of my journey), nor hast "thou heard news of me I have been travelling to "the land of Paniragana (?) since the month of Siwan, "pray, therefore, to Bêl and Bêlit on my behalf. "Give greetings to Iddina-Marduk, my father, Ina-"Esagila-ramat, my mother, also to Šullumu, my "father, and Damka, my mother, also to Dumuk, my "brother

"Why hath news of thee to me been delayed, and "why have I not seen a single answer to all the "letters I wrote thee? For I wrote unto thee thus "'From the day that I start, send unto me whatever "(taketh place) in my (?) house.' Why, then, have "I heard no news of thee? . . ."

No. 40 comes from a man to his wife, the lady Epirtum, congratulating her on an expected increase in his family. "By the tribulations of the gods (?) "why have I heard no news of thee? My heart "rejoiceth that thou art about to become a mother.

"Now matters are going badly [with me], so send "me a mana of silver. It is the King's command "that stamped (?) silver shall not be sent (by "messenger), so get some tested (?) silver; arrange "this, I pray thee Send it by some traveller. Give "greeting to the ladies Bazitu, Ḫaninâ, Ana- . . . , "and Aa-enkit"

On the other hand, we find letters from women in very much the same strain. No. 221 comes from the lady Amtia ("my handmaiden") to Bêl-etir: "Now, "if thou art ready, put the meat which hath been "sent thee into salt, but if thou art not ready give the "meat to Nasir after the ninth day." No 224 is written by the lady Mušezibtum to Balaṭsu, her son "... The woman Nanâ- . . abideth yonder "with you, yet didst not thou thyself say to the "mistress of my slave-women, 'When I go, I will send "her to thee'? Now why hast thou not sent her "with some traveller? The lady Mušezibtum sendeth "greeting to the lady Sirâ, her daughter."

The lady Pukâ writes to Iddina-Nabû in the following words (No. 225): "When I heard that thou "hadst come in (to the city), I hastened, but now "I am greatly troubled, I am greatly distressed (?). "Let not a messenger from thee be wanting."

No. 222, from the lady Gagâ to Ša-pî-Bêl, relates a story of minor oppression. "Why, pray, am I and "my daughters to pass the time thirsting for a letter "from thee? Now, gather thy wits together, and "then, by Šamaš, observe! Why, pray, hath Bêl-"uballit taken away all my dates? When I spoke to "Bêl-upaḫḫir (about it), he answered, 'See, thy dates "belong to Bêl-uballiṭ,' but Bêl-uballiṭ hath not given "me back a single one. When I told them that the "dates were our own produce, they said to me, 'Get "thee gone, and speak to the son of Dakuru about it' "When I spoke to them a second time (they said), "'Go away, and call on the gods.' Now do I put my "faith in my lord—let me have a letter with my lord's "directions, whatever they may be."

Of the remaining letters, one, in duplicate (No. 1), is from a king, and the two others (Nos 247 and 248), entirely different in size and shape from the remainder, are written by officers to the King. The first contains concise directions to the recipient, who lives in Borsippa, to take certain people mentioned by name, together with "such people of Borsippa as thou knowest," to seek out all possible tablets which may be of use to the Royal Library. "Seek out the rare

" tablets such as are to be found on your route, but do " not exist in Assyria, and send them to me. I am " sending the authority for the *šatam* and *šaku* " officials. Thou shalt put them in thy strong-box. " No one shall withhold tablets from thee; and if there " be any tablet or spell which I have not made " mention of to you (*sic*), and thou shalt learn of (it), " and it is good for my palace, search for it and get it " and send it to me."

Now from the contents of this letter, as well as from the fact that it exists in duplicate, it is not at all an improbable theory that this letter is a copy of one that was sent by Aššurbanipal, King of Assyria B.C. 668–626, to further the search for new books for his great library at Nineveh.

The remaining two letters are of probably later date. No. 247 describes a military expedition, and its contents are worth noting. After mentioning the land of Assyria and Karanduniaš, the writer goes on: " Without thee I had not taken the city of Urizu, by " thy seal and signet[1]! Without thee I had not " taken the city of Rimizḫû, by thy seal and signet! " Without thee I had not taken the city Šad . . " u . . mandaru, by thy seal and signet! The " son of Zikri, who dwelleth in Ur—a servant!— " hath insulted me! (Though I told the King, my

[1] The exact meaning of the phrase "thy seal and signet" is doubtful.

" lord, yet he did not do me justice.) I and Uzubšîḫu " are the officers of the King, my lord, yet me he put in " ward, and had my brothers beaten with rods. Though " I besought the King, yet he did not do me justice."

No. 248 is even more interesting, for it appears to contain a description of a successful campaign against Assyria by the Babylonians.

" . . . 'Set his cities on fire, set his cities on " fire; bring woe upon city and field.' According as " the King, my lord, commanded, so did I; I set his " cities on fire, I set his cities on fire, I brought woe " on city and field; I scattered the spoil of Assyria " over the land . . ."

Naturally, the defeated people clamoured against their commander, "Why hast thou not delivered thy land?" A reinforcement of spearmen is apparently demanded, but to no avail, for the successful general continues:—

" After I had captured the . . . , they were " defeated, their house [I destroyed (?), and] I cut " off the head of the prince, and send it to the King, " my lord. Then I turned my attention to the " fortresses; then the officers of the fortresses (said), " 'Tell us, where is the King! Tell us, where is the " King! Set us on our way (back)!' Now the King " had pitched his advance camp in Baghdad . . ."

Certain of the phrases found in these letters are peculiar to this period. Frequently a letter ends with "Let me hear the news and greeting of my lord," or simply "Let me hear news from my lord," that is to say, directions or further orders. Another ending often met with, which is discussed in a footnote on p. 20, occurring often when a messenger has been sent with the letter and the writer desires his early return, is "Speedily set him on his return journey" Asseverations are frequently used: "May Bêl and Nabû know" (i.e., I call them to witness), or simply "By Bêl and Nabû," followed by the conjunction *kî*, "whether," implying a negation in the dependent sentence which follows. Another writer uses "By Šamaš and Marduk" (No. 35, 31, and No. 36, 10). The phrase for asking after the welfare of a person is usually done in the third person—"Iddina-apli asks after the health of Dumuk, his brother" (No. 6, 16)—and is of frequent occurrence. In apologies for troubling the recipient, the phrase used is *kî naḳutti altappar*, "although I am sending (what is) an importunity," while in directions not to be slack or to omit anything, the phrases are *bêl la isilli*,[1] "let not my lord be neglectful," or *la tušetikšu*, "omit it not"

Another phrase with similar meaning is *nubatti la ibâta*, "he shall not hold holiday," *nubatti* being the word for "festival," and *bâtu*[2] probably meaning "to pass the time," the same as the Arabic بات, "to pass the night." It occurs, for instance, in No. 222, l. 6 ff., *ammeni ina panika anaku u mârâti-ia ina ṣummê ša*

[1] For *salû*, compare Late Heb. סְלָא, Syriac ܣܠܐ.

[2] It is quite possible that the word *nubattu* is to be referred to this root.

šipirtu abâta, "Why, an't please you, am I and my daughters to pass the time in thirst for a letter?"

Again, *alla* is a word on the meaning of which these texts throw considerable light, and a comparison of the phrases in which it occurs will show that it is the equivalent of the Syriac ܐܠܐ in its meanings of "but" and "except."

The remainder of Part XXII, Plates 48–50, is composed of a small series of maps and plans, all from tablets of about the same date The most interesting is the Map of the World, according to Babylonian ideas, with the divisions of land and sea marked. L. 10 of the obverse was misread in a previous publication of this text, and should show, as in the present copy, the well-known names of Šamaš-napištim, Sargon, and Nûr-Dagan. Plate 49 contains a map of the city Tuba, or less probably Tuma, with the river which flows along it, and the "Great Gate of the Sun" or "East"; a map of Sippar with the Euphrates and a canal marked; and a map, possibly of part of Babylon with a diagram of the Temple of Bêl and the main street. The last plate is an architect's plan of a building, with the dimensions of the chambers and courts marked in cubits.

This Introduction is but a brief sketch of the contents of this class of letter tablets, and it is hoped that students of history, archæology, and language will find points that are worthy of interest in an almost entirely new branch of Assyriological study.

Transliterations

and

Translations.

Transliterations.

No. 1.—Obv.: (1) *A-mat šarri a-na* ^{m}*Ša-du-nu* (2) *šul-mu ia-a-ši lib-ba-ka lu-u-ta-ab-ka* (3) *ûmi(mi) dup-pi ta-mu-ru* ^{m}*Šu-ma-a* (4) *mâri-šu ša* ^{m}*Šuma-ukina(na)* $^{m\ ilu}$*Bêl-eṭir(ir) aḫi-šu* (5) ^{m}*Apla-a mâri-šu ša* ^{m}*Ar-kat-ilâni*^{pl} (6) *u* ^{am}*um-ma-nu ša Bar-sib*^{ki} (7) *ša at-ta ti-du-u ina ḳatâ*^{II}*-ka ṣa-bat-ma* (8) *duppi*^{pl} *ma-la ina bîtâti*^{pl}*-šu-nu i-ba-aš-šu-u* (9) *u duppi*^{pl} *ma-la ina E-zi-da šak-nu* (10) *ḫi-pi-ir-ma duppi*^{pl} *ša* TIG^{pl} *ša šarri* (11) *ša na-ra-a-ti ša ûmi*^{pl} *ša* ^{arḫu}*Nisanni* (12) ^{abnu}TIG *ša nâri*^{pl} *ša* ^{arḫu}*Tašriti ša bît sa-la-'-a*^{pl} (13) ^{abnu}TIG *ša nâri*^{pl} *ša di-ni ûmu(mu)* (14) *IV* ^{abnu}TIG^{pl} *ša rîš maial šarri u . . . šarri* (15) *urkarinnu erinu ša rîš maial šarri* (16) *šiptu* ^{ilu}*E-a* ^{ilu}*Marduk ni-me-ḳa* (17) *li-gam-me-ru-ni pu-uḫ-ḫu-ru* (18) KU-KAR *taḫazi ma-la ba-šu-u* (19) *a-di giṭṭâti*^{pl}*-šu-nu at-ra-a-ti* (20) *ma-la i-ba-aš-šu-u* (21) *ina taḫazi kanû ana ameli la iteḫḫi(e).* Rev.: (22) EDIN-NA DIB-BI-DA E-GAL TUR-RA (23) *ni-pi-ša-a-nu*

---

[1] L. 12. The Incantation *Bît-sala'* is known from K 2,832, a list of incantations published in King's *Babylonian Magic and Sorcery*, p xcx.

3

Translations.

No. **1.**—The word of the King unto Šadunu: I am well, mayst thou be happy. The day that thou seest this letter of mine, take with thee Šumâ, the son of Šuma-ukina, Bêl-eṭir, his brother, Aplâ, the son of Arkat-ilâni, and such people of Borsippa as thou knowest, and seek out all the tablets which are in their houses, and all the tablets laid up in the Temple of Ezida, and collect the tablets of the . . . of the King, of the tablets for the days of the month Nisan, the stone . . . of the month Tisri, of the series *Bit Sala'*,[1] the stone . . . for "reckoning the day,"[2] the four stone . . . for the head of the royal bed and the royal . . . the woods *urkarinnu* and cedar for the head of the royal bed, the series "Incantation:—May Ea and Marduk complete wisdom," all the series that there are relating to war, besides all their copious documents that there are, the series "In battle a staff (?) shall not come near the man," the series EDIN-NA DIB-BI-DA E-GAL TUR-RA,

[2] L. 13. On the phrase "reckoning the day," see my *Reports of the Magicians and Astrologers*, p. XIX. It refers to the calculation of the duration of the month, as to whether it will consist of twenty-nine or thirty days.

ŠU-IL-LA-KAN-*a-nu* (24) *mal-ta-ru ša abni*[pl] *u* (25) *ša a-na šarru-u-ti ta-a-bi* (26) *tak-pir-ti ali* IGI-NIGIN-NA (27) *ki-i na-kut-ti u mimma(ma) ḫi-šiḫ-ti* (28) *ina ekalli ma-la ba-šu-u u duppi*[pl] (29) *aḳ-ru-tu ša mi-tak-ku-nu-šim-ma* (30) *ina* [mâtu]*Aššuri*[ki] *ia-'-nu bu-'-a-nim-ma* (31) *šu-bi-la-a-ni a-du-u a-na* (32) [am]ŠA-TAM *u* [am]ŠA-KU *al-tap-ra* (33) *ina bît ḳatâ*[II]*-ka tal-tak-nu man-ma* (34) *dup-pi ul i-kil-la-ka u ki-i* (35) *mimma(ma) dup-pi u ni-pi-šu ša a-na-ku* (36) *la aš-pu-rak-ku-nu-šu u ta-bar-ra-ma* (37) *a-na ekalli-ia ṭa-a-bu* (38) *it-ti-'-im-ma i-ša-nim-ma* (39) *šu-bi-la-a-ni.*

[Nos. 25,676 and 25,678.]

NO **2**.—OBV.: (1) *Duppi* [m]*E-babbara(ra)-ša-du-nu* (2) *a na* [am]*ki-i-pi* (3) *abi-ia* [ilu]*Bêl u* [ilu]*Nabû šu-lum* (4) *ṭu-ub lib-bi tu-ub šeri* (5) *arak ûmu(mu) ša abi-ia* (6) *lik-bu-u a-na ḳime ša* (7) *bêl iš-pu-ra XL gur kime* (8) *ina XLII šaḳ-ḳa-a-ta* (9) *at-ta-da-aš-ša-ka* (10) *u ak-ta-na-ku . . .* (11) *. . . ul-te-li . .* (12) *. . al-tap-tar-ra* (13) *šaḳ-ḳa-a-ta bêl li-mur* (14) *man-ma ša-la beli-ia* (15) *la i-bat-ti* (16) *ḳime ṭabti* (17) *bit-li-e.* REV.: (18) *ina katâ*[II] [m ilu]*Bêl-iddin u*

[1] L. 17. *Bitlî* occurs in the following passages in contract tablets:—

(1) In a list of house furniture, in *eštên bît tâbti u bitlî*, "a box for salt and *bitlî*" (Strassmaier, *Nebukadnezar*, No. 441).

(2) A contract mentioning six and ten *gur* of *bitlî* (ibid., *Cyrus*, No. 54)

(3) A contract mentioning the large quantity of six hundred and twenty-five *gur*, four *pi* of ŠE-BAR *ša bitlî* ("corn of *bitlî*"), (ibid., No. 34, l. 20).

Peiser, in his *Babyl. Vertr.*, p. 287, translated it in the first passage

spells, prayers, stone inscriptions and those that are excellent for (my) royalty, the series (?) *Takpirti ali* IGI-NIGIN-NA (although this is a trouble) and whatever may be necessary in the palace, and seek out the rare tablets such as are to be found on your route, but do not exist in Assyria, and send them to me. I am sending the authority for the *šatam* and *šaku* officials. Thou shalt put them in thy strong-box. No one shall withhold tablets from thee; and if there be any tablet or spell which I have not made mention of to you, and thou shalt learn of (it), and it is good for my palace, search for it and get it and send it to me.

No. **2.** — Letter from Ebabbara - šadunu to the Governor, my father. May Bêl and Nabû grant peace, happiness, health, and long life unto my father.

With regard to the flour, concerning which my lord hath sent unto me, I am now forwarding unto thee forty *gur* of flour in forty-two sacks, having sealed them . . . I am sending up . . . and despatching . . . Let my lord see the sacks himself, that none open them without the authority of my lord. I am sending flour, salt, and *bitlî*[1] unto my lord by the

as "plates of ointment," but in the second passage he compared the Heb בדלח *bdellium* (*Zeits. fur Alttestamentliche Wissenschaft*, XVII, p. 346). But neither of these explanations is satisfactory, and if it were not for the enormous quantity mentioned in the third passage quoted above, the phrase "a box of salt and *bitlî*" would seem to point to some condiment. See also Demuth, *Beitrage zur Assyriologie*, III, p. 436.

(19) ^{m}*Ardi-ia V ma-na kaspi* (20) *ina ḳatâ*^{II} ^{m}*Bêl-ziri u* (21) $^{m\,ilu}$*Bu-ne-ne-ibni* (22) *a-na bêli-ia* (23) *ul-te-bi-li* (24) *mit-ḳa ša dul-li-ka ina lib-bi* (25) *bêl li-is-bat a-na eli* (26) *parzilli ša bel iš-pu-ra* (27) *parzilli ki-ru-bu-tu* (28) *ia-a-nu a-mur u-ba-'-ma* (29) *na-aš-am-ma a-na* (30) *bêli-ia u-še-bi-li* (31) *ṭe-im u šu-lum* (32) *ša bêli-ia* (33) *lu-uš-me.*

[No 79,327]

No **3**—Obv.: (1) [*Duppi* ^{m}*E-babbara*](*ra*)-*ša-du-nu* (2) [*a-na* ^{am}]*ki-i-pi abi-ia* (3) [^{ilu}*Bêl u*] ^{ilu}*Nabû šu-lum* (4) [*ša bêli*]-*ia lik-bu-u* (5) [^{am}]*ri'i*^{pl} *ša ṣi-e-ni* (6) [. . . *ma-na*] *kaspi id-di-nu* (7) *u* ^{am}*damkari*^{pl} (8) *ša ina ḳa-ti-šu-nu i-bu-ku* (9) *ina* ^{alu}*U-pi-ia maṣṣarti* (10) *ša bêli-ia i-na-aṣ-ṣa-ru* (11) *bêl la is-si-'-us* (?) . . . (Remainder of obv and top of rev. broken off.) Rev (13) *ṭa-a-bi* . . . (14) *nu-ḳar-ri-ib* . . . (15) *bêl i-di ša šarru a-na eli* (16) *iš-mu-*[*u* . . .]-*mu-ma* (17) *man-ma* [*ul iš*]-*pur-ru* (18) *ki-i na-ḳut-ti* (19) [*nu-še*]-*e-li-ka bêl ra-šu-u* (20) . . . *šarru te-e-mu* (21) [*a-na eli*] *bêli-ia il-ta-kan* (22) [*um-ma*] ^{am}*ri'i*^{pl} (23) [*a-na pani*]-*ia ab-ka* (24) [*a-mur*] *it-tal-ku* (25) . . . (26) [*lu-uš-me* ?] (27) *te-e-mu ša bêli-ia.*

[No. 50,204]

No. **4**—Obv.: (1) *Duppi* ^{m}*E-babbara*(*ra*)-*ša-du-nu* (2) *a-na* ^{am}*ki-i-pi* (3) *abi-ia* ^{ilu}*Bêl u* ^{ilu}*Nabû* (4) *šu-lum ṭu-ub lib-bi* (5) *ṭu-ub šeri*^{pl} *ša abi-ia* (6) *lik-bu-u a-na eli* (7) *parzilli ša bêli iš-pu-ra* (8) ^{ilu}*Bêl u* ^{ilu}*Nabû ki-i a-ki-i ša* (9) ^{am}*apil-šipri ša bêli-ia* (10) *ši-pir-ti iš-ša-am-ma* (11) *id-di-nu a-ka-lu*

hands of Bêl-iddin and Ardia, (and) five manas of silver by the hand of Bêl-ziri and Bunene-ibni, for the despatch of thy commission. May my lord receive (it) for this purpose.

With regard to the iron, concerning which my lord hath sent; there is no iron ore (?). Lo, I have sought to get it and send it to my lord. Let me hear the news and welfare of my lord.

No. **3.**—[Letter from Ebabba]ra-šadunu [to] the Governor, my father. May [Bêl and] Nabû grant health unto my [father].

The shepherds of the flocks have paid [. . mana] of silver, and the husbandmen by whom they sent them are now watching on behalf of my lord in the city of Opis . . . (*Remainder of obv. and top of rev. broken off.*) . . . My lord knoweth that the King hath heard thereto . . . and no one hath sent . . . Though it be a care to thee, (nevertheless) we have sent up to thee, my lord, [for thou art?] a creditor. The King hath commanded thus, "Send the shepherds [to] my [presence]." [Behold,] they have gone. [Let me hear] news of my lord.

No. **4.**—Letter from Ebabbara-šadunu to the Governor, my father. May Bêl and Nabû grant peace, happiness, and health unto my father.

Concerning the iron about which my lord hath sent, by Bêl and Nabû, after the messenger of my lord had brought (his) letter and given it (to me),

(12) [*ak*]-*lu me-e al-ṭi-me* (13) . . . *bilti parzilli a-na kaspi* (14) [*la*] *aš-ša-am-ma* (15) [*ana pani*] *bêli-ia* (16) *la u-še-bi-la.* REV.: (17) *ḫi-tu a-na bêli-ia* (18) *ul aḫ-ṭu a-na* (19) *eli mi-nu-u* (20) *ki-i ḫa-an-na-ḳa-ta* (21) *u pa-ni ša bêli-ia* (22) *a-na lib-bi-ia* (23) *bi-i-šu-'* (24) *ḫi-šiḫ-ti ša bêli-ia* (25) *ša i-na-šu-u* (26) *bêl liš-pu-ra* (27) *ṭe-im u šu-lum* (28) *ša bêli-ia lu-uš-me*

[No. 49,181]

NO. **5**. — OBV.: (1) *Duppi* ᵐ *U-bal-liṭ-su-* ⁱˡᵘ *Marduk* (2) *u* ᵐ *Ši-riḳ-tum* (3) *a-na* ᵐ *Šarru-lu-da-ri* (4) ᵃᵐ TIL-LA-GID-DA *E-babbara*(*ra*) (5) ᵐ ⁱˡᵘ *Bêl-iddin u* ᵐ ⁱˡᵘ *Nabû-aḫi* ᵖˡ*-ukin* (6) ᵃᵐ *dup-šar E-babbara*(*ra*) (7) *abi* ᵖˡ *-nu* ⁱˡᵘ *Bêl u* ⁱˡᵘ *Nabû* (8) *šu-lum u balaṭi ša abi* ᵖˡ *-nu* (9) . . . REV.: (10) . . . (11) *a-na-aš-ši ki-i ṣi-ba-tu-nu* (12) *III at-tu-nu* ᵃᵐ *mâr-banûti* ᵖˡ (13) *al-ka-nim-ma* ⁱˢᵘ *elippi-a-an* (14) *šu-ti-iḳ ḳa-aš ia-a-nu* (15) *ki-i mi-ik-su ta-nam-din* (16) *in-na-' a-mur V VI ûmi* ᵖˡ (17) *a-gan-na dul-la-an-na* (18) *ûmu*(*mu*)*-us-su te-lit-tum* (19) *nu-še-e-li.* (Left-hand edge) (20) . . . *-us ina muḫ-ḫi-ku-nu* (21) . . . *-na-aṣ ša buši-'.*

[No. 84,940]

NO. **6**.—OBV.: (1) *Duppi* ᵐ *Iddina*(*na*)*-apli ana* ˢᵃˡ *Ku-da-šu* (2) *bêlti-ia ûmu*(*mu*)*-us-su* ⁱˡᵘ *Bêl u* ⁱˡᵘ *Nabû* (3) *a-na balat napšâti arak ûme*(*me*) (4) *tu-ub lib-bi ša bêlti-ia u-ṣal-la* (5) *ina ṣilli ša ilâni* ᵖˡ *šu-lum a-na-ku* (6) *u a-na man-ma*

I neither ate food nor drank water until I had obtained . . talents weight of iron for the money and sent it to my lord. I have in no wise cheated my lord ; what is the reason that thou art angry and the face of my lord is unkindly turned against me? Let my lord send whatever my lord may require Let me hear of the news and welfare of my lord.

No. **5.**—Letter from Uballiṭsu-Marduk and Širiḳtum to Šarru-ludari, the warden of Ebabbara, Bêl-iddin, and Nabû-aḫi-ukin, the scribe of Ebabbara, our fathers. May Bêl and Nabû [grant] peace and long life to our fathers . . .

. . . I will receive. So, if it be according to your will (for ye be three gentlefolk), go and send a ship. There is no straw; if ye will pay the dues, send (some).[1] Lo, our work here hath lasted for five or six days, as each day we have been sending up the produce (?) . . . to you . . .

No. **6.**—Letter from Iddina-apli to the lady Ḳudašu, my sister. Daily I pray Bêl and Nabû daily for the long life and length of days, and happiness for my sister.

---

[1] *Inna'*. From the passages in which this word occurs it must have the meaning of "to send." No. 31, 6: *IX gur saluppi ana* ^{m}*Suḳâ* ^{am}PA *ša* ^{am} . . . ^{pl}*inna'*. No. 33, 10: *XII gur* AŠ-A-AN *ana* ^{m}*Ardia inna'*. No. 14, 10: *ana* ^{m}*Dumuk inna'*. No. 20, 10: ŠE-KUL *u kiššat ana* $^{m\,ilu}$*Šamaš-upaḫḫir inna-ma.*

ma-la ıt-tı-ıa (7) *na-ḳut-ta-a la ta-rı-ša-'* (8) *ša ṭe-ma-a la ta-ša-ma-'* (9) *ul-tu* *arḫu* *Sımâni a-na* *mâtu* *Pa-ni-ra-ga-na* (10) *at-ta-la-ak* *ilu* *Bêl u* *ilu* *Bêlti-ıa* (11) *a-na muḫ-ḫı-ıa ṣu-ul-lı-ıa* (12) *m* *Iddına-aplı šu-lum ša* *m* *Iddına-* *ilu* *Marduk abı-šu* (13) *u* *sal* *Ina-E-Sagıla-ra-mat ummı-šu* (14) *ı-ša-a-lu* *m* *Iddına-aplı šu-lum ša* (15) *m* *Šul-lu-mu abı-šu* *sal* *Dam-ḳa-a* (16) *ummi-šu i-ša-a-lu* *m* *Iddına-aplı šu-lum* (17) *ša* *m* *Du-muḳ aḫı-šu ı-ša-a-lu* (18) *nıš* (?) *ša ilânı* *pl* *mi-na-a* (19) *te-en-ka la-pa-ni-ıa* REV: (20) *ı-ri-ıg-ga-am* (21) *m* *Šı-ir-ku la ta-sıl-lu* (22) *ul-tu* . . . *-ka-nu la i-* . . . *-da* (23) *m* *Iddına-aplı šu-lum ša* *m* *Ḫa-ba-ṣi-ru* (24) *m* *Šad-dın-nu u* *sal* *I-mat aḫı* *pl* *-šu ı-ša-a-lu* (25) *m* *Iddına-aplı šu-lum ša* *m* *Itti-* *ilu* *Nabû-balaṭu aḫı-šu* (26) *i-ša-a-lu mı-na-a te-en-ka* (27) *la-pa-nı ıa ı-rı-ık u ši-pır-tum* (28) *ma-la a-šap-pa-rak-ka gab-rı ši-pır-tum* (29) *ul am-mar al-ta-pa-rak-ka* (30) *um-ma ul-tu muḫ-ḫi ûmu(mu) ša al-lı-ku* (31) *mı-nu-u kı-ı ına bıt* (?)*-tum* (?)*-šu šu-bu-u* (32) *mı-na-a te-en-ka ul aš-me* (33) *m* *Pur-ku-u a-na pur-kı ša* *ilu* *Taš-me-tum* (34) [*ı*]*-tı-lı-' šu-pur* *m* *Iddına-aplı* (35) *šu-lum ša* *sal ilu* *Taš-me-tum-tab-nı* (36) *sal* *Ina-E-Sag-ıla-be-lıt* (37) *m* *Sı-ır-ku* *m* *Lıb-luṭ* *m* *Pur-ku-u* (38) [*m ilu*] *Na-na-a* . . . (39) . . . . . . (Left-hand edge) (40) *bît gab-bı ı-ša-a-lu a-na* *m ilu* *Bel-su-pı-e-mu-ḫu-ur* (41) *mı-na-a ına arḫı eštenıt(it) šı-pır-ta-ka ul am-mar.*

[No 31,121]

No. **7**.—OBV. (1) *Duppi* *m* *Iddına-* *ilu* *Bêl* (2) *a-na* *m* *U bar aḫı-ıa* (3) *ilu* *Bêl u* *ilu* *Nabû šu-lum u balaṭı* (4) *ša aḫı-ıa lıḳ-bu-u* (5) *a-na-ku me-e ša* (?) . . . *tam-tım* (6) ŠE-KUL *pl* *ša iṣ-ṣur me-e* (7) *bîtâtı* *pl* *gab-bı ša* *alu* *Za-mat u* ŠE-KUL *pı*

For my own part, I am well, by the grace of the gods, as also are all that are with me, but thou hast not asked of my troubles, nor hast thou heard news of me. I have been travelling to the land of Paniragana (?) since the month of Siwan; pray therefore to Bêl and Bêlit on my behalf. Iddina-apli asks after the health of Iddina-Marduk, his father, and Ina-Esagila-ramat, his mother; also of Šullumu, his father, and Damka, his mother; also of Dumuk, his brother. [In the name] of the gods, why has news of thee to me been delayed? Be not neglectful of Širku—from the . . . Iddina-apli asks after the health of Ḫabaṣiru, Šaddinnu, and the lady Imat, his brothers; also of Itti-Nabû-balaṭu, his brother. Why has news of thee to me been delayed, and why have I not seen a single answer to all the letters I wrote thee? For I wrote unto thee thus: "From the day that I start, send unto me whatever (takes place) in my (?) house." Why have I heard no news of thee? Send (if) Purkû has been promoted to the *purki* of Tašmetum. Iddina-apli asks after the health of the lady Tašmetum-tabni, the lady Ina-Esagila-belit, Širku, Libluṭ, Purkû, Nana . . . and all the household. Unto Bêl-supi-muḫur. Why have I nọt seen a single letter from thee for a whole month?

No. **7**.—Letter from Iddina-Bêl to Ubar, my brother. May Bêl and Nabû grant peace and life to my brother. I the water . . . the corn for the

i-šaḫ-i-pu gab-bi (8) *a-ka-* . . *-ni.* (Remainder of obv. and top of rev broken off) REV (9) *tu-še-ti-iḳ* . . . (10) *ᵃᵐ ṣabi*ᵖˡ *ul ta-ad-din-nu* (11) *u* GIŠ-BARᵖˡ*-šu nu a-na* (12) *bît šarri* (13) *ul ta-ad-din ⁱˡᵘ Bêl u ⁱˡᵘ Nabû* (14) *lu-u-i-du ki-i a-di* (15) *a-na muḫ-ḫi da-a-ta kurummati* (16) *u-ḳar-u-ba-ka* (17) ŠE-BAR GIŠ-BARᵖˡ *ša ᵃᵐ ṣabi*ᵖˡ*-a-an* (18) *XXVIII ul-tu bîti-ka* (19) *a-maḫ-ra-u-ka.*

[No. 36,525]

NO. **8**—OBV.. (1) *Duppi ᵐ Iddina - ⁱˡᵘ Marduk* (2) *a - na ᵐ ⁱˡᵘ Daîan-bêli-usur* (3) *aḫi-ia ⁱˡᵘ Bêl u ⁱˡᵘ Nabû* (4) *šu-lum u balaṭ ša aḫi-ia* (5) *liḳ-bu-u a-mur ba-ṭi-il* (6) *ina šûmi u šammi ša ⁱˡᵘ Nergal* (7) *at-tu-ka u* (8) *ᵃᵐ ikkari*ᵖˡ*-ka.* REV.: (9) *a-na arḫu* . . . (10) *pa-ni-ia* (11) *ta* (?)*-di-gi-il* (12) (at foot of rev., upside down) *ni-ḳu-du.*

[No. 31,417]

NO **9**—OBV.: (1) *Duppi ᵐ Iddina - ⁱˡᵘ Marduk* (2) *a - na ᵐ ⁱˡᵘ Marduk-ri-man-ni* (3) *ᵐ ⁱˡᵘ Nergal - ri - ṣu - u - a* (4) *u ᵐ Ina-silli - ⁱˡᵘ Bêl ilâni*ᵖˡ (5) *šu-lum-ku-nu lik-bu-u* (6) *tal-te-ma-' um-ma* (7) *ta-mir-tum ta-mir* (8) *mi-na-a ᵃᵐ apil-šipri-ku-nu* (9) *ul a-mur en-na al-[tap]-rak-ka-ki-nu-šu* (10) *ᵐ ⁱˡᵘ Bêl-šu-lim-an-ni* . . . (11) *u ᵐ ⁱˡᵘ Nergal-e*(?)*-du-uṣur* (12) *it-ti ᵐ Iddina*(*na*)*-apli* (13) *šup-ra-a-nu.* REV.: (14) *u mi-nu-u* (15) *ki-i ᵐ Lu-aḫu-u-a* (16) *i-ḳa-ba-ki-nu-šu* (17) *a-na muḫ-ḫi šu-gar-ru-u* (18) *ip-ša-'* (19) *ᵐ Iddina*(*na*)*-apli* (20) *ša aš-pur-ak-ki-nu-šu* (21) *šu-di-da-aš* (22) *u u-du-ra-aš.*

[No 34,557]

NO. **10**—OBV.: (1) *Duppi ᵐ Aḫu-u* . . . (2) *u ᵐ Na-din a-na ᵐ ⁱˡᵘ Marduk-šuma-iddin* (3) *ᵃᵐ šangi Sip-par*ᵏⁱ *bêl-ni-e*ᵖˡ

water birds, all the houses of the city Zamat, and the corn they have spoilt . . .

. . . Thou hast not given men nor hast thou paid their wages for the King's house. I call Bêl and Nabû to witness whether, since I gave thee the present of the food, I have ever received of thee corn and wages for the men, (who number) twenty-eight from thy house.

No. **8.**—Letter from Iddina-Marduk to Daîan-bêl-uṣur, my brother. May Bêl and Nabû grant peace and life unto my brother.

Lo, now, there is a deficiency in the garlic and vegetables for Nergal; wherefore do thou and thy gardeners until the month of . . . wait for me.

No. **9.**—Letter from Iddina-Marduk to Marduk-rimanni, Nergal-riṣua, and Ina-ṣilli-Bêl. May the gods grant peace unto you. Have ye heard thus: "Thou hast sent (?) a present"? Why have I not seen a messenger from you? Now I am sending unto you; send back to me Bêl-šuḷim-anni and Nergal-edu (?)-usur with Iddina-apli; do according as Lu-aḫûa shall direct you in the matter of the *šugarrû* (of dates). As for Iddina-apli, whom I send you, befriend and respect him.

No. **10.**—Letter from Aḫu . . and Nadin to Marduk-šuma-iddin, the priest of Sippar, our lord.

ᵢˡᵘBêl u ᵢˡᵘNabû (4) šu-lum u balaṭi ša bêl-ni-e-nu (5) lik-bu-u tu (SIC) lib-bi (6) u a-ra-ku ûmu(mu) a-na (7) bêl-ni-e-nu li-ki-šu-' (8) en-na ša bêl iš-par-na-a-šu (9) um-ma ᵐ(?)Ki-di-u (10) [ši-pir?]-ta-a-šu ina mât-su (11) . . . ki am-mu-u (12) . [ᵐ] Ka-ru-ḫi-ia (13) . . . [šup]-ra-' (14–15 broken). REV : (16) . (17) ru-u-du-' (18) ki-i gu-mu-ta-nu (19) ina katåᴵᴵ ᵐKa-ru-ḫi-ia (20) la nu-kul-li-li (21) u ᵐKa-ru-ḫi-ia (22) ina katåᴵᴵ-ni-i-ni (23) la i-ḫal-lik-an-ni-in-ni ᵖˡ (24) ša a-na pa-ni bêl-ni-eᵖˡ (25) la ni-iš-mu ki-[i] (26) ṣi-bu-tu an-ni-tu (27) ra bi-e-ti (28) a-gan-na i-ba-aš-[ši] (29) a-mur gab-ri (30) ši-pir-tum (31) a-na bêli-ia (32) . ni-il-par-ri.

[No. 64,899.]

NO 11 —OBV (1) Duppi ᵐAḫiᵖˡ-iddin-ᵢˡᵘMarduk a-na (2) ᵐAḫiᵖˡ-iddin-ᵢˡᵘMarduk (3) ᵐᵢˡᵘBêl-iddin u ᵐᵢˡᵘNabû-aḫiᵖˡ-ukin (4) aḫiᵖˡ-e-a ᵢˡᵘNabû u ᵢˡᵘMarduk (5) a-na aḫiᵖˡ-e-a lik-ru-bu (6) ša ta-aš-pu-ur-an-ni um-ma (7) II C ŠE-BAR bêli lu-še-bi-il-an-na šu (8) ŠE-BAR bêli la i-kal lu (9) ŠE-BAR-u ki-i a-na ᵢˡᵘŠamši (10) a-kal-lu-u mi-nam-ma (11) ni-ba-šu ša saluppi (12) ša ta-ad-di-na-' . . . (13) ta-aš-pu-ur-an-na-[šu] (14) u ni-ba . . (15) . . . (Remainder of obv. and top of rev broken off) REV : (16) ᵐ . . . (17) ša ᵐᵢˡᵘNabû-šuma(?)-ikiša(?) (18) nap-ḫariš V C LXXIX . . . (19) ul-te-bi-lak-ka . . . (20) ki-ma-' ki-i . . . (21) eli ta-na-aš-[šu-u] (22) u ak-ka-' . . . (23) ki-i ina eli GIŠ-DA (24) ša ᵢˡᵘŠamši tu-ša-az-zi-za-' (25) šu-up-ra an-ni (26) ia-a-nu-u al-la (27) a-ga-a a-na eli (28) ŠE-BAR (29) la ta-aš-par-ra-ni

[No 75,762.]

NO. 12 —OBV : (1) Duppi ᵐAḫiᵖˡ-iddin-[ᵢˡᵘMarduk] (2) a-na ᵃᵐšangi UD-KIB-NUN-[KI] (3) abi-ia ᵢˡᵘNabû u ᵢˡᵘMarduk (4) a-na abi-ia lik-ru-[bu] (5) a-mur XXV gur

May Bêl and Nabû grant peace and life to our lord, (and) may they bestow upon our lord happiness and length of days. Now, concerning what our lord sent unto us, saying: "Kidiu . . ." (*Hiatus of eight lines*) since we shall not complete the *gumutanu* in the hands of Karuḫiya, and Karuḫiya at our hands shall not escape us. Of that which concerneth our lord, we have not heard that this is the great wish here. Lo, we send answer to my lord.

No. **11**.—Letter from Aḫi-iddin-Marduk to Aḫi-iddin-Marduk, Bêl-iddin, and Nabû-aḫi-ukin, my brothers. May Nabû and Marduk bless my brothers.

Concerning that which thou didst send me, saying: "Let my lord despatch to us two hundred (measures) of corn—let not my lord withhold the corn." How should I withhold corn from Šamaš? What is the amount of dates which thou hast given? Thou hast sent to us, and the amount . . .

. . . a total of five hundred and seventy-nine . . . I have sent thee. When thou receivest the flour . . . when thou hast decided about the tithe of Šamaš, send me (if) there be none, but do not send to me this about the corn.

No. **12**.—Letter from Aḫi-iddin-[Marduk] to the Priest of Sippar, my father. May Nabû and Marduk bless my father.

Behold, I am delivering twenty-five gur of corn to Šamaš-aḫi-ukin, the keeper of the birds, according to

ŠE-BAR (6) *a-ki-i ši-pir-tum ša bêli-[ia]* (7) *a-na* [m ilu] *Šamšu-aḫi*[pl]*-ukin* (8) [am] *ri'i iṣṣuri*[pl] *ad-dan bêli* (9) *lu-uš-mu* . . . (10) *maḫ-ri-tum a-* . . . (11) *buši at-ta-din* . . . (12) *a-na* [am] *dupšarri*[pl] . . . (13) *a-šap-par-ma um-ma* (14) *ina eli li-'* (15) *ša* [ilu] *Šamši* ŠE-BAR. REV.: (16) *la li-ik-ru-bu* (17) *u ak-ka-[']* (18) *ki-i tu-ša-az-za-az* (19) *ši-pir-ta-ku-nu lu-mur* (20) *II-ta III-ta ši-pir-tum* (21) *ki-i aš-pur-ra-aš-šu-nu-tu* (22) *ul i-man-gur-ma* (23) *ul u-ša-az-za-az* . . . (24) ŠE-BAR *ma-la bêli* . . . (25) *bêli liš-pur-am-[ma]* (26) *lu-ud-din* . . . (27) *man-ma a-na* . . . (28) *ik-ku* (?) . . .

[No. 84,973 + 84,987.]

NO **13**. — OBV.: (1) *Duppi* [m] *Etir-*[ilu] *Marduk a-na* (2) [m ilu] *Nabû-šuma-ešir* (3) [m ilu] *Nabu-zira-ešir u* [m] *Ki-i-*[ilu] *Bêl* (4) *aḫi*[pl]*-e-a* [ilu] *Nabû u* [ilu] *Marduk* (5) *a-na aḫi*[pl]*-e-a lik-ru-bu* (6) [m] *Šit-kul apil-šu ša* [m ilu] *Šamšu-aḫi-iddin* (7) *il-tap-par um-ma dul-lu* (8) *ša ni-bi-ḫu ša* [ilu] *Samši* (9) [ilu] *Bu-ne-ne u* (10) *ša lu-bu-uš ša* [arḫu] *Addari* (11) *u* [arḫu] *Nisanni il-la-'* (12) *šipâtu ta-kil-tum ba-aṭ-il* (13) [*ta* ?]*-mur-ru-' mi-nu-u* (14) . . . *ša ni-bi-ḫu* (15) . . . (Perhaps two lines wanting) REV.: (18) . . . *iš-ši-'-ma* (19) . . . *ni-bi-ḫu* (20) *ša* [ilu] *Šamši u* [ilu] *Bunene u* (21) *lu-bu-uš ša* [arḫu] *Addari* (22) *u* [arḫu] *Nisanni li-pu-uš* (23) *dul-lu-šu la i-baṭ-il* (24) *kap-du šipâtu ta-kil-tum* (25) *in-na-ni-iš-ši.*

[No. 65,295.]

[1] *Kapdu* The reading *kapdu*, and not *kabdu*, is proved by the two passages. *kapâdi ḫarrana* [II] *ana šepâ* [II]*-šu šukun* (No. 52) and *ana kapadaia* (No. 129, 11). From the following passages in which it occurs, it appears to have some such meaning as "without fail," or "speedily":—

my lord's instructions. My lord, let me hear . . . The former . . . for the goods I will give. I have also sent unto the scribes, saying: "Touching the matter of the Šamaš-tithe, let no corn come near you. Let me see a letter from you saying how ye have arranged." Although I have written two or three letters to them, they will not obey nor have they arranged. All the corn which my lord [desireth] let my lord send word of, and I will deliver it . . .

No. **13.**—Letter from Etir-Marduk to Nabû-šuma-ešir, Nabû-zira-ešir, and Kî-Bêl, my brothers. May Nabû and Marduk bless my brothers.

Šitkul, the son of Šamaš-aḫi-iddin, has sent, saying: "There is work on the stoles of Šamaš and Bunene, and the robes for the months of Adar and Nisan, (but) blue cloth is wanting." Hast thou seen what [is necessary?] for the stoles? . . .

. . . Let him complete the stoles for Šamaš and Bunene, and the robes for the months of Adar and Nisan; his work shall not cease, and speedily[1] the blue cloth shall be sent.

No. 59, 26: *kapdu tême ša bêlia nišme.*
No. 62, 10: *kapdu ina izkata idišima.*
No. 105, 24: *kî kaspi kapdu ul tušebilu.*
No. 117, 8: *kapdu XX marri L ṣabbillum šubilanu.*
No. 148, 16: *kapda innašu'.*

Kapdu in classical Assyrian is an adjective meaning "planning," and doubtless assumes an adverbial form like *lu ma'adu*, "especially."

NO. **14**—OBV.: (1) *Duppi* ^{m}*Eṭir*-^{ilu}*Marduk a-na* $^{m\ ilu}$*Nabû-šuma-ešir* (2) $^{m\ ilu}$*Bêl-apli-iddin* $^{m\ ilu}$*Nabû-zira-ešir* (3) ^{m}*Ba-la-ṭu u* ^{m}*Ki-i-*^{ilu}*Bêl* (4) *aḫi* ^{pl}*-e-a* ^{ilu}*Nabû u* ^{ilu}*Marduk* (5) *a-na aḫi*^{pl}*-e-a lik-ru-bu* (6) *I ma-na kaspi ša a-na iṣ-ṣur-ru* (7) *šu-bu-lu-u-ma a-na ku-tal-la* (8) *i-ḫi* (?) . . . *u* $\frac{5}{6}$ *ma-na kaspi* (9) *ana* [*eli*]*-ia a-na saluppi* (10) *na-ša-' a-na* ^{m}[*Ta*]*-kiš* (11) *in-ha-'-ma* . . . *-šu* (12) *li-pu-uš dul-la-šu* (13) *la i-bat-il a-na* (?) . . . (14) . . . *-it u* ^{m}*Šu* (?)*-mu* (?) (15) . . . *-'-ma* (16) REV.: . . . *kaspi ša* (17) . . . ^{pl} *lu-u-ši-bu* . . . (18) . . *-mur bîtâti*^{pl} (19) . . . *šup-ru-u-ni* (20) *a-* . . . ^{arḫu}*Âbi* (21) *ḳa-ta ki-i a-na muḫ-ḫi* (22) GIŠ-DA *eš-šu ša ina* ^{arḫu}*Âbi* (23) *a-ga-a si-in-ḳa ša i-di* (24) *bîtâti*^{pl} *ša eli ka-a-ri* (25) *al-tap-par-rak-ka-šu-nu-tu* (26) ^{m}*Gu-za-nu ša bît ḳatâ*^{II} *it-ti* (27) ^{m}*Su-ḳa-a-a liš-ša-' u* (28) *lil-lik-ku* GAR-MEŠ *ri-iḳ-ḳu* (29) *la i-li-ḫi-im*

[No. 67,355]

NO **15**—OBV.: (1) [*Duppi* ^{m}] *Etir-*^{ilu}*Marduk* (2) [*a*]*-na* $^{m\ ilu}$*Nabû-šuma-ešir* (3) *u* $^{m\ ilu}$*Bêl-apli-iddin aḫi*^{pl}*-a* (4) ^{ilu}*Nabû u* ^{ilu}*Marduk a-na aḫi*^{pl}*-a* (5) *lik-ru-bu II-ta* (6) *u-il-tim*^{pl} *ša* ŠE-BAR (7) *eštenit*(*it*) *ša XXX* . . (Remainder of obv. and top of rev. broken off) REV.: (8) *lu-* . . . (9) *ina pani-ka bêl liš-kun* (10) *u gab-ra-ni-e* (11) *ku-nu-uk u šu-bi-la* (12) *ša-ta-ri ša par-ṣu* (13) *ša* ^{ilu}*A-nu-ni-tum* (14) *ša* ^{abnu}*kunukki*^{pl} *ša* ^{am}*ki-pa-ni* (15) *it-ti-i* (16) [*lu*]*-ṭu-ub-bu-'* (Left-hand edge) (17) [*te*]*-e-mu šu-kun u a-ša-* . . . (18) [*šu-bi*]*-la.*

[No. 93,089]

NO **16**—OBV.: (1) *Duppi* ^{m}*Etir-*^{ilu}*Marduk* (2) *a-na* $^{m\ ilu}$*Nabû-šuma-ešir* (3) $^{m\ ilu}$*Nabû-zira-ešir* ^{m}*Balati* (4) *u* ^{m}*Ki-i-*^{ilu}*Bêl aḫi*^{pl}*-e-a* (5) ^{ilu}*Nabû u* ^{ilu}*Marduk a-na* (6) *aḫi*^{pl}*-e-a lik-ru-bu* (7) *II bilat šipâti a-na* (8) *dul-lu ša* . . .

No. **14**.—Letter from Etir-Marduk to Nabû-šuma-ešir, Bêl-apli-iddin, Nabû-zira-ešir, Balaṭu, and Kî-Bêl, my brothers. May Nabû and Marduk bless my brothers.

Send one mana of silver for the birds, and in return . . . receive and five-sixths of a mana of silver on my account for dates. Send unto Takiš also that he may do his work and it may not come to an end . . . . . . if it be for a new tithe in this month of Ab. As for the clamps (?) of the wall of the houses along the rampart, I send thee them ; let Guzanu of the chest with Sukâ receive them and let them come ; they do not knead the spiced bread (here ?).[1]

No. **15**.—[Letter] from Eṭir-Marduk to Nabû-šuma-ešir and Bêl-apli-iddin, my brothers. May Nabû and Marduk be gracious unto my brothers.

Two promissory notes for corn, one for thirty . . . . . . unto thee, my lord, let him direct, and seal thou the answers, and send the decision of Anunit. Of the governors' seals, let the impressions be deeply made. Give orders and send . . .

No. **16**.—Letter from Etir-Marduk to Nabû-šuma-ešir, Nabû-zira-ešir, Balatu, and Kî-Bêl, my brothers. May Nabû and Marduk bless my brothers.

[1] The reverse of this text is very difficult, and the sense is doubtful. *Sinka* is probably to be connected with *sanâḳu*, "to press together, tie, shut up." In the last sentence *ilihim* may be connected with לחם "bread."

(9) *ša* (?) $^{m\ ilu}$*Bêl-* . . . (10) . . . [*la*]*-mu-ta-nu* (Remainder of obv. and top of rev broken off) REV.: (11) *ki-ra-* . . . (12) *in-na-' dul-la-šu* . . . (13) *la i-baṭ-il šu-u* . . . (14) *a-na muḫ-ḫi aḳ-tak-bi-šu-nu-ti.*

[No 65,294.]

NO. **17**.—OBV.: (1) [*Duppi* ^{m}]*Eṭir-*^{ilu}*Marduk* (2) [*a*]*-na* ^{am}*šangi*^{pl} (3) *aḫi*^{pl} ^{ilu}*Nabû u* ^{ilu}*Marduk* (4) *a-na aḫi*^{pl} *lik-ru-bu* (5) *ulṭu lib ša te-en bêli* (?) (6) ^{arḫu}*Kisilimi šatti XIV*^{kam} (7) *mi-nu-u* [*dul*]*-lu* (8) *a-na* ^{am}MU^{pl} (9) *ta-ad-din-nu-'* (10) *šu-tur-ra-'* (11) [*u ina*] *ḳatâ*^{II} $^{m\ ilu}$*Šamšu-ibni* (12) [*u* ^{m} *Tal*]*-la-â* REV: (One or two lines wanting) (13) [*en*]*-na a-na* $^{m\ ilu}$ *Šamšu-ibni* (14) *u* ^{m} *Tal-la-a* (15) *ta-ad-din-nu šup-ni* (16) *u ku-un-ta-'* (17) *u šu-bi-la-'* (18) *ḳi-ma-' kaspi ḫa-tu* (19) *u ḳi-ma-' kaspi* (20) *ša šipâti šup-ra-'* (21) [*kap*]*-du ḫarrana*^{II} (22) [*ana šepâ*]^{II}*-šu-nu* (23) [*šu-kun*]*-na-'.* (Left-hand edge) (24) . . . *i-bi-tu-'.*

[No 55,859.]

NO. **18**—OBV: (1) [*Duppi*] ^{m} *Eṭir-*^{ilu}[*Marduk*] (2) *a-na* $^{m\ ilu}$*Nabû-šuma-*[*ešir*] (3) $^{m\ ilu}$*Bêl-apli-iddin* ^{m} *Eṭir-*^{ilu} *Marduk* (4) *u* ^{m}*Ki-i-*^{ilu}*Nabû* (5) *aḫi*^{pl}*-e-a* ^{ilu}*Bêl u* ^{ilu}*Nabû* (6) [*šu*]*-lum ša aḫi*^{pl}*-e-a* (7) [*liḳ-bu*]*-u I ma-na kaspi* (8) [*šu*]*-bi-la-nu* (9) . . . *ia-a-*[*nu*]. (Remainder of obv and top of rev. broken off) REV.: (11) . . *dul-lu a-gan-*[*na*] (12) *ina*

[1] *Kapdu ḫarrana*^{II} *ana šepâ*^{II}*-šunu šukunna'*. This phrase is very common in this class of tablets. The more usual form is (*kapdu*) *ḫarrana*^{II} *ana šepâ*^{II}*-šu šukun*, but it is amplified here [*kap*]*du ḫarrana*^{II} [*ana*] *šepâ*^{II}*-šunu* [*šukun*]*na'*, and similarly *kapdu ḫarrana*^{II} *ana šepi-šunu šukun* in No 61, 15. Further instructive additions are to be found in No 19, 27, *ḫarrana*^{II} *ana šepâ*^{II} *ša* ^{m} *Mu*[*ra*]*nu šukun*; No. 87, 29, *kapdu ḫarrana*^{II} *ana šepâ*^{II}*-šu ša* ^{am}BUR-LA *bêl liškun*; No. 131, 21, *ḫarrana*^{II} *ana šepâ*^{II} *ša* ^{m}*Luddu-ana-sabi šukna'*; No. 214, 21, *kapdu ḫarrana*^{II} *ana šepi ša* ^{am} *lamutanu šukun*; No. 100, 13, *ḫarrana*^{II} *ana šepi-šu ina pani-*

Two talents weight of wool for the execution of the work on . . .

. . . his commission shall not lie idle, for I have spoken to them about the matter.

No. **17.**—[Letter] from Etir-Marduk to the Priests (of Šamaš), my brothers. May Nabû and Marduk bless my brothers.

Why have ye entrusted work to the . . . -men ever since my lord's (?) instructions of Kislew of the fourteenth year? Write, [and] by the hand of Šamaš-ibni [and Tal]lâ . . .

. . . Now ye shall give unto Šamaš-ibni and Tallâ . . . and send flour: the money is wrong, and (so) is the flour; send money for the wool. Speedily set them on their way.[1]

No. **18.**—[Letter] from Eṭir-[Marduk] to Nabû-šuma-[ešir], Bêl-apli-iddin, Eṭir-Marduk, and Kî-Nabû, my brothers. May Bêl and Nabû grant peace unto my brothers.

Send us a mana of silver, as there is no . . . The work here is being done before my eyes; (ye

kunu liškun. The word *kapdu* (which is not essentially a part of the phrase) appears to mean "speedily" or something similar (see footnote to No. 13); *ḫarranu* may have the special meanings of "expedition," or even, at this period, "business," but the most probable meaning here is the ordinary one of "road," the whole phrase being literally "determine the road for his feet," *i.e.* arrange his route for him, and set him on it

pani-ia ip-pu-uš (13) *iḫ-te-li-iḳ-'* (14) *mi-nam-ma a-na-ku* (15) [*a*]-*gan-na a-ba-a-ta* (16) *u at-tu-nu* (17) *a-gan-na-ka* . . . (18) *III IV al-lu-*[*ḫap pu* (?)] (19) *a-gur-ru* . . . (20) [*šu*]-*bi-il-nu.* (Left-hand edge) (21) . . . *ud* . . .

[No. 84,915]

No. **19.**—Obv.: (1) *Duppi* [*m Etir*]- *ilu Marduk a-na* (2) *m* . . . *-apli aḫi-ia* (3) *ilu Nabû u ilu Marduk a-na* (4) *aḫi-ia lik-ru-bu* (5) *a-mur m Mu-ra-nu u* (6) *am*[*sabi* ?]*pl a-na aḫi-ia* (7) . . . *u a-mir-tum ša* ŠE-BAR (8) . . . *ul-te-bi-lak-ka* (9) . . . ŠE-BAR *ina ḳatâ II* (10) . . . *a-na* (11) . . . *nadnat* (*na-at*) (12) . . . *a-na* (13) . . . (14) . . . *nadnat* (*na-at*) (15) . . . GUR ŠE-BAR (16) [*a-na*] *E-babbar*(*ra*). Rev.: (17) [*nadnat*] (*na-at*) *ri-ḫi-it* (18) *XV* GUR ŠE-BAR *e-lat* (19) *ḳi-ba-a-ta a-na* (20) *m Mu-ra-nu i-din* (21) *mi-nam-ma ḫa-di-ra-nu* (22) *ina eḳli ša ilu Šamši* . . . (23) *u at-ta ši-ti-iḳ-e-tu* (24) *a-ga-' ša a-na* -[*ku*] (25) *u m ilu Nabû-si-lim ni-*[*iḳ-bu-u*] (26) *um-ma ekli ša ilu*[*Šamši*] (27) *paḳ-dak-ka ḫarrana*[*II*] (28) *a-na šêpâ II ša m Mu-ra-nu* (29) *šu-kun.*

[No 84,936 + 84,960]

No **20**—Obv.: (*a*) [*Duppi m Etir-ilu Marduk a-na*] . . . (1) *m Ki-i-ilu Nabû* [*aḫi-e-a*] (2) *ilu Nabû u ilu Marduk a-na aḫi-e-a* (3) *lik-ru-bu* ŠE-KUL *bit-* . . . (4) *ša apli-šu m Li-šir* . . . (5) *muš-šir u kurummati* (6) *ul ir-riš al-ka-ma* (7) *i-na i-ni-ku-nu* (8) *a-mu-ra-' ki-ma-'* (9) *ki-i* ŠE-KUL *mu-šu-ru* (10) ŠE-KUL *u kiš-šat* (11) *a-na m ilu Šamšu-upaḫḫir*(*ir*) (12) *in-na-ma* ŠE-KUL (13) *la u-ta-ab-bal.* Rev.: (14) *II ma-na kaspi* (15) *a-na m ilu Bêl-apli-iddin* (16) *u m ilu Bêl-uballiṭ*(*it*) (17) *šu-bi-la-nu kaspi* (18) *ša ina pani-šu-nu* . . .[1]

[No. 56,029]

[1] There are properly traces of three characters here

ask) will it fail? Why am I spending time here, while ye are . . . over yonder? Send three or four loads (?) of burnt brick . . .

No. **19**.—Letter from [Eṭir]-Marduk to . . . -apli, my brother. May Nabû and Marduk bless my brother.

Behold, [I am sending?] Muranu and the [work]-men unto my brother, and I am despatching the full amount (?) of corn . . . of corn by the hand of . . . hath been given . . . *gur* of corn hath been given to the Temple of E-babbara. The rest of the fifteen *gur* of corn, besides (what) thou hast said, give to Muranu. Why are there green shoots (?) in the field of Šamaš and thou art careless (?). This is what I and Nabû-silim [spake unto thee]· "The field of [Šamaš] hath been entrusted to thy charge." Speedily set Muranu on his way.

No. **20**.—[Letter from Eṭir-Marduk to Nabû-šuma-ešir and?] Kî-Nabû [my brothers]. May Nabû and Marduk bless my brothers.

Leave the seed corn of the house of . . . of the son of Lišir . . . and I will not ask for maintenance. Come and see with your own eyes the flour, how much seed corn is left. I have sent corn and cucumbers to Šamaš-upaḫḫir, and I have not taken away corn. Send unto us two manas of silver for Bêl-aplı-iddin and Bêl-uballıt, the money which is due to them.

No. 21—Obv.: (Top broken) (1) . . . $^{m\,ilu}$Bêl-aplı-ıddın
(2) . . . [^{m}]^{ilu}Bêl-uballıt(ıṭ) (3) [$u\,^{m}Ki$]-i-^{ilu}Nabû aḫı^{pl}-e-a
(4) ^{ilu}Nabû u ^{ilu}Marduk a-na aḫi^{pl}-e-a (5) lik-ru-bu ^{ilu}Bêl
^{ilu}Nabû lu-u-i-du-u (6) kı-i ûmu(mu) a-ga-a ši-pır-tum (7) al-
tap-par-ak-šu-nu-tu a-di-ı (8) ša ir-ru-bu . . . -ku-nu uš-
mar-[ra] (9) ul ka-lak-ku ki-i ta-pat-ta-' (10) ul pı-i-su-u-tu ki-ı
(11) tu-uš-ša-an-na-' ul ıl-ḳı (12) kı-ı ına kı-sal-lu i-ba-aš-šu-u
(13) ⅔ ma-na kàspi u GIŠ-DA maḫ-ru-u (14) ıt-ti-ku-nu i-ša-
an-ni u (15) lıl-kan-nim-ma dul-lu a-na . . . (16) ıp-ša-'
u mi-nu-u ša ^{ilu} . . . (17) ki-i la u-ḳu (?)-ra (?) . . .
(A few lines wanting between obv. and rev.) Rev.: (18) . . .
mıt ki-ı taḳ-ḳa-ba-['] (19) [um]-ma (Erasure.) la . .
(20) ^{am}ŠA-KU ul nı-ıl-lak-ku (21) bu-ud ^{am}ŠA-KU na-ša- . . .
a-di elı (22) ša a-na ku-tal-la ta-at-ta· . . . (23) . . .
-šu ul im-mar-ka šu-nu . . . (24–26 oblıterated.) (27) u ina
muḫ-ḫi-ku-nu šup-[ra] . . . (28) e-lat ša ^{am}ŠA-KU ina muḫ-
ḫı-ku-nu (29) uš-mar-ra- . . . lu-u (30) . . . lu
rabu(u) (31) . . . (32) (Left-hand edge) (33) . . ıd-nı i
. . . muḫ-ḫı-ku-nu . . . [No 56,028.]

No. 22.—Obv.: (Top broken) (1) $^{m\,ilu}$Bêl-aplı-iddın . . .
(2) ^{m}Na-ṣır u ^{m}Eṭir-^{ilu}[Marduk] (3) aḫı^{pl}-e-a ^{ilu}Nabû u
^{ilu}Marduk (4) a-na aḫi^{pl}-e-a lık-ru-bu (5) [^{m}]^{ilu}Šamšu-ri'u-u-a
(6) [u ^{m}]Pu-ṣa-a-a i-ḳab-ba-' (7) [um]-ma šattu (8) . . . -u
gab-bi-e. (Remainder of obv. and top of rev broken off;
rev. too mutilated for insertion) [No. 59,092.]

No. 23—Obv.: (1) Duppı [^{m}] . . . (2) a-na $^{m\,ilu}$Nabû-
šuma-[ešır] (3) $^{m\,ilu}$Bêl-uballıṭ(ıṭ) ^{m}Na-sir (4) u ^{m}Ki-i-
^{ilu}Nabû aḫı^{pl}-e-a (5) ^{ilu}Nabû u ^{ilu}Marduk a-na (6) aḫı^{pl}-e-a
lik-ru-bu (7) mimma(ma) ma-la . . . (8) rı-iḫ-tum . . .
(9) mu-ḫur-šu ṣab-tu (10) ša ı-sab-ba-tu (11) la ta-paṭ-ṭar-'
(12) šu-ut-ṭir-a-ma (13) ına elı ^{isu}li-e (14) šu-uz-zı-za-'.
Rev: (15) ^{isu}li-e (16) su- . . . (Remainder too mutilated
for insertion.) [No. 56,036.]

No. **21.**—[Letter from Etir-Marduk to Nabû-šuma-ešir . . .], Bêl-apli-iddin, . . . Bêl-uballit, [and] Kî-Nabû, my brothers. May Nabû and Marduk bless my brothers.

I call Bêl and Nabû to witness that from to-day when I send you my letter until the time when your . . . shall arrive . . .[1] ye shall not open a single cellar, ye shall not change a single . . . nor shall a single order be given for the Temple. Send unto me from you two-thirds of a mana of silver and the former tithe, that it may reach me and do the work for . . . , and what is for [Šamaš] . . .

No **22.**—[Letter from Eṭir-Marduk (?) to . . .] Bêl-apli-iddin . . . Naṣir, and Eṭir-[Marduk], my brothers. May Nabû and Marduk bless my brothers.

Šamaš-ri'ua [and] Puṣâ have spoken thus: "For a year all . . ."

No. **23.**—Letter [from . . .] to Nabû-šuma-[ešir], Bêl-uballiṭ, Naṣir, and Kî-Nabû, my brothers. May Nabû and Marduk bless my brothers.

All that . . . the remainder . . . receive it. What hath been taken (which they have taken) do not ye let go. Write, and arrange about the tithe; the tithe . . .

[1] L. 8. The word *ušmarra* occurs also on rev. 29.

No. **24**—Obv.: (1) *Duppi* ^{m}*Mušallim*-^{ilu}*Marduk* (2) *a-na* ^{m}*Eṭir*-^{ilu}*Marduk* (3) *u* ^{m}*Na'id*-^{ilu}*Marduk* (4) *aḫi*^{pl}*-e* ^{ilu}*Bêl u* ^{ilu}*Nabû* (5) *šu-lum u balati ša aḫi*^{pl}*-e-a* (6) *lik-bu-u a-mur* (7) *V alpi šu-nu-'-i* (8) *I šu-lu-u* (9) *XX immeri ina lib-bi* (10) *X ka-lu-me-e* (11) [*ina*] *ḳatâ*^{II} $^{m\,ilu}$*Nabû-ba-a-di* . . . (12) *al-tap-rak-ku-nu-šu.* Rev.: (13) *alpi ša ûmi XX*^{kam} (14) *ša* ^{arḫu}*Simani* (15) *ḫi-iṭ* [*aḫ-ṭu*] (16) *a-na-ku* [*kap*]*-du* (17) *al-tap-*[*par*]*'a-na* (18) ^{m}*Ta-kiš* (19) *ki-ba-'-ma* (20) *ina muḫ-ḫi* (21) *dul-lu-šu* (22) *la i-sil-li.* [No. 64,901]

No **25**—Obv.: (1) *Duppi* ^{m}*Mušallim*-^{ilu}*Marduk* (2) *a-na* ^{m}*Eṭir*-^{ilu}*Marduk* (3) *u* ^{m}*Na'id*-^{ilu}*Marduk* (4) *aḫi*^{pl}*-e-a* ^{ilu}*Bêl u* (5) [^{ilu}*Nabû*] *šu-lum u balaṭi* (6) [*a-na aḫi*^{pl}]*-e-a* (7) [*lik-bu*]*-u* (8) . . . *gi-iz-zi* (9) . . . *-ku-'*. (Remainder of obv. lost; rev. blank.) [No. 64,901.]

No **26**—Obv.: (1) *Duppi* ^{m}*Mušallim*-^{ilu}*Marduk a-na* (2) ^{m}*Mu-še-zib*-^{ilu}*Marduk* (3) $^{m\,ilu}$*Nabû-bani-ip-ša-ri* (4) *u* ^{m}*Na'id*-^{ilu}*Marduk* (5) *aḫi*^{pl} *-ia* ^{ilu}*Nabû u* ^{ilu}*Marduk* (6) *a-na aḫi-ia lik-ru-*[*bu*] (7) ½ *III ḳa ša* ½ *III ḳa* . . . (8) . . . *lu-na* . . . (Remainder of obv. and top of rev. broken off.) Rev.: (9) *ki-i ku-na* . . . (10) *a-na kaspi mu-ki* . . . [No. 84,912]

No. **27**.—Obv.: (1) *Duppi* ^{m} . . . *-gi*-^{ilu} . . . (2) . . . *-uṣur a-na* (3) ^{m}*Ki-i*-^{ilu}*Bêl u* $^{m\,ilu}$*Bêl-šuma-ešir* (4) *u* ^{m}*Ḫa-ba-si-ru* (5) *abi*^{pl}*-e-a-a* ^{ilu}*Bêl u* ^{ilu}*Nabû* (6) [*šu*]*-lum u balati ša abi-e-a-a* (7) [*lik*]*-bu-u ûmu(mu)-us-su* (8) . . . ^{ilu}*A-nu-ni-tum* (9) [*a*]*-na balat napšâti*^{pl} *a-ra-ku ûmu(mu)* (10) *ṭu-ub lib-bi ṭu-ub širi* (11) *ša abi-e-a-a* (12) *nu-ṣal-la* (13) *II-e bil-la* . . . (14) *ina ḳatâ*^{II} ^{m} . . . Rev.: (15) *abi-e-a-a* (16) *lu-še-bu-ku-un-nu* (17) *kap-du te-e-mu* (18) *ša abi-e-a-a* (19) *ni-šim-mu.*

[No. 64,898.]

No. **24**.—Letter from Mušallim[1]-Marduk to Etir-Marduk and Na'id-Marduk, (my) brothers. May Bêl and Nabû grant peace and life unto my brothers.

Behold, I am sending you five humped bullocks, one *šulû*-bullock, twenty sheep and therewith ten lambs, by the hand of Nabû-bâdi . . . I omitted the bullock for the twentieth of Siwan, so speedily I will send it. Speak unto Takiš that he may not be slack over his work.

No. **25**.—Letter from Mušallim-Marduk to Eṭir-Marduk and Na'id-Marduk, my brothers. May Bêl and [Nabû] grant peace and life to my brothers.

Concerning the fleeces . . .

No. **26**.—Letter from Mušallim-Marduk to Mušezib-Marduk, Nabû-bani-ipšari, and Na'id-Marduk, my brothers. May Nabû and Marduk bless my brothers.

No. **27**.—Letter from . . . gi . . . [and] . . . -usur to . . . Kî-Bêl, Bêl-šuma-ešir, and Ḫabasiru, my fathers. May Bêl and Nabû grant peace and life unto my fathers. Daily unto . . . Anunitum, for the preservation of the life, for the lengthening of the days, for the happiness and health of my fathers, we pray.

Let our fathers send us two . . . by the hand of . . . Speedily let us hear news from our fathers.

[1] L 1. The reading GI = *Mušallim* is shown by Delitzsch, *Notizen zu den neubabylonischen Kontrakttafeln*, *Beitrage zur Assyriologie*, III, 388.

No. **28**—Obv.: (1) *Duppi* ^{m}*Mušallim-* ^{ilu}*Marduk* [*a-na*] (2) ^{m}*Mu-še-zib-* ^{ilu}[*Marduk*] (3) *aḫi-ia* ^{ilu}*Nabû u* ^{ilu}[*Marduk*] (4) *a-na aḫi-ia lik-ru-bu* (5) *IV ma-na kaspi šu-bi-*[*la*] . . . (6) *II* ^{am}*mâr-ba-ni-tu* (7) . . . *nu* . . . (Remainder of obv. and top of obv. broken off.) Rev.: (9) *li-lik-ki.*

[No 84,922]

No. **29**.—Obv.: (1) *Duppi* $^{m\,ilu}$ . . . *-šuma* . . . (2) *a-na* ^{m} . . . *-a* (3) *aḫi-ia* ^{ilu}*Marduk* (4) *u* ^{ilu}*Sar-pa-ni-tum* (5) *šu-lum u balati ša aḫi-ia* (6) *lik-bu-u mi-na-a* (7) *aš-me-e-ma pi-iš-ki* (8) *ina* . . . *eburi*^{pl} *ša* ^{ilu}*Bêl* (9) *ša* [*Bar*?]*-sip*^{ki} (10) . . . *ip-pu-uš* (11) . . . *lu* (12) . . . *ti.* (Remainder of obv. and top of rev. broken off.) Rev.: (13) *ki-i* . . . *ina* (?) *lib-bi* (14) *ta-ap-te-ki-id* (15) *a-na* ^{am}*piḫati* (16) *a-na muḫ-ḫi-ka* (17) *a-kab-bi* (18) *man-ma te-ik-ti* (19) [*ina lib*]*-bi-ka* (20) . . . *te-e-ka* (21) . . . *ka* (22) [*la i*]*-ba-aš-ši.*

[No. 46,729.]

No. **30**.—Obv.: (1) *Duppi* ^{m}*A-na-a-mat-* ^{ilu}*Bêl-ad-dan* (2) *a-na* ^{am}*šangi* UD-KIB-NUN-KI (3) *bêli-ia ûmu*(*mu*)*-us-su* ^{ilu} . . . (4) *a-na balaṭ napšâti*^{pl} *ša bêli-ia* (5) *u-ṣal-la ina* ^{arḫu}*Šabati* (6) *ul-tu a-na* TIN-TIR-KI (7) *it-ti bêli-ia al-li-ki* (8) *bêl bîti ina* TIN-TIR-KI (9) . . . *-ti il-la-ak* (?) . . . (10) . . . *gi* (?) . . . (Remainder of obv. and top of rev. broken off.) Rev.. (11) *a-na muḫ-ḫi* . . . (12) *ša* ^{m}*Bêl-šu-nu at-* . . .

[No. 63,028.]

No **31**—Obv.: (1) *Duppi* ^{m}*Ina-E-sag-ila-lil-bur* (2) *a-na* $^{m\,ilu}$*Bêl-iddin u* (3) $^{m\,ilu}$*Nabû-aḫi*^{pl}*-ukin* (4) *aḫi*^{pl}*-a* ^{ilu}*Bêl u* ^{ilu}*Nabû* (5) *šu-lum u balati ša aḫi*^{pl}*-a* (6) *lik-bu-u IC gur*

No. **28.**—Letter from Mušallim-Marduk to Mušezib-[Marduk], my brother. May Nabû and [Marduk] bless my brother.

Four manas of silver . . . two nobles . . . (*only one word visible on reverse*, "let him go").

No. **29.**—Letter from . . . -šuma . . . to . . . -a, my brother. May Marduk and Ṣarpanitum grant peace and life to my brother.

What is this I have heard, that there is blight on the crops of Bêl in Borsippa? Send (?) . . . . . . how thou hast arranged in this matter. I will speak about thee to the governor. No one shall [make] an ending[1] . . .

No. **30.**—Letter from Ana-amat-Bêl-addan to the Priest of Sippar, my lord. Daily for the life of my lord I pray unto . . .

In the month of Sebat (after I went to Babylon with my lord) a householder in Babylon came . . . . . . of Bêl-šunu I have given (?).

No. **31.**—Letter from Ina-Esagila-lilbur to Bêl-iddin and Nabû-aḫi-ukin, my brothers. May Bêl and Nabû grant peace and life to my brothers.

---

[1] L 18 · *tiktu.* This word occurs in the following passages —
No. 43, 20. *tektum ana bêlia la ippal.*
No. 60, 13: *tekti ina libbi bêlia la išakkan.*
No. 133, 21: *tektum* ^{m} *Bakû ina libbikunu la išakkan.*
B.M No. 84,962. *mimma tiktum la tašakkan.*
It is probable that it should be referred to the root *kîtu*, "to end"

saluppi (7) *a-na* ^{m}*Suḳa-a-a* ^{am} PA (8) *ša* ^{am} . . ^{pl} *in-na-'* (9) *u saluppi* $^{a\,an}$ (10) *IC ina ma-aš-ša-ra-a-ta-šu* (11) *ti-ni-it-ra-'* (12) *kap-du ḫarrana* ^{II} (13) *a-na šepâ* ^{II} *-šu* (14) [*šu*]-*kun-na*-['].

[No. 60,627]

No **32**—Obv.: (1) *Duppi* ^{m}*Ap-la-a* (2) *a-na* ^{m}*Ša-du-u-nu* (3) *abi-ia* ^{ilu}*Nabû u* ^{ilu}*Marduk* (4) *a-na abi-ia lik-ru-bu* (5) *am-me-ni ši-pir-tum* (6) *ma-la a-na bêli-ia* (7) *a-šap-par-ra gab-ri* (8) *ši-pir*-[*ta ul*] *a*-[*mur*?]. (Remainder of obv. and top of rev. broken off) Rev.: (9) $^{m\,ilu}$*Nabû-šuma-ešir* . . . (10) *bêl lu-še-sa-a* (11) *u a-gur-ru* (12) *ša* (?)[1] *muḫ-ḫi-ia* (13) *kal*(?) *ši-tu* (14) *ad-da-ni-ka* (15) *muḫ-ḫi bêl* (16) *la i-sil-li* (17) *ṭe-e-mu u šu-lum* (18) *ša bêli-ia lu-uš-mu*.

[No 46,924]

No. **33**—Obv.: (1) [*Duppi*] ^{m}*Iṣ-ṣur* (2) *a-na* ^{m} *Tâbti-*^{ilu}IB (3) ^{m}*Ka-ṣir* (4) *u* ^{m}*Itti-* ^{ilu}*Nabû-gu-zu* (?) (5) *aḫi* ^{pl} *e-a* (6) ^{ilu}*Bêl u* ^{ilu}*Nabû* (7) *šu-lum u balati ša* (8) *aḫi* ^{pl} *-e-a* (9) *lik-bu-u* (10) *XII gur* AŠ-A-AN (11) *a-na* ^{m} *Ardi-ia* (12) *in-na-'*. Rev.: (13) *kap-du ḫarrana* ^{II} (14) *a-na šêpâ* ^{II}*-šu* (15) *šu-kun-nu-'*.

[No 47,363]

No. **34**—Obv.: (1) *Duppi* ^{m}*Eri-ba-* . . (2) *a-na* ^{am} E-BAR UD-KIB-NUN-KI (3) *bêli-ia* ^{ilu}*Nabû u* ^{ilu}*Marduk* (4) *a-na bêli-ia lik-ru-bu* (5) *u mimma*(*ma*) *ma-la bêl* (6) *ip-pu-šu ina muḫ*-[*ḫi ša*] *šarri* (7) *ur* (?)-*di* (?) *u* (?) ^{am} *ṣabi* ^{pl} (8) *al-tap-par-ki* . . . (One or two lines wanting) Rev.: (12) *a-mur* . . (13) *a-na na-da-nu* (14) *ša bêli-ia u-ḫi* (?)-*it* (15) ^{ilu} *Šamšu ina lib-bi* (16) *a-na bêli-ia* (17) *ad-dan-'*.

[No 4,902]

No **35**—Obv.: (1) *Duppi* ^{m} *Eri-ba-* ^{ilu}*Marduk* (2) *a-na* ^{am}*ki-i-pi* (3) *bêli-ia* ^{ilu}*Nabû u* ^{ilu}*Marduk* (4) *a-na bêli-ia*

[1] *Ša* is a possibility.

Send a hundred *gur* of dates to Sukâ the PA-officer of the . . . -men, and for each of those hundred *gur* of dates thou shalt be paid at the monthly rate. Speedily set them on their way.

No. **32**.—Letter from Aplâ to Šadûnu, my father. May Nabû and Marduk bless my father.

Why [have I seen no] answer to any of the letters which I have sent unto my lord? . . .

. . . Let my lord send forth Nabû-šuma-ešir, for of the burnt bricks I will give thee all which have been rejected (?) with me.

Let not my lord be neglectful of this. Let me hear the news and of the welfare of my lord.

No. **33**.—[Letter] from Iṣṣur to Ṭâbti-Ib, Kasir, and Itti-Nabû-guzu, my brothers. May Bêl and Nabû grant peace and life to my brothers.

Send twelve *gur* of corn to Ardia. Speedily set it on its way.

No. **34**.—Letter from Eriba-[Marduk?] . . . to the Priest of Sippar, my lord. May Nabû and Marduk bless my lord, and whatever my lord may do.

Concerning that which the King ordered (?), soldiers I will send thee . . .

. . . Lo . . . for the gift of my lord, the . . . of Šamaš thereto unto my lord I give.

No. **35**.—Letter from Eriba-Marduk to the Governor, my lord. May Nabû and Marduk bless

lik-ru-bu (5) *ûmu(mu)-us-su* ^{ilu} *Šamšu* (6) *u* ^{ilu} *A-a a-[na] ṭu-ub* (7) *lib-bi tu-ub [šeri arak]* (8) *ûmu(mu) ša bêli-ia u-[ṣal-la]* (9) *šu-lum ina ali ekurri u bîti* (10) *ša bêli-ia ša-kin ma- . . . -a* (11) *ûmu(mu) ša* ^{am} *apil-šipri i-ru-[bu-ma]* (12) *bêl la i-mu-ru . . .* (13) *ma-'-diš at-tal-la-ka(?)* (14) . . . *-te-šu* (15) . . . ŠE-BAR (16 to 19 broken.) REV.: (20) . . . *-kap* GIŠ-BAR (21) . . . *id-dan-nu* (22) . . . [TIN]-TIR-KI *ki-i* (23) *[it]-ta-šu-u ûmu(mu)* (24) . . . *te(?)* ^{am} ŠA-TAM (25) . . . (26) . . . ^{alu} . . . (27) *ul id-din-nu u* ŠE-BAR (28) *at-tu-nu ša ina* TIN-TIR-KI (29) *gab-bi la i-aš-ša-'* (30) *ICL gur* ŠE-BAR . . . *bêl* (31) *lu-u-i-di* ^{ilu} *Šamšu u* ^{ilu} *Marduk* (32) *mimma(ma) ma-la ina bi-ib-lu* (33) *lib-bi-ka dul-la a-na* (34) *šarri bêli-ka te-ip-pu-uš* (35) *dum-ḳi-šu lu-kal-lim-mu-ka* (36) *te-e-mu u šu-lum* (37) *ša bêli-ia lu-uš-mu* (38) *ša(?)-ti-im-ia* (39) *ri-ḫi-e-ti.* (Left-hand edge) (40) . . . *-e katâ* ^{II} *u ki-din-ni-e* (41) . . . ^{pl} *ša bêli-ia ana bêli-ia ul-te-ḫi-* . . .

[No. 49,909]

NO. **36**.—OBV: (1) *[Duppi* ^{m} *Eri]-ba-* ^{ilu} *Marduk* (2) *[ana* ^{am} *ki]-i-pi* (3) *[bêli-ia]* ^{ilu} *Bêl* ^{ilu} *Nabû* ^{ilu} *Samšu* (4) ^{ilu} *A-a šu-lum ṭu-ub* (5) *lib-bi ṭu-ub šeri* (6) *a-ra-ku ûmu(mu) ša bêli-ia* (7) *liḳ-bu-u šu-lum ina ali* (8) *ekurri u bîti ša bêli-ia ša-kin* (9) *a-na eli kaspi ša e-bu-ra-nu* (10) *ša bêli iš-pur-ru* ^{ilu} *Šamšu* (11) *u* ^{ilu} *Marduk ki-i ul-tu eli* (12) *ša* ^{am} *šangi Sip-par* ^{ki} *bêli* (13) *i-mu-ru a-di-i eli* (14) *ša en-na lu ma-a-du* (15) *la mar-ṣu lu la dib-bi* (16) *ma-ṣu-u a-na eli* (17) *a-la-ku ša* TIN-TIR-KI (18) *ša bêli iš-pur-ru* (19) *lu la dib-bi* (20) *it-ti-ia.* REV.: (21) *ul ma-ṣu* (22) *a-mur* ^{m} *Ki-na-a* (23) *bêl li-ša-al a-na eli* (24) *alpi* ^{pl} *ša bêli iš-pur-ru* (25) *a-di la* ^{am} *apil-šip-ri ša bêli-ia* (26) *am-ma-ru* ^{alpu} *litti-ka*

my lord. Daily I pray to Šamaš and Âa for the happiness, health, and long life of my lord. Peace be upon the city, temple, and household of my lord.

The day that (my) messenger entered (the city) he did not see my lord; (so) I will come myself especially . . . unto the city of . . .

. . . They have not given, and (as for) the corn belonging to all of you who are in Babylon, not (one) hath received the hundred and fifty *gur* of corn. May my lord now be advised of this. By Šamaš and Marduk, whatever is the desire of thy heart, the work for the King, thy lord, thou shalt do, that he may show thee his favour. Let me hear the news and welfare of my lord. The rest of the . . . and the *kidinnî* [and the] . . . for my lord unto my lord I will send (?).

No. **36.**—[Letter from Eri]ba-Marduk [to] the Governor, [my lord]. May Bêl, Nabû, Šamaš, and Âa grant peace, happiness, health, and long life unto my lord. Peace be upon the city, temple, and household of my lord.

In the matter of the money for the labourers on the harvest, about which my lord hath sent, by Šamaš and Marduk, from the time when the Priest of Sippar saw my lord until now, they have not in any way been sick or quarrelsome, and in the matter of the Babylonian caravan, about which my lord hath sent, neither have there been quarrels with me. Behold, let my lord question Kinâ in the matter of the oxen about which

(27) *kur-ba-nı-tum ki-ı a-bu-ku* (28) *a-na bêli-ıa al-tap-ra*
(29) ^{ilu} *Šamšu u* ^{ilu} *Marduk mimma(ma)* (30) *ma-la ḳatâ*^{II} *-ka
ina eli* (31) *šak-na-at gab-bı* (32) *a-na dum-ḳi lu-tır-ra*
(33) *ṭe-e-mu u šu-lum* (34) [*ša*] *bêli-ıa lu-uš-mu*.

[No. 79,323.]

NO. 37.—OBV : (1) *Duppi* ^{m} *Arad-* ^{ilu} *Bêl a-na* ^{milu} *Marduk
- šuma - iddin* (2) *bêli - ia ûmu(mu) - us* ^{ilu} *Bêl* ^{ilu} *Nabû*
(3) ^{ilu} *Ûmu(mu)* ^{ilu} *Nergal a-na balaṭ napšâti*^{pl} (4) *a-ra-ku
ûmu(mu) ṭu-ub lib-bı ṭu-ub šîri* (5) *bu-nı pa-ni ša šarri ḫa-
du-tu itti bêli-ia* (6) [*u*]-*ṣal-la bêl lu-u-i-di ul-tu* (7) . . *šu*(?)
ši-pir-tum ^{milu} *Šamšu-upaḫḫir(ır) a-na pani* (8) . . . *ka
šı-i* [^{m}]^{ilu} KA (9) . . . *karanı* . . . *-ḫi*
(10) . . . (Remainder of obv. and top of rev broken off)
REV.: (11) . . . (12) . . . *mimma(ma) ina lıb-bi ul
id-nu* (13) [*ana* ^{m}] ^{ilu} *Šamšu-ıt-ta-du-u kurummati* (14) [*lıd*]-
din-nu-nu šad-da-gıš II BAR *ma - na kaspi* (15) . . *su
suk' si-ıb-ma I gur* ^{išu} *karanı* (16) *la-bi-ru u immeru* . . .
-ma-ta ub-lu (17) *u ḫaltıkki*^{pl} ŠE-BAR *šamaššammı gap-nu*
(18) *a-na* ^{milu} *Šamšu-upaḫḫir(ır) ıd-dan-nu·' bêl* (19) *lu-u-ı-di
kap-du ṭe-e-mu* (20) *ša bêli-ia lu-uš-me-'-ma lu-še-taḳ.*

[No. 84,963]

NO. 38.—OBV.: (1) *Duppi* ^{m} *Arad-* ^{ilu} *Bêl a-na* (2) ^{am} *šangi
Sıp-par*^{ki} *bêli-ia* (3) *ûmu(mu)-us-su* ^{ilu} *Bêl* ^{ilu} *Nabû* ^{ilu} *Šamšu*
(4) *u* ^{ilu} *Nergal ana balaṭ napištim(tim)* (5) *a-ra-ku ûmu ṭu-ub
lıb-bi* (6) *u ṭu-ub šîri ana bêli-ia u-ṣal-la* (7) *a-na eli* ŠE-BAR
u ^{išu} *karani ša a-na* (8) *pa-ni* ^{milu} *Šamšu-upaḫḫir(ır) ša bêl
iš-pur-ru-an-nı* (9) ^{išu} *karani ina pa-na-tu-u-a ṣa-ḫı-id* (10) *u*

my lord hath sent; before ever I saw the messenger of my lord, I had fetched and sent unto my lord thy cow, which is thy temple-gift.

May Šamaš and Marduk bring luck to everything to which thy hand is put! Let me hear the news and welfare of my lord.

No. **37**.—Letter from Arad-Bêl to Marduk-šuma-iddin, my lord. Daily I pray Bêl, Nabû, Ûmu (= Šamaš) and Nergal for the life, long days, happiness, and health, and that the light of the King's countenance may be favourable unto my lord.

May my lord be advised that ever since the letter of Šamaš-upaḫḫir unto . . .

. . . nothing thereto have they given. Let them give (his) sustenance to Šamaš-ittadû. Of old, two and a half mana of silver . . . send one *gur* of old wine and a . . . sheep; and *ḫaltikki*, corn, sesame, grapes, unto Šamaš-upaḫḫir they shall give. May my lord be advised of this. Speedily let me hear news of my lord, that I may not omit (anything).

No. **38**.—Letter from Arad-Bêl to the Priest of Sippar, my lord. Daily I pray unto Bêl, Nabû, Šamaš, and Nergal for the life, long days, happiness, and health of my lord.

In the matter of the corn and wine which are due to Šamaš-upaḫḫir, about which my lord hath sent me; the wine is being fermented before me, and the corn

ŠE-BAR *a-na kaspi nadnat* (*na-at*) (11) *bêl lu-u-i-di X gur* ^{išu}*karani* (12) . . . ŠE-BAR *u* ^{išu}*karani* (13) . . . (Remainder of obv. and top of rev. broken off.) REV.: (14) *ul* . . . (15) *u* ^{m}*Ta-kiš a-na pa-ni bêli-ia* (16) *al-tap-par ṭe-e-mu ša bêli-ia* (17) *a-na ka-pa-du lu-uš-me* (18) *a-na eli* ^{m}*Ri-mut-*^{ilu}KA *u* $^{m\,ilu}$*Šamšu-udannin* (?) (19) *ša bêl iš-pur-ra-an-ni ki-i u-ba-'-u* (20) *ul a-mur-šu-nu-tu bêl lu-u-i-di* (21) *a-na eli* ŠE-BAR *ša* $^{m\,ilu}$*Nabû-uballiṭ*(*iṭ*) ^{am}*ir-ri-ši* (22) *ša bêl iš-pur-ra-an-ni* ^{am}*mâr-banûti*^{pl} *ul-te-zi-iz* (23) *u* ^{m}*Itti-*^{ilu}*Nabû-pani-ia ina pa-ni-šu-nu uk-ti-in* (24) *um-ma IV-ta bâbi*^{pl} $^{m\,ilu}$*Nabû-uballiṭ*(*iṭ*) (25) *i-te-riš a-na* $^{m\,ilu}$*Šamšu-upaḫḫir*(*ir*) (26) *ki-i a-ḳab-bu-u um-ma* (27) *mi-ri-is* ^{išu}*karani ina pa-na-tu-u-a* (28) . . . *ṣa-ḫa-ad.* (Left-hand edge) (29) . . . *um-ma la-pa-ni* ^{am}*nakri ni-ip-ta-*[*laḫ*] (30) . . . *iṣ-ṣa-ḫa-id a-mur ri-ḫi-tu a-bil* . . .

[No. 65,387]

NO. **39**. — OBV.: (1) *Duppi* ^{m}*Arad-*^{ilu}*Bêl a-na* (2) $^{m\,ilu}$*Šamšu-aḫi-iddin abi-ia* (3) ^{ilu}*Nabû u* ^{ilu}*Marduk a-na abi-ia* (4) *lik-ru-bu ina ṣilli ša ilâni*^{pl} (5) *šu-lum a-na-ku a-ga-a-'-i* (6) *gab-bi ša aḳ-bak-ka um-ma* (7) *a-na ka-pa-du ṭe-en-ku* (8) *u mi-nu-u* [*ša*] *te-pu-uš* (9) *šu-pur en-na* [*mi*]*-nam lu-di* . . . (10) . . . (11) . . (12) . . . *u-a* (13) . . . *u ki-i* (14) . . *-ḳab-bu-u* (15) . . . *ki-i* [*ta*? *-dib*]*-bu-ub-'* (16) *su-ut-tir id-di-nu ši-i-mu* (17) *šu-pur a-na* ^{m}*La-ki-pi ḳi-bi* (18) *um-ma la tap-laḫ ki-i* (19) ^{am}*šangi Sip-par*^{ki} ^{am}*ki-i-pi* (20) ^{am}*šangi*^{pl} *i-mur* . . . (21) *um-ma ḳi-ma-' kaspi a-na* REV.: (22) [*pani* (?)] $^{m\,ilu}$*Bêl-lu-u-aḫu-u-a* (23) *li-din ḳi-bi um-ma kaspi* (24) *ul a-mur ki-i a-na eli gap-nu* (25) *šamaššammi*

has been sold. May my lord be advised; ten *gur* of wine . . . corn and wine . . .

. . . and I send Takiš unto my lord, that I may speedily hear news of my lord.

Concerning Rimut-ka and Šamaš-udannin, about whom my lord hath sent unto me; although I have searched, I have not been able to see them, so let my lord take note of this.

Concerning the corn of Nabû-uballiṭ, the gardener, about which my lord hath sent unto me; I appointed (certain) nobles, and Itti-Nabû-pania hath certified before them that Nabû-uballiṭ hath sown the four gates. After I had told Šamaš-upaḫḫir that the must of the wine was fermenting with me, [he said] "We shall fear (any) enemy, (now that) . . . it is fermenting." Lo, the rest an answer (?) . . .

No. **39.**—Letter from Arad-Bêl to Šamaš-aḫi-iddin, my father. May Nabû and Marduk bless my father. As for myself, I am well by the grace of the gods.

Was not this all that I spake unto thee, saying, "Speedily send news of thyself and tell me what thou hast done?" Now . . .

. . . Do thou write according as thou hast arranged; (and) send (whether) they have given the price. Speak unto Lakipi thus. "Fear not that the Priest of Sippar, the Warden, or the Priests have seen." [They have spoken (?)] thus: "Let him pay the money to Bêl-lû-aḫûa for the flour." Speak thus: "I have not seen the money." If he give thee (?) the

. . . *-nik-ka* (26) *ḳi-bi-šu-nu ina ki-* . . *-ka* (?) *up-te-ḫi-ir-ru* (27) *u ina* GIŠ-BAR *ki-i an* . . . *du* (28) [$^{m\ ilu}$ *Bêl*]*-lu-u-aḫu-u-a* ^{m}*Itti-* ^{ilu} *Nabû-pani-ia* (29) . . . *-bu-di-ia at-ta-din* (30) . . . *lib - bi* . . . *ul iš - ši* (31) . . . *ša šamaššammi ul i-mu-ur* (32) . . . (33) . . . (34) *šup* (?) . . . *-ma* (?) *ul a-ka-lu* (?)*-su* (35) . . . *la* . . . $^{m\ ilu}$ *Bêl-aḫi*^{pl} *-iriba* (?) (36) *u* ^{m}*Kal-ba* (?) . . . *a-na pani-ka mu-* . . . (37) *su-ut-ṭir-ma ina pani-šu-nu i-ši-ma* (38) 30 *ka saluppi V tab-bu* (?)- . . . *eš* (?)*-gi* (?)*-tu* (39) *a-na* $^{m\ ilu}$*Nabû-naṣir i-din mi-nu-u* (40) ^{m}*Aḫi*^{pl}*-a-a šu-pur šu-* . . . (41) *ša* (?) ^{m}*Arad-* ^{ilu} *Bêl šu-lum* (42) ^{sal}*Ba-zi-tum bêlti-šu* (43) *i-ša-al.*

[No 84,928.]

No. **40**—Obv: (1) *Duppi* ^{m}*Arad-* ^{ilu} *Bêl a-na* (2) ^{sal}*E-pir-tum aḫati-ia* (3) ^{ilu} *Bêl* ^{ilu} *Nabû šu-lum balati ša aḫati-ia* (4) *liḳ-bu-u ik-ki-bi ša ilâni*^{pl} . . . (5) *mi-nam-ma ṭe-e-mu-ku-nu* (6) *ul aš-me lib-bu-u-a il-ṣi* (7) *ki-i ta-ri-' en-na* (8) *dib-bi gab* (?) *- bi* (?) . . . *bi* (9) *bi - šu-'-a I ma - na kasbi*(*bi*) (10) *in-ni-i u a-mat šarri ši-i* (11) *kaspi ša gi-i-ni ul in-na-'* (12) *kaspu mu-ru-ḳu i-ši-i* (13) *šu-šir-a-am a-ša-li-ka* (14) *ina ḳatâ*^{II} *man-ma al-la-ka šu-bi-lu* (15) ^{m}*Arad-* ^{ilu} *Bêl šu-lum ša* ^{sal}*Ba-zi-tu* (16) ^{sal}*Ḫa-ni-na-a* ^{m}*A-na* (?) . . . (17) *u* $^{sal\ ilu}$ *A-a-en-ḳit* (18) *i-ša-al-la.* Rev.: (19) *pa-ni* ^{sal} *Ba-zi-*

[1] *Ginû* and *muruku.* What the difference is between these two sorts of silver is very difficult to determine; *ginû* occurs in the following passages in contract-tablets.—*XVI* TU *kâspi ša gini ša nadanu u maḫari,* "sixteen shekels of *ginu*-silver, for selling and buying" (Peiser, *Bab. Vertr.*, No. xlviii, ll. 1–2); *XII mana kaspi ša ginu ša nadanu u maḫari,* "twelve mana of *ginu*-silver, for selling and buying" (Strassmaier, *Inschr von Darius,* No. 134, l. 1).

grapes and sesame, tell him I have collected . . . and as wages I will give . . . to Bêl-lû-aḫûa, Itti-Nabû-pania, [and] . . . budia . . . hath not received . . . the . . . of the sesame he hath not seen . . . Bêl-aḫi-iriba and Kalba . . . unto thy presence ; write, and receive in their presence. Give thirty *ḳa* of dates, five . . . to Nabû-nasir. Why Aḫiâ . . . ? Arad-Bêl asks after the welfare of Bazitum, his sister.

No. **40**.—Letter from Arad-Bêl to the lady Epirtum, my sister. May Bêl and Nabû grant health (and) life unto my sister.

By the tribulations of the gods (?) why have I heard no news of thee? My heart rejoiceth that thou art about to become a mother.

Now, matters are going badly [with me . . .], (so) send one mana of silver. Now it is the King's command that stamped (?)[1] silver shall not be sent (by messenger), so get some tested (?)[1] silver; arrange (this), I pray thee. Send it by some traveller.

Arad-Bêl asks after the welfare of the lady Bazitu, the lady Ḫaninâ, Ana- . . . , and the lady Aa-enkit.

On *nadanu u maḫaru*, see Meissner, *Zeits. fur Assyr.*, vol. ix, p. 275. With regard to *muruḳu*, the root *marâku* occurs in the contracts with the meaning "to prove a claim to" (Peiser, *Bab. Vertr*, p 260), and with a further meaning at the end of a contract-tablet (Strassmaier, *Nebuchadnezzar*, No 64, ll. 21–22), *kaspu ina ṣêri ul immarriḳḳi*, "The silver in the desert could not be proved," which seems to indicate that some sort of testing was in use

tum (20) *la i-bi-šu-'* (21) *a-na* ᵐ ⁱˡᵘ *Šamšu-aḫi-iddin aḫi-ia* (22) ⁱˡᵘ *Nabû* ⁱˡᵘ *Marduk a-na aḫi-ia* (23) *lik-ru-bu mi-nam-ma ṭe-en-ka* (24) *ul aš-me ina eli ka-si-ia* (25) *ša aš-pur-rak-ka la ta-sil-li* (26) *I ka ka-si-ia ina ḳatâ* ᴵᴵ *man-ma* (27) *la tu-maš-šir IC XCVII* . . . (28) *saluppi i-na libbi-ka ina eli* (29) *saluppi la ta-sil-li* (30) *u ina ḳatâ* ᴵᴵ *man-ma la tu-maš-šir* (31) *ḫu-ṣa-bi* . . . *-at bi ina* ⁱˢᵘ *kiri-ka* (32) *u* . . . *-ka man-ma* (33) *la im-mar* ᵃᵐ *ki-i-pi* (34) *a-gan-na di-na-a ta-[din]* (35) *a-na* ᵃᵐ *šangi Sip-par* ᵏⁱ . . . (36) *a-gan-na a-na e* . . . (37) *aḳ-ta-bi* . . .

[No 64,781.]

NO. **41**.—OBV.: (1) *Duppi* ᵐ *Arad-* ⁱˡᵘ ME-ME (2) *a-na* ᵃᵐ *šangi Sip-par* ᵏⁱ (3) *bêli-ia ûmu(mu)-us-su* (4) ⁱˡᵘ *Bêl u* ⁱˡᵘ *Nabû a-na balaṭ* (5) *napištim(tim) ša bêli-ia* (6) *u-ṣal-la* (7) *kap-du* ᵃᵐ *mâr-šip-ri* (8) *bêl liš-pur-am-ma* (9) *saluppi as-ni-e* (10) *liš-ši* (11) . . . *ṣa-ar* . . (Remainder of obv. and top of rev, perhaps two lines, broken off) REV.: (12) *ina lib-bi i-na-aš-[ši]* (13) *ina ḳatâ* ᴵᴵ *-šu-nu bêl* . . . (14) *lu* (?)-*u* (?)-*še-bi-la* . . . (15) *a-mur pani* ᵃᵐ *mâr-šip ri* (16) *ša bêli-ia [a]-da-gal.*

[No. 60,686.]

NO **42**.—OBV.: (1) *Duppi* ᵐ *Arad-* ⁱˡᵘ *Bunene* (2) *u* ᵐ ⁱˡᵘ *Marduk-na-sir* (3) *a-na* ᵃᵐ*[šangi] Sippar* ᵏⁱ (4) *aḫi-ni* ⁱˡᵘ *Nabû u* ⁱˡᵘ *Marduk* (5) *a-na aḫi-ni lik-ru-bu* (6) [ᵐ] ⁱˡᵘ *E-a-mudammiḳ[iḳ]* (7) *[apil] - šu ša* ᵐ ⁱˡᵘ *E - a - šuma* (?) *- epuš* (8) GIŠ-DA-*a ša* ⁱˡᵘ *Nin-ib* (9) *ina pani* ⁱˡᵘ *Šamši* (10) *ma* (?)-*gal - li - lu* (?) (11) ᵃᵐ ŠA-TAM. REV: (12) *u* ᵃᵐ ŠA-KU (13) *iḳ-ta-bu-[u]* (14) *um-ma a-[mat-ni]* (15) *ši-i* . . .

[No. 75,598.]

The lady Bazitu doth not (I pray) look with disfavour on Šamaš-aḫi-iddin, my brother; may Nabû (and) Marduk be gracious unto my brother. Why have I heard no news of thee?

Concerning my cassia, of which I did send thee, be not neglectful (and) entrust not a single *ḳa* of cassia to the hands of anyone else. There are a hundred and ninety-seven measures of dates in thy care(?); in the matter of the dates be not neglectful (and) entrust them not to the hands of anyone else. None seeth the date-palms . . . in thy garden.

The Warden here shall judge(?) my case; unto the Priest of Sippar here I have spoken . . .

No. **41.**—Letter from Arad-Meme unto the Priest of Sippar, my lord. Daily I pray unto Bêl and Nabû for the life of my lord.

Speedily let my lord send a messenger to take the *asni*-dates . . .

. . . therein shall he take. Let my lord send [it] by their hands. Behold, I await my lord's messenger.

No. **42.**—Letter from Arad-Bunene and Marduk-naṣir unto the [Priest] of Sippar, our brother. May Nabû and Marduk be gracious unto my brother.

Ea-mudammiḳ, the [son] of Ea-šuma(?)-epuš, hath [converted ?] the tithe of Ninib to Šamaš. The *šatam* and the *šaku* have spoken thus: "This [is our will ?]."

No. 43 —Obv. : (1) *Duppi* ᵐ *Itti-* ⁱˡᵘ *Nabû-balatu a-na* (2) ᵐ *Iddina-(na)-apli aḫi-ia* (3) ⁱˡᵘ *Bêl u* ⁱˡᵘ *Nabû šu-lum u balati* (4) *a-ra-ka ûmu(mu) ša aḫi-ia* (5) *liḳ-bu-u ti-i-di* (6) *ša abi u aḫi al-la-nu-uk-ku* (7) *la dag-lak-ku ûmu XVI* ᵏᵃᵐ (8) *ša-la pani-ka al-li-ik-ku* (9) *ib-bi-ru-u a-na ši-il-lu* ᵐ *Šarru-di* . . . (10) *a - ta - mar - šu* . . . *- ti il - ḳa - an - ni* (11) ⁱˡᵘ *Nabû* (?) *ki-i aš-mu-u* (12) *a-na Babili* ᵏⁱ (13) *it-tal-lak-ku ša bêl* (14) *im-ma-ru-šu bêl* (15) *la u-maš-šir-šu* (16) *mar-šip-ri.* Rev. : (17) *ša bêli-ia lu-mur-'-ma* (18) *a-na Dil-bat* ᵏⁱ (19) *lu-li-ik-ki* (20) *te-ik-tum a-na* (21) *bêli-ia la i-ip-pal* (22) *a-na șeri i-ḫal-liḳ* (23) *ṭâbti-ka ra-bi-tum* (24) *ša abu-u-tu u aḫu-u-tu* (25) *ina muḫ-ḫi-ia šu-kun* (26) ᵐ *Šad-din-nu lu-ki-il-lim-ma* (27) *it-ta-aḫ-ḫa-aš-šu* (28) *lu-u-aš-ši-ib* (29) *a-di eli ša ana-ku* (30) *al-la-ka* (31) . . *-mi-tum* (32) . . *la i-pa-aš-šu.*

[No 30,778]

No. 44 —Obv. : (1) *A-na* ᵐ *Ba-si-ia* (2) *u* ᵐ ⁱˡᵘ *Šamšu-ri'i-šu-nu en-na* (3) *a-mur* ᵐ *Ni-din-tum-* ⁱˡᵘ *Bêl* (4) *apil-šu ša* ᵐ ⁱˡᵘ *Bêl-a-su-u-a* (5) *u* ᵐ ⁱˡᵘ *Ad-da-iddina(na)* (6) *ki-li-šu II C gur* (7) *saluppi ina muḫ-ḫi-ka* (8) *u-ši-ti-ku-nu* (9) *a-na* ⁱˢᵘ *elippi-šu* (10) *la ta-el-li* (11) *me-ik-su ša II C gur* (12) *[i]-na ka-an-da-ki-šu* (13) *al-la ki-i.* Rev. : (14) *e-ti-ik-šu* (15) *i-ba-aš-šu-u* (16) *ina ma-ši-ḫu-šu mu-ḫur-šu* (17) *u ša-ṭa-ri it-ti-šu* (18) *šu-ṭu-ru ša it-ti* (19) ᵐ *Kud-da-a-a u-ša-za-zu-ma* (20) *i-nam-da-ka* (21) *ḫu-sab eli* (?) . . . *-ta* ⁱˢᵘ *elippi* (22) *la ta-maḫ-ḫar-šu* (23) *kap-du ḫarrâna* ⁱⁱ *a-na šepi-šu* (24) *šu-kun.* (Seal-impression.)

[No. 79,395.]

No. **43**.—Letter from Itti-Nabû-balatu unto Iddina-apli, my brother. May Bêl and Nabû grant health and life (and) long days unto my brother.

Thou knowest that I have not set eyes on father or brother for a long time, so I set out without thy knowledge on the sixteenth day. Shall I cross over to the booth[1] of Šarru-di . . . [and] see him? . . . hath taken me. By Nabû (?) when I had heard that he had gone to Babylon that my lord might see him, (I knew) my lord would not desert him. Let me see my lord's messenger, and let him come to the city of Dilbat. The end for my lord he will not see, unto the desert he hath gone away. Do thou bestow thy great fatherly and brotherly kindness upon me. Let me shew Šaddinnu and let me sit . . .[2] until I come. He will make no . . .

No. **44**.—Unto Basia and Šamaš-re'i-šunu.

Now, behold, Nidintum-Bêl, the son of Bêl-asûa, and Adda-iddina, his . . . have despatched two hundred *gur* of dates unto thee. Go not up into his boat, the customs-dues for the two hundred *gur* are in his *kandaku*; but if he pass (the customs without paying), there it is; receive it according to its measure, and write him a receipt. What I have arranged with Kuddâ, he will give unto thee, but as for the logs . . . from the boat, do not receive them. Speedily set him on his way.

---

[1] *Šillu*, possibly the same as *šîlu* To this day the natives of Mesopotamia erect shelters of boughs in the gardens on the river banks for a watchman to live in. [2] *Ittaḫḫaššu* = *ina taḫḫaššu*?

No. **45**.—Obv.: (1) *Duppi* *m ilu* *Bêl-aḫi-ibašši(ši)* (2) *u* *m* *Šu-la-a a-na* (3) *m ilu* *Nabû-zira-ešir* (4) *u* *m ilu* *Nabû-ukin-ziri* (5) *aḫi pl -e-ni* (6) *ilu* *Bêl u* *ilu* *Nabû šu-lum* (7) *ša aḫi pl -e-a lik-bu-u* (8) *III C sab-bi-lu* (9) *ina katâ II* *m ilu* *Nabû-bêl*(?)*-ibašši* (10) *am* *išpar-iṣi* (11) *VII* *m ilu* *Šamšu-iddin apil-šu ša* (12) *m ilu* *Bêl-ib-ni* (13) *VII* *m ilu* *Šamšu-šuma-epuš* (14) *XI* *m* *Ardi-ia* (15) *apil-šu ša* *m ilu* *Bêl-ibni* Rev.: (16) *IV* (?) *m* *Tab-ni-e-a* (17) *apil-šu ša* *m ilu* *Nergal-iddin* (18) *X* *m* *Bêli* (?)-*ia apil-šu ša* (19) *m ilu* *Nabû-ki-ṣir* (20) *X* *m ilu* *Bêl-šuma-ukin* (21) [*apil-šu ša* *m* . . . *-uballit*] (*it*) (?) (22) [. . *m* . .]-*ni* (23) . . . *-ki* (24) . . . *-mu* (25) . . . [*m ilu*] *Marduk-mušallim* (26) . . . *ša* *m* *Mu-še-zib-* *ilu* *Bêl* (27) *apil-šu ša* *m* *Ukin-ziri* (28) *a-na ṣabi pl* (29) *maḫ-ru-tu* (30) *ki-i ni-ik-bu-u* (?). (Left-hand edge) (31) . . . *-iš-šu-nu* . . . *iṣu* (32) *ia-a-nu bêli pl lu-u-i-du-u.*

[No 60,075 + 84,923]

No. **46**—Obv.: (1) [*Duppi* *m*] . . . *u* *m ilu* *Bêl-aḫi pl-iddin* (2) [*a-na* *m*] *ilu* *Bêl* (?)*-šuma* (?)*-iddin aḫi-i-ni* (3) [*ilu* *Nabû*] *u* *ilu* [*Marduk a-na*] *aḫi-i-ni* (4) [*lik*]*-ru-bu* . . . [*E*]*-sag-ila* (5) . . . *tu* (?) *u* . . (6) [*a*]*-na aḫi-i-ni ni* . . . (7) *X alpi šuk-lu-lu pl ma* . . . *IV-u V-u* (8) *ša i-na bît u-ri-e* . . . *muḫ-ḫi* (9) *a-na e-ri-tu ša šarri* . . . (10) *liš-pur-an-na-a-šu a-na bît u-ri-e* (11) *nu-še-iḫ-lu ia-a-nu-u* (12) *šarru i-šim-me-e-ma ina muḫ-ḫi-ni* (13) *iḫ-ḫa-an-na-ak u ki-i* (14) *alpi pl-ka ša a-na* UD-AB-AB (15) . . *arḫu* *Nisannu* (16) . . . (17) . . . Rev: (18) . . . *ûmu*(*mu*) *ša ta-*[*am-ma-ru*] (19) *ša* *ilu* *Šamšu i-te-ib-bu-u* (20) *šu-pur-an-na-ši-ma* (21) *alpi pl ku-um kaspa-'-a* (22) *ni-iš-pur-rak-ka*

No. **45**.—Letter from Bêl-aḫi-ibašši and Šulâ unto Nabû-zira-ešir and Nabû-ukin-ziri, our brothers. May Bêl and Nabû grant health unto our brothers.

Three hundred baskets by the hand of Nabû-bêl-ibašši (?), the basket-maker[1]; seven for Šamaš-iddin, son of Bêl-ibni; seven for Šamaš-šuma-epuš; —— for Ardia, son of Bêl-ibni; four for Tabnêa, son of Nergal-iddin; ten for Bêlia, son of Nabû-kiṣir; ten for Bêl-šuma-ukin . . .

. . . Marduk-Mušallim, of Mušezib-Bêl, son of Ukin-ziri. After we had spoken to the former workmen . . . there was no wood, so may our lords be advised (of this).

No. **46**.—[Letter from] . . . and Bêl-aḫi-iddin [unto] Bêl (?)-šuma (?)-iddin, our brother. May [Nabû] and [Marduk] be gracious unto our brother.

[Cattle] are wanting in [E]-Sagila, [so we send] unto our brother, that he may send us ten perfect bulls . . . four or five which in the stalls . . . for the pregnant cow (?) of the King, and we will put them into the stalls, (for) should there be none, the King will hear (of it) and be wroth against us; and when thy oxen which [have been settled ?] for the festival in Nisan . . .

. . . the day thou seest (?) that the sun is bright, send unto us and we will send thee the oxen for the money. Should, however, we change towards thee,

[1] Literally "wood-weaver."

(23) *ša-nu-u ki-i ni-ša-an-nu-ka* (24) ^{ilu}*Bêl u* ^{ilu}*Nabû ki-i a-di-i* (25) *alpi*^{pl} *ša a-na la alpi*^{pl}*-ka* (26) *ba-nu-u ni-šap-par-rak-ka* (27) *u ki-i ia-a-nu-u lu-u* (28) *[ma]-tu-u mimma(ma) ša eširti ša* (29) . . . *ši-ḫu šup-ra-am-ma* (30) . . *nu-še-bi-lak-ka* (31) . . . *i-ni sal-ḳu-ut-ti-ia* (32) . . . *iḫ-ḫi-su.*

[No. 56,022.]

No. **47**.—Obv.: (1) *Duppi* $^{m\ ilu}$*Bêl-aḫi*^{pl}*-iddin* (2) *[a]-na* ^{am}*ki-i-pi* (3) *[u* ^{am}*] šangi* UD-KIB-NUN-KI (4) *[aḫi]*^{pl}*-e-a* (5) *[*^{ilu}*Nabû] u* ^{ilu}*Marduk* (6) *[a-na] aḫi*^{pl}*-e* (7) *[lik-ru]-bu* (8) . . . *ma-na* (Remainder of obv. broken off, what remains of the rev. is blank)

[No. 84,941.]

No. **48**.—Obv.: (1) *Duppi* $^{m\ ilu}$*Bêl-aḫi*^{pl}*-iddin* (2) *a-na* ^{m}*Iddina-*^{ilu}*Marduk abi-ia* (3) ^{ilu}*Nabû u* ^{ilu}*Marduk a-na abi-ia* (4) *lik-ru-bu a-na eli* (5) *abi-ia ki-i* . . . (6) *u-di-e a-na bîti-'* (?) (7) *ul-te-ti-ik a-mat-ka* (8) *it-ti-ia la ta-ša-an-ni* (9) *ši-pir-ti ši-i* (10) *ša ina ḳatâ*^{II} ^{m}*Tar-ḫu-ru* (11) *taš-pu-ru mi-nu-u ši-i* (12) *en-na a-mur* (13) ^{m}*Ḳud-da-a u* ^{m}*Bêl-usur.* Rev: (14) *a-na abi-ia al-tap-par* (15) *u-il-tim it-ti* (16) ^{m}*Ḳud-da-a bêl li-'-il-šu* (17) *u ši-pir-tum* (18) *bêli liš-pur-ra-am-ma* (19) *u-di-e-šu lu-še-ṣu* (20) *u mi-nu-u ki-i ša kunukki* (21) *it-ti-šu bêl ip-pu-šu* (22) *u ina muḫ-ḫi-šu il-la-'* (23) *a-na-ku gab-bi* (24) *a-na bêli-ia id-dan.*

[No. 31,155.]

No. **49**.—Obv.: (1) *Duppi* $^{m\ ilu}$*Bêl-aḫi*^{pl}*-iddin a-na* $^{m\ ilu}$*Bêl-uballit(it)* (2) *aḫi-ia* ^{ilu}*Bêl u* ^{ilu}*Nabû šu-lum u balati ša aḫi-ia liḳ-bu-u* (3) *ša at-ta u* ^{m}*Mu-šal-lim at-ri-ia* (4) *tu-ša-an-na* . . . *ina pani* $^{m\ ilu}$*Bêl* . . . (5) *XI bilat* . . . *a-na* . . . (6) *a-na I ma-na kaspi at ta-nak-* . . . (7) . . . *šiḳli kaspi ša nad-nu ta-* . . . (8) . . .

then by Bêl and Nabû will we return the contracts for the oxen (which were created without thy bulls); and should there be none or should there be too few, then do thou send whatever is needful (?) in the Temple and we will forward thee [the money ?] . . .

No. **47.**—Letter from Bêl-aḫi-iddin unto the Warden (and) Priest of Sippar, my [brothers]. May [Nabû] and Marduk be gracious [unto] my brothers . . . mana . . .

No. **48.**—Letter from Bêl-aḫi-iddin unto Iddina-Marduk, my father. May Nabû and Marduk be gracious unto my father.

I have omitted the furniture for the house according as . . . unto my father. Change not thy orders to me—this letter which thou hast sent by the hand of Tarḫuru—what is it? Now, behold, I am sending Ḳuddâ and Bêl-usur unto my father, let my lord give a promissory note to Ḳuddâ, and let my lord send a letter that I may send out his furniture, and my lord shall arrange according to the agreement with him, and it shall come up to him. I will give it all to my lord.

No. **49.**—Letter from Bêl-aḫi-iddin unto Bêl-uballiṭ, my brother. May Bêl and Nabû grant health and life unto my brother.

Of that which thou and Mušallim my . . . did change (your minds about) . . . I have given eleven talents of [wool ?] for the . . . to Bêl . . . for one mana of silver. The . . . shekels

kaspu pişû(u) II . . . (9) . . . ${}^{m\ ilu}$*Sin-* . . . (10) . . . *iddina u* . . . REV.: (11) [^{m}] *Mu-šal-lim ina pani* . . . (12) . . . *III ma-na XI šiķli kaspi* . . . (13) *ši-me šipâti ša ina pani pa-ni-* . . . (14) *ri-ḫi VII šiķli kaspi ši-me šipâti* (15) *VII šiķli kaspi ši-me immeri ša ki-na na-a-tu* (16) *ina pani-ka a-ga-a gab-bi* (17) *at-ta u* ^{m} *Na-şir te-te-ša-in-ni.*

[No. 78,094]

NO. **50**.—OBV.: (1) [*Duppi*] ${}^{m\ ilu}$ *Bêl-aḫi*^{pl}*-iķiša(ša) a-na* (2) ^{m} . . . ^{m}*Na-şir* (3) *u* ^{m}*Ki-i-*^{ilu}*Nabû aḫi-ia*^{pl} (4) ^{ilu}*Nabû u* ^{ilu}*Marduk a-na* [*aḫi*]^{pl} *lik-ru-*[*bu*] (5) *III gur saluppi* . . . *-a* (6) ^{am}*riķķi* (?)^{pl} *ša* ^{arḫu}*Du'uzi u* ^{arḫu}*Âbi* (7) *ina ķatâ*^{II} ^{m}*Na-din šu-bil-la-* . . . REV.: (8) *III gur saluppi ina kurummati* (9) ^{am}*şabi*^{pl} *ša* ^{am} *ki-i-pi* (10) ^{arḫu} *Du'uzi u* ^{arḫu}*Âbi* . . . (11) . . . *be* (?) *-ri ša* ^{am}*ki-i-pi* (12) . . . ^{arḫu}*Simanu šattu XVII*^{kam} . . .

[No. 75,635]

NO. **51**—OBV.: (1) *Duppi* ${}^{m\ ilu}$*Bêl-apli-iddin* ^{m}*Na-şir u* ^{m}*Ki-i-*[^{ilu}*Nabû*] (2) *a-na* ^{m}*A-na-a-mat-*^{ilu}*Bêl-ad-gal aḫi-i-ni* (3) *XCI gur 20 ķa saluppi ina pap-pa-su* (4) ^{am} . . . *-u-tu a-na eli* ^{m}*Mušallim-*^{ilu}*Marduk* (5) *a-na* ^{m}*Šit-ķul apil* ${}^{m\ ilu}$*Šamšu-aḫi-iddin i-din* (6) *XII gur saluppi kurummati* ^{m}*Šit-kul ša šatti XV*^{kam} (7) *u VI gur kurummati* ${}^{m\ ilu}$*Bunene-šarri-usur* ^{am}*išpari* (8) *napḫariš IC IX gur 20 ķa saluppi* (9) *a-na* ^{m}*Šit-kul i-din.* REV.: (10) ^{arḫu}*Kisilimu umu XVIII*^{kam} *šatti XV*^{kam} (11) ${}^{m\ ilu}$*Nabû-na'id šar E*^{ki}. (Three seal-impressions.)

[No. 75,734]

of silver which hath been paid . . . "white" silver, two . . . Sin- . . , . . -iddina and . . . ; Mušallim in the presence of . . . three mana, eleven shekels of silver as the price of the wool which was left over from the former ; seven shekels of silver as the price of the wool ; seven shekels of silver the price of the sheep for the servants with thee ; all this thou and Naṣir have asked me (?).

No. **50.**—[Letter] from Bêl-aḫi-iḳiša unto . . . Naṣir and Kî-Nabû, my brothers. May Nabû and Marduk bless my brothers.

Send three *gur* of dates [as the food of] the *riḳḳu*-officials for the months of Tammuz and Ab, by the hand of Nadin. (*Seal.*)

Three *gur* of dates as the food for the men of the Warden for the months of Tammuz and Ab . . . -riša, the Warden ; Siwan, the seventeenth year.

No. **51.**—Letter from Bêl-apli-iddin, Nasir, and Kî-[Nabû] unto Ana-amat-Bêl-adgal, our brother.

Give ninety-one *gur*, twenty *ḳa* of dates as payment for the . . . work towards Mušallim-Marduk, to Šitkul, the son of Šamaš-aḫi-iddin : twelve *gur* of dates as the food for Šitḳul for the fifteenth year ; and six *gur* as the food for Bunene-šarri-uṣur, the weaver ; total, one hundred and nine *gur*, twenty *ḳa* of dates, which thou art to give to Šitḳul.

Kislew, the eighteenth day, the fifteenth year of Nabû-na'id, King of Babylon. (*Three seals.*)

No. **52**—Obv.: (1) *Duppi* ${}^{m\ ilu}$ *Bêl-uballit(it)* (2) *a-na* ^{am} *šangi* NUN-KIB-KI (3) *aḫi-ia Bêl u* ^{ilu} *Nabû šu-lum u balati* (4) *ša aḫi-ia liḳ-bu-u* (5) ^{m} *Šul-lu-ma-a ša a-na* (6) *pa-ni bêli-ia il-li-ka* (7) *ina pani bêli-ia la e-ka-aš-ši* (8) *ka-pa-a-di ḫarrana* ^{II} *a-na* (9) *šepâ* ^{II}*-šu šu-kun* (10) *dul-lu-šu a-ka-[an-na]* (11) *i-ba-aš-ši* (12) *pap-pa-aš-su šu* . . . (13) *la tu-ša-par-ka* (14) *a-ga-a lu-ta-bat-ka* (15) *ḫarrana* ^{II} *a-na šepâ* ^{II}*-šu* Rev.. (16) *bêl li-iš-ku-nu* (17) *ḫuraṣi ša tu-še-bi-lu* (18) *ša-pi-il a-mur* (?) (19) *dul-lu ša nam-* . . . (20) *e-te-pu-uš-su* (21) *a-mur* ^{m}*Kal-ba-a* (22) *al-tap-rak-ka* (23) *ḫuraṣi ina eli liš-kun* (24) *u I ma-na ḫuraṣi* (25) *sa-a-mu* (26) *šu-bi-lu.*

[No. 56,277]

No **53**—Obv: (1) *Duppi* ${}^{m\ ilu}$ *Bêl-uballit(it)* (2) *a-na* ^{am} *šangi Sip-par* ^{ki} (3) *bêli-ia ûmu(mu)-us-su* (4) ^{ilu}*Bêl u* ^{ilu}*Nabû a-na balaṭ napšâtim(tim)* (5) *tu-[ub] lib-bi tu-ub šeri* (6) *ar-[kat ûmi] u bu-un-nu pa-ni* (7) *ša šarri ḫa-du-tu ša it-ti* (8) *bêli-ia u-sal-la ina ṣilli ša ili* (9) *dul-lu ša bêli-ia in-ni-ip-šu* (10) ^{am} *sabi* ^{pl} *a-na ṣa-pi-tum* (11) *ki-i uš-ri-du* (12) *iḳ-kab-bu-u-um-ma* (13) . . *ni* (?) *i-bi* (?)*-na* . . . (14) . . *u mas-tig* (?) . . (15) [*ul* (?)*-te* (?)]*-bi-la* (16) . *ri-ša* (Remainder of obv. and top of rev broken off) Rev · (17) [${}^{m\ ilu}$ *Nabû* ?]*-na'id* (?) *šarri* . . . (18) . . . (19) *bêl lu-še-bi-lam-ma* (20) *a-na* ^{m} *Ni-din-[tum]* (21) ^{am} *ardu* . . *-din* (22) *ina la mu-zib-tum* (23) *ina muḫ-ḫi dul-lu ul i-di-na.*

[No 56,021.]

No **54**—Obv. · (1) *Duppi* ${}^{m\ ilu}$ *Bêl-uballit(it)* (2) *a-na* ^{am}*šangi Sip-par* ^{ki} (3) *aḫi-ia* ^{ilu}*Nabû u* ^{ilu}*Marduk* (4) [*a*]*-na aḫi-ia lik-ru-bu* (5) *saluppi-'* (6) *ša bêl iḳ-ba-a* (7) *a-di eli en-na* (8) *a-na* ^{am}*gal-la* (9) *bêl ul id-din* (10) *en-na-'*

No. **52**.—Letter from Bêl-uballiṭ unto the Priest of Sippar, my brother. May Bêl and Nabû grant peace and life unto my brother.

Šullumâ (who comes into my lord's presence) before my lord doth not . . . Speedily set him on his road, for there is work here for him. Do not cease giving his pay for the . . . May this arrangement be pleasing unto thee; let my lord set him on his road.

The gold which thou didst send is too little. Lo, I am doing the work on the . . . Lo, I am sending Kalbâ unto thee to settle the matter of the gold in this case, and do thou send a mana's weight of "red" gold.

No. **53**.—Letter from Bêl-uballiṭ to the Priest of Sippar, my lord. Daily I pray unto Bêl and Nabû for the life, happiness, health, long days, and that the King's countenance may be favourable unto my lord.

The commission of my lord is progressing under the favour of heaven. After I had despatched the workmen for the *ṣapitu* they spake thus . . . . . . Let my lord send and give (it) unto Nidintum, the servant of . . . , for he hath not given it unremittingly for the work.

No. **54**.—Letter from Bêl-uballiṭ unto the Priest of Sippar, my brother. May Nabû and Marduk bless my brother.

Is it not true that up to this present time my lord hath not given the slave the datés as he promised?

(11) *šat-ti.* REV.: (12) *ta-at-ta-rak* (13) *en-na saluppi* (14) *a-na* ^{am}*gal-la* (15) *bêl lid-din bi-riš* (16) *lid-di u te-e-me* (17) *ša bêli-ia lu-uš-me* (18) *kap-du . . . -gi* (?)-' (19) *bêl lu-še-*[*bi-la*] (20) *dul-la . . .* (21) *ba-ti* (?)-[*il* ?].

[No. 74,881]

NO. **55**.—OBV.: (1) *Duppi* $^{m\ ilu}$*Bêl-uballit*(*iṭ*) *a-na* (2) ^{m}*Iddina-*[^{ilu} *Marduk*] *aḫi-ia* (3) ^{ilu} *Bêl* ^{ilu} *Nabû šu-lum balaṭi ša aḫi-*[*ia*] (4) *lik-bu-u a-mur* ^{m} *Ri-*[*mut-ili*] (5) *a-na pa-ni-ka* (6) *al-tap-par it-ti-*[*šu*] (7) *a-lik-ma maḫiri* (8) *a-na ḫu-ṣab* (?) . . . *si* (?) . . . (9) . . . (10) *lu-u-ri-du a-na* (11) *eli di-li- . . .* REV.: (12) [*ma*]*ḫiri a-na* (13) [^{m} *Ri*]*-mut-ili* (14) . . . *u bu* . . .

[No. 64,812.]

NO **56**.—OBV.: (1) *Duppi* $^{m\ ilu}$*Bêl-iddin a-na* (2) ^{m} *Mu-še-zib-*^{ilu}*Marduk aḫi-ia* (3) ^{ilu} *Bêl u* ^{ilu}*Nabû šu-lum balaṭi* (4) *ša aḫi-ia lik-bu-u* (5) ^{am}ŠU-ḪA^{pl}*-ku-nu a-gan-na-ku* (6) *a-na bit* ^{m} *Mu-še-zib-* ^{ilu}*Bêl* (7) ^{am}*sabi katâ*^{II}*-ia ki-i* (8) *ir-ru-bu-' u* ^{subatu}*mu-sip-pi-e-ti* (9) *di* (?)*-i-na ul-tu* (10) *lib-bi it-ta- . . .* REV. (11) . . . *pur* . . . (12) . . . *ki-i* . . . *u-ta* (13) *a-na pa-ni-ka al-tap-par* (14) *a-šar* ^{subatu} *mu-ṣip-pi-e-ti* (15) *id-din-nu-' i-šam-ma* (16) *a-na Kal-ba-a* (17) ^{am}*apil-šip-ri-ia i-din* (18) *ia-a-nu-um-mu* (19) *a-šar id-din* . . . (20) *a-na e-* . . . (21) . . . *ši.*

[No. 56,005.]

NO. **57**.—OBV.: (1) *Duppi* $^{m\ ilu}$ *Bêl-iddin* (2) *a-na* $^{m\ ilu}$*Nabû-id-dan-na* (3) *abi-ia* ^{ilu}*Bêl* ^{ilu}*Nabû u* ^{ilu} IB (4) *šu-lum u balati ša abi-ia* (5) *lik bu-u* ^{am} *išparu bir-mu* (6) ^{am} *išpar iṣi ina*

Is it not a year that thou hast delayed? Now let my lord give the dates unto the slave—let him deliver them in plenty, and let me hear news of my lord. Speedily let my lord send . . . (for) the work [on the . . .] hath ceased.

No. **55**.—Letter from Bêl-uballiṭ unto Iddina-[Marduk], my brother. May Bêl (and) Nabû grant peace and life unto my brother.

Behold, I am sending thee Rimut-[ili]; go with [him] and [tell him?] the market rates for palm-logs (?) . . . let him come down. [Speak to?] Rimut-ili concerning the . . . of the market rates.

No. **56**.—Letter from Bêl-iddin unto Mušezib-Marduk, my brother. May Bêl and Nabû grant peace and life unto my brother.

When your fishermen yonder had entered the house of Mušezib-Bêl, my servant, they took therefrom some turbans (?).[1] Judgment shall be given (?) thereon (in the courts) . . .

. . . I am sending thee. Find out where they have put the turbans (?) and give (them) to Kalbâ, my messenger, for they are not here. Where they put (them) . . .

No. **57**.—Letter from Bêl-iddin unto Nabû-iddanna, my father. May Bêl, Nabû, and Ib grant peace and life unto my father.

[1] *Musippêti*, perhaps to be referred to the same root as the Chald. **מצנפת**.

pani ia (7) *ia-a-nu al-la* (8) *ûmu V* ^{am} *naggaru* (9) *ina pani-ia ia-a-nu* (10) *ûmu XVIII* ^{kam} ^{am} *sabi* ^{pl} (11) *ina muḫ-ḫi du-* . . . Rev.: (12) *i-nam-din-nu* (13) . . . *ûmu XVIII* ^{kam} (14) *ûmu XX* ^{am} *sabi* ^{pl} (15) *id-dan-na um-ma* (16) *kurummati in-na-aš-šu-nu-tu* (17) *ia a-nu* (18) *man-ma it-ti-ia* (19) *ul i-lam-ma-'* (20) *te-e-mu ša bêli-ia* (21) *lu-uš-me.* (Left-hand edge) (22) *ia-a-nu u dul-lu* (23) *i-baṭ-ṭi-il.*

[No 47,397.]

No **58**—Obv · (1) *Duppi* $^{m\,ilu}$*Bêl-iddin a-na* (2) ^{am}*šangi* UD-KIB-NUN-KI (3) *aḫi-ia* ^{ilu} *Nabû u* ^{ilu} *Marduk* (4) *a-na aḫi-ia lik-ru-bu* (5) ^{am} ŠA-TAM *ša* E-ZI-DA (6) *a-na eli imera-a-'* (7) *iš-tap-ri um-ma* (8) *kaspi a-na eli* (9) *it-tal-ku ki-i* (10) *pani-ka maḫ-ri* (11) *at-ta bêl* (12) *li-bu-uk-šu.* Rev.: (13) *u ki-i a-a-nu-u* (14) *a-di la a-na gi-iz-zu* (15) *al-la-ku šup-ra-aš* (16) *u a-na-ku ki-i a-mu-ru* (17) *ra-bi u pani-ia* (18) *ul ma-ḫi-ir a-mur* (19) ^{m} *Suka-a-a a-na pani aḫi-ia* (20) *al-tap-ri imeri* (21) *u u-di-e imeri* (22) *ina ḳatâ* ^{II}*-šu bêl* (23) *liš-pu-ru.*

[No. 84,932]

No **59**—Obv.: (1) *Duppi* $^{m\,ilu}$ *Bêl-bul-liṭ-su* (2) *a-na* ^{m} *Ḫa-aš-da-a-a* (3) *bêli-ia* ^{ilu} *Marduk u* (4) ^{ilu} *Sar-pa-ni-tum šu-lum* (5) *u ba-la-ṭu ša bêli-ia* (6) *lik-bu-u* [*šu*]*-lum* (7) *a-na* E-[SAG]-ILA (8) *u* TIN-TIR-[KI] *šu-lum* (9) *a-na* . . . *-ri-in-du* (10) *a-*[*na eli ša*] *ta-ḳab-bi* (11) [*um-ma*] . . . *kaspi ša bêl iš-pu-ru* (12) . . . [*a*]*-gan-na* (13) . . . *-an-ḫi dan - nu* (14) . . *kaspi* (15) . . *iš.* Rev.: (16) [*a*]*-na muḫ-ḫi dib-bi* (17) *ša bêl iš-pu-ru* (18) *dib-bi a-na la* (19) *ša maḫ-ru-u* (20) *ul iš-nu-u u* (21) ^{am} *ṣabi* ^{pl} *gab-bi* (22) *ul-tu Šu-ša-an* ^{ki} (23) *i-tir-bu-ni* (24) *mimma*(*ma*) *a-na ša*

I have no weaver of coloured stuffs or basket-weaver here with me, nor for five days have I had a carpenter. Eighteen days they paid the workmen for the . . . (Now?) it is the eighteenth day; for twenty days the workmen he must pay, and deliver to them their sustenance, (or) there will be none (and) no one will join with me. Let me hear news of my lord, for there is no work going on here, it has ceased.

No. **58.**—Letter from Bêl-iddin unto the Priest of Sippar, my brother. May Nabû and Marduk bless my brother.

The *šatam* of the temple Ezida hath sent for an ass, saying: "The money is coming for it, so as soon as it is convenient to thee, do thou, my lord, send it; and if there should be none until the sheep-shearing, send it (by) a traveller." And when I saw (this) it was too much (to ask) and it was not convenient. Wherefore I send Sukâ unto my brother, that he may send an ass and its trappings by his hand.

No. **59.**—Letter from Bêl-bulliṭsu unto Ḫašdâ, my lord. May Marduk and Ṣarpanitum grant peace and life unto my lord. Peace upon E-Sagila and Babylon; peace upon . . . *rindu*.

Concerning that which thou didst say, that "the money which my lord hath sent . . . ."

Concerning the matter which my lord sent, nothing has changed from the former conditions. All the workmen have come back from Susa, (and) there is

la taš-mu-u (25) *dıb-bi ul ıš-nu-u* (26) *kap-du ṭe-e-me* (27) *ša bêli-ia ni-ıš-me* (28) *a-mur ûmu(mu)-us-su* (29) ^{ilu}*Bêl u* ^{ilu} *Bêlti-ıa* (30) *a-na ba-la-ṭi-ka* (31) *u-ṣal-la.*
[No. 79,582.]

No. 60 — OBV.: (1) *Duppi* $^{m\,ilu}$*Bêl-zıra-ıbni* (2) *a-na* ^{am}*šangi* UD-KIB-NUN-KI (3) *abi-ia* ^{ilu}*Bêl u* ^{ilu} *Nabû* (4) *šu-lum u balati ša abi-ia* (5) *lık-bu-u* [^{m}*Arad* (?)] ^{ilu}*Gu-la* (6) *ša a-na* . . . (7) *aš-pur-ra X šikli kaspı* (8) *ina kurummatı-šu in-na-aš-šu* (9) *ki-sa-ti ul-tu ra-man-ni-šu* (10) *u-ša-ak-ka-lu* (11) *kap-du ḫarrâna* ^{II} *a-na* (12) *šepâ* $^{II\,pl}$ *šu šu-kun* (13) *te-ik-ti* REV.: (14) *ina lib-bı bêlı-ia* (15) *la ı-šak-kan* (16) ^{imeru} *sısi* ^{pl} (17) *ša šarri muš-šu-ru.*
[No 64,184 + 84,966.]

No. 61 — OBV.: (1) *Duppı* $^{m\,ilu}$*Bêl-zıra-ıbnı* (2) *a-na* ^{am}*šangı* UD-KIB-NUN-KI (3) *abi-ia* ^{ilu}*Bêl u* ^{ilu} *Nabû* (4) *šu-lum u balatı ša abı-ıa* (5) *lık-bu-u a-mur* (6) $^{m\,ilu}$*Nabû-si-lım u* (7) ^{m}*Su-ḳa-a-a a-na* (8) *pa-nı abı-ıa al-tap-rak* (9) [*ıl?*]-*li-ku bîtı pa-nı-e* (10) . . . -*u* (?). (Remainder of obv. and top of rev. broken off) REV : (11) . . . -*aš-šu-nu-tu* (12) . . . -*ka* (13) *u-ṣur* (?) *a-na bâbi u* (14) *u bıt-an-nu a-šaṭ-ru* (15) *kap-du ḫarrana* ^{II} *a-na šepi-šu-nu* (16) *šu-ku-un.*
[No. 79,583]

No. 62. — OBV.: (1) *Duppi* $^{m\,ilu}$*Bêl-zira-ıbni* (2) *a - na* $^{m\,ilu}$*Šamšu-ba-ni* (3) *aḫı-ıa* ^{ilu}*Bêl u* ^{ilu}*Nabû* (4) *šu-lum u balatı ša aḫi - ıa* (5) *lık - bu - u mi - na - a* (6) $^{m\,ilu}$*Bêl - da - a - nu* (7) *u* $^{m\,ilu}$*Šamšu-aḫı-ıa* (8) *ak-ka-ba-u ına pani-ia* (9) *en-na al-tap-par.* REV.: (10) *kap-du* (11) *ina ıs-ka-a-ta* (12) *ı-di-ši-ma* (13) *a-na* $^{m\,ilu}$*Nabû-lı* (?)- . . . (14) *ı-ḳa* (?)-*aš* (?)-*šu* (?) - *tu - šu - nu* (15) . . . (16) ^{ilu}*Nabû* [*u* ^{ilu}*Marduk lu*]-*ı-di* (17) *kı-*[*i* . . .]-*i* (18) *ıa-*[*a-nu*] (19) *a-na* ^{am}*mar šarrı* (20) *a-na muḫ-ḫi-ka* (21) *a-ḳa-bu-u.*
[No. 60,766]

nothing in addition to that which thou hast heard; nothing has changed. Let us speedily hear news of my lord; lo, I pray daily unto Bêl and Bêlit for thy life.

No. **60**.—Letter from Bêl-zira-ibni unto the Priest of Sippar, my father. May Bêl and Nabû grant peace and life unto my father.

Arad-Gula, whom I sent unto . . . I delivered to him ten shekels of silver for his sustenance. I have made him eat his own vegetables (?).[1] Speedily set him on his way, that my lord may not bring about a cessation (of the work). The King's horses are left behind.

No. **61**.—Letter from Bêl-zira-ibni unto the Priest of Sippar, my father. May Bêl and Nabû grant peace and life unto my father.

Behold, I am sending Nabû-silim and Sukâ unto the presence of my father. They have started. The former house . . . for the gate and palace I have written. Speedily set them on their way.

No. **62**.—Letter from Bêl-zira-ibni unto Šamaš-bani, my brother. May Bêl and Nabû grant peace and life unto my brother.

What are Bêl-dânu and Šamaš-aḫia saying against me? Now I send; speedily put them in ward and unto Nabû-li (?) . . . them . . . By Nabû [and Marduk], if this (?) is not done I will speak to the King's son about thee.

[1] *Kisati* occurs in the phrase *šammu kisat ṣiri* as an equivalent of *šammu zir ḳulḳullâna*: *Cuneiform Texts*, xiv, pl. 18, rev., cols. i–ii, l. 18.

No. **63**—Obv: (1) *Duppı* [m]*Ba-lat-su* (2) *a-na* [am]TIL-LA-GID-DA (3) *bêlı-šu* [ilu]*Šamšu u* [ilu]*Bu-ne-ne* (4) *šu-lum u balatı ša bêlı-ıa* (5) *lık-bu-u mâr šarri* (6) *ša a-na bîtı ıl-te-par-ku* (7) *šı-zıb il-ta-ti* (8) *ına su-li-e-šu ša* [ilu]*Šamšu* (9) *pa-ni-šu ba-nu-u* (10) *ki-i u-sat-tı-ru* (11) *ına pani-šu at-ta-zız* (12) *nı-sip ša ḫı-me-tı* (13) *ša u-kır-rı-ba-aš* (14) *a-na mâr* [am]*ka-ṣır* (15) *ul-te-bı-li.* Rev: (16) *a-na mâr* [am]*ša-kın* (17) *ša ıl-lı-ku* (18) *ıl-tar um-ma* (19) *bîti ba-nı-i* [am]*ša-kın* (20) *ık-ta-ba-aš-šu* (21) *um-ma bîtu ba-nu* (22) *pa-ni ša mâr* [am]*ka-ṣır* (23) *ina muḫ-ḫı ib-ta-nu u* (24) *ešten(en) dan-nu ša maḫ-rat* (25) *ešten(en) dan-nu ša pa-ṣı-e* (26) *ešten(en)* . . . 54 *ḳa kurummatı* (27) *102 ḳa* ŠE-BAR *ul-te-rı-bı-šu* (28) *ina šı-ın-dı-ka* (29) *ın-da-ḫar-an-nı* (30) *u pa-ni-šu* (31) *ba-nu-u* (Left-hand edge) (32) *mâr* [am]*ka-ṣır il-tar-par-ra-šu um-ma* (33) *kurummatı la ta-ak-ta a-dı elı ša ana pani-ka* (34) *al-la-ku.* (Between obv. and rev) (35) *maḫıra šı-pir-tum* (36) *ša bêlı-ıa* (37) *lu-uš-mu.*

[No 50,294]

No **64**—Obv: (1) *Ardı-ka* [m]*Balat-su a-na* (2) [am]*šangı Sıp-par bêlı-šu* (3) *lu-u šu-lum a-na bêli-ia* (4) [ilu]*Nabû u* [ilu]*Marduk a-na bêlı-ia* (5) *lık-ru-bu a-mur ILX immerı* (6) *ša* [m]*Il-ta-la* [am]*rab-ešrıtu(tu)* (7) *XXVII ımmerı ša* [am]*ešrıtu(tu) ša* [ilu]*A-a* (8) *napḫarıš LXXXVII ımmeri ûmu I* [kam] (9) *ša* [arḫu] . . . *bêli-ıa.* (Remainder of obv. and top of rev. broken off.) Rev: (10) *VI* [m] . . . [am] . . .

No. **63**.—Letter from Balaṭsu to the Governor, his lord. May Šamaš and Bunene grant peace and life to my lord.

The King's son (who sent thee unto the house) desireth some goat's (?)[1] milk for prayers to Šamaš. He was willing that I should write, (as) I stand in his presence (i.e. am his secretary). I have sent a *nisip* of cream, which I have presented to him, to the son of the guard. He wrote unto the son of the prefect (who has arrived) and spoke concerning the built house of the prefect, thus: "The son of the guard desireth the built house; he will send into it one cask of *maḫrat*, one cask of *paṣû* beer, one . . . fifty-four *ḳa* of flour, one hundred and two *ka* of corn; in thy mark he has received it from me, and he is agreeable." The son of the guard sent to him thus: "Cease not the sustenance until I come unto thee."

Let me have an answer from my lord.

No. **64**.—Thy servant Balaṭsu unto the Priest of Sippar, his lord. May there be peace upon my lord; may Nabû and Marduk bless my lord.

Lo, sixty sheep belonging to Iltala, the Chief Priest.

Twenty-seven sheep belonging to the Priest of Âa.

Total, eighty-seven sheep on the first day of the month . . . my lord . . .

Six belonging to . . . the officer of . . .

[1] *Illati*, from a singular *iltu*, perhaps a feminine of *âlu*, "ram."

(11) *V*[m] [*ša* [m]*Arad*] - [ilu]*Gu-la* (12) *II*(?) . . . [ilu]*Nabû* (13) . . . [[m]] *Bêli-šu-nu* (14) *IV* [m ilu]*Bêl-aḫi*[pl]*-eriba* (15) *II* [m]*Ki-ra-am-ma* (16) *napḫariš I LX ša* [m]*Il-ta-la-a* (17) *VIII immeri* [m ilu]*Bu-ne-ne-ibni* (18) *V* [m]*Ad-ra-a* (19) *V* [m ilu]*Nabû-rim-an-ni* (20) *V* [m ilu]*Nabû-zira-ibni.* (Left-hand edge) (21) [. . .]-[ilu]*A-a napḫariš XXVII immeri ša* [am]*rab-ešritu(tu)* (22) *ša* [ilu]*A-a.*

[No 50,524]

No. **65**—Obv.: (1) *Duppi* [m ilu]*Bêl-ki-ṣir* (2) *a-na* [am]*šangi Sip-par*[ki] (3) *bêli-ia ûmu(mu)-us-su* (4) [ilu]*Bêl u* [ilu]*Nabû a-na balat napšâti*[pl] (5) *a-ra-ku ûmu(mu)* (6) *ṭu-ub lib-bi ṭu-ub šeri* (7) *a-na bêli-ia* (8) *u-ṣal-la ul-tu eli* (9) *ša bel iš-pur-ra-an-ni* (10) *di-ra-a-ta gab-bi.* (Remainder of obv. and top of rev. broken off.) Rev.: (11) *ina lib-bi a-* . . . (12) *ul id-din* (13) *a-mur a-na-ku* (14) *gu-li-in-ni* (15) *um-ma ṭi-pi* (16) *it-ti mu-ša-ni-tum* (17) *ti-pi* [am]*ir-ri-še-e* (18) *gab-bi un-da-aš-šir-'* (19) *u iḫ-te-liḳ-'.*

[No 64,857]

No. **66**.—Obv.: (1) *Duppi* [m ilu]*Bêl-ki-ṣir* (2) *a-na* [m]*La-ba-a-ši* (3) *bêli-ia ûmu(mu)-us-su* (4) [ilu]*Bêl u* [ilu]*Nabû a-na ba-la-tu* (5) *napšâtim(tim)*[pl] *ša bêli-ia* (6) *u-ṣal-la* [m]*Mu-še-zib-*[ilu]*Bêl* (7) *ma-'-diš pir-ki it-ti-ia* (8) *it-te-dib-bu-ub* (9) *mimmu(mu)*

---

[1] It is possible to compare the Aramaic *ṭ'phaḥ*, "extend," "spread," with *tipi*.

[2] On *mušanitum*, see Peiser, *Bab. Vertr*, p. 305, and Jastrow, *Hebr.*, x, 193, and compare the Chaldee משׁנית "rock wall."

Five belonging to [Arad ?]-gula.
Two (?) [belonging to . . .]-Nabû.
Forty-one (?) [belonging to] Bêli-šunu.
Four belonging to Bêl-aḫi-iriba.
Two belonging to Kiramma.
Total, sixty belonging to Iltalâ.
Eight sheep belonging to Bunene-ibni.
Five belonging to Adrâ.
Five belonging to Nabû-rimanni.
Five belonging to Nabû-zira-ibni.
[Four belonging to . . .]-Âa.
Total, twenty-seven belonging to the Chief Priest of Âa.

No. **65**.—Letter from Bêl-Kiṣir unto the Priest of Sippar, my lord. Daily I pray unto Bêl and Nabû for the life, long days, happiness, and health of my lord.

Ever since my lord sent unto me, all the . . . thereto . . . he hath not given. Lo, order me thus: "Go on (?), go on (?)[1] with the embankment."[2] If I leave all the gardeners, they will run away.

No. **66**.—Letter from Bêl-Kisir unto Labâši, my lord. Daily I pray unto Bêl and Nabû for the life of my lord.

Mušezib-Bêl has been threatening[3] me greatly, and will not cease (?).

[3] *Pirki dabâbu*. This phrase occurs also in No. 210. *Pirku* might be referred to *parâku*, "do violence."—*Inadid*. For *nadâdu* cf. Heb. נָדַד "wander, retreat," but the passage is doubtful.

ka-la-mu (10) ul i-na-di-id (11) a-mur ^{m} Mu-še-zib-^{ilu} Bêl ina E^{ki} (12) it-ti-šu bêl li-dib-bu-ub (13) ši-pir-ta-šu a-na pa-ni (14) $^{m\,ilu}$ Nabû-id-dan-nu (15) u ^{m} [Su (?)]-la-a (16) bêl li-iš-ša-am-ma. Rev.. (17) bêl (?) lu-še-bu-lu (18) a-na ^{m} Šul-lu-u-a (19) aḫi-ia ^{ilu} Bêl u ^{ilu} Nabû (20) . . . aḫi-ia (21) . . . (22) ši-pir-tum siḫirtum (23) ina ḳatâ^{II} ^{m} Šad-din-nu ul-te-bi-lu (24) a-na $^{m\,ilu}$ Nabû-ad-dan-nu i-din (25) gab-ru-u ši-pir-tum (26) a-ki-i siḫirtum i-ša-am-ma (27) lu-še-bu-lu eštenit(it) ši-pir-tum (28) ša ^{am} daiani i-ša-am-ma (29) a-na pa-ni ^{m} Am-bu-lu (30) ^{am} TU-u ša bît-^{ilu} Nergal (31) ša muḫ-ḫi u-il-tim-ma (?) (32) [tu]-pat-ta ina pa-ni-šu (33) . . . -dak-ka i-ša-am-ma (34) šu-bu-lu

No. **67**.—Obv: (1) Duppi $^{m\,ilu}$ Bêl-ri-man-ni (2) a-na ^{am} ki-i-pi aḫi-ia (3) lu-u šu-lum a-na (4) aḫi-ia ^{ilu} Bêl u ^{ilu} Nabû (5) šu-lum ša (6) aḫi-ia [liḳ-bu-u]. (Remainder lost.)

[No. 51,200]

No **68**—Obv. (1) Duppi $^{m\,ilu}$ Bêl-šarri-uṣur (2) a-na ^{m} Mu-še-zib-^{ilu} Marduk ilâni^{pl} (3) šu-lum-ka liḳ-bu-[u] (4) a-mur ^{m} Bêli-šu-nu u ^{m} . . . (5) ^{am} MAS-MAS^{pl} a-na [eli-ka] (6) al-tap-par ḫi-ši-[iḫ-ti] (7) ša dul-lu ša ni-[bi-ḫu ša] (8) ^{ilu} Bu-ne-[ne] . . . (Remainder of obv and top of rev. broken off) Rev: (9) ul-te-[bi-la] . . . (10) si-ip-pi . . . (11) gab-bi lu . . . [No. 73,469]

No. **69**—Obv.: (1) Duppi $^{m\,ilu}$ Bêl-ibni . . . (2) a-na $^{m\,ilu}$ Nabû- . . . (3) $^{m\,ilu}$ Bêl-apli-iddin ^{m} Ki-i-[^{ilu} Nabû] (4) u $^{m\,ilu}$ Šamšu-eriba aḫi^{pl}-e-a (5) ^{ilu} Bêl u ^{ilu} Nabû šu-lum u balati (6) ša aḫi^{pl}-e-a lik-bu-u (7) ina eli ka-ba-as (8) ša ^{šipâtu} ra-am-mu (9) la ta-sil-la-' (10) ^{šipâtu} ra-am-mu a-na (11) ^{isu} narkabti ša ^{ilu} Šamši (12) dib-bi ša šad-da-giš (13) šipâti us-sa-an-na (14) ša ina lib-bi ta-kan . . (15) ša ^{ilu} Šamši . . . (16) . . . ša ^{m} . . (Remainder of obv. and top of rev. broken off, about four

Behold, Mušezib-Bêl is in Babylon—let my lord speak with him. Let my lord take his letter before Nabû-iddannu and Su(?)lâ, and send it.

Unto Šullûa, my brother, may Bêl and Nabû [grant peace and life unto] my brother . . . I am sending a short letter by the hand of Šaddinnu; give it unto Nabû-iddannu. Obtain an answer, even although it be only a short one, and let him bring it. Obtain one letter from the Judge and open it in the presence of Ambulu, the treasurer (?) of the Temple of Nabû, who is in charge of the debt-accounts. Obtain thy . . . and send it (to me).

No. **67**.—Letter from Bêl-rimanni unto the Warden, my brother. May there be peace upon my brother; may Bêl and Nabû [grant] peace [unto my brother] . . .

No. **68**.—Letter from Bêl-šarri-uṣur unto Mušezib-Marduk. May the gods grant thee peace.

Lo, I am sending unto [thy presence] Bêlišunu and . . . the soothsayers; whatever thou desirest for the work on the robes of Bunene [tell them] . . .

No. **69**.—Letter from Bêl-ibni unto Nabû- . . . Bêl-apli-iddin, Kî-[Nabû], and Šamaš-eriba, my brothers. May Bêl and Nabû grant peace and life unto my brothers.

Concerning the fulling of the *rammu*-wool, be not neglectful; the *rammu*-wool is for the chariot of Šamaš . . . the matter which was in times past. I have changed the wool . . .

lines) REV.: (17) *u* . . . (18) *a-ra-tum* (?) . . . (19) ^{isu} *narkabti ša* ^{ilu} *Samši* . . . (20) *šu-up-ra-'* (21) *la ta-sil-la-'* (22) *ši-pir-ta-[ka] lu-uš-mu* (23) *u* . . *ši* . . . (24) *ša šad-da-giš* . . . *-il* (25) *ša al-tap-par it-ti* (26) *re'i atudi ša* ^{ilu} *Šamši* (27) *ta-al-lak* (?). [No. 60,102.]

No **70**.—OBV.: (1) *Duppi* $^{m\ ilu}$ *Bêl-uballit(it)* (2) *a-na* $^{m\ ilu}$ *Bêl-etir aḫi-ia* (3) *ilâni*^{pl} *šulum-ka liḳ-bu-u* (4) *en-na a-mur* ^{m} *Ba-la-ṭu* (5) *ul-te-bi-ka* (6) *ki-i immeri* . . . (7) *kaspa*$^{a\ an}$ ^{m} *Ba-la-[ti]* 8) *i-din-' immeri* (?) (9) *šu* (?)*-bi-lu* . . . (Remainder of obv. and top of rev. broken off.) REV.: (10) *ina lib-bi immeri* . . . (11) *ša a-na bît u-ru-[u]* (12) *ba-nu-u* (13) *šu-bi-lu*. [No 47,627.]

No. **71** —OBV.: (1) . . . (2) *a-na* ^{am} *re'i* . . (3) ^{ilu} *Bêl* ^{ilu} *Nabû* ^{ilu} *Sin u* ^{ilu} *[Šamšu]* (4) *šu-lum balaṭi arak ûmi*^{pl} (5) *ša abi-ia liḳ-bu-u* (6) *ša bêl iš-pu-[ru]* (7) *um-ma šu-pur-am-ma* (8) *kaspi lu-še-bi-lak-ka* (9) *a-mur* $^{m\ ilu}$ *Sin-na-din-aḫi* (10) *a-na bêli-ia al-tap-ra* (11) *V ma-na kaspi bêl* (12) *lu-še-bi-la* (13) *ki-i a-na ṣi-bu-ti-ia* (14) *al-tak-nu-uš* (15) *ina* ^{arḫu} *Araḫšamni* REV.: (16) *kaspi a-na bêli-ia* (17) *lu-še-ib-bi-la* (18) *u ia-a-nu-u* (19) *kaspi ul i-ša-an-ni* (20) *ina kunukki-šu* (21) *a-na bêli-ia* (22) *u-šib-bi-la*

[No. 26725.]

No **72**—OBV.: (1) *Duppi* ^{m} *Ba-ni-ia* (2) *a-na* ^{m} *Arad-*^{ilu} *Bêl* (3) *aḫi-ia* ^{ilu} *Bêl u* ^{ilu} *Nabû* (4) *šu-lum u balaṭi ša aḫi-ia* (5) *liḳ-bu-u a-mur* (6) ^{m} . . . *-ia* . . . (7) . . . *-lu a-na* (8) . . . (9) . . . (10) ^{am} *šangi* . . . (11) *a-na* ^{m} . . . (12) *ip-te-* . . . REV.: (13) . . . (14) . . . *ša* ^{ilu} *Šamši* . . . (15) GIŠ-BAR . . . (16) *ba-ab-tum* (17) *XV* ŠE-BAR *a-na* (18) ^{m} *Ardi-ia i-din a-di-i* (19) *maḫ-ri-tum* (20) *niš-mu-u* ^{am} *sabi*^{pl} (21) ^{m} *Ardi-ia a-na bîti* (22) *ki-me i-nam-din* (23) *[kap]-da harrana*^{II} (24) *[a-na] šepâ*^{II} *-šu* (25) *šu-kuṇ-* . . . [No. 75,895]

. . . send the . . . for the chariot of Šamaš; be not neglectful, but let me hear thy report . . . which I sent, with the shepherd of the goats of Šamaš thou shalt go.

No. **70**.—Letter from Bêl-uballiṭ unto Bêl-etir, my brother. May the gods grant thee peace.

Now see, I am sending thee Balaṭu; when [he shall give thee] a sheep, pay unto Balatu the money . . . . . . with regard to the matter . . . send the . . . which have been built for the stalls.

No. **71**.—[Letter from . . .] unto the Shepherd . . . May Bêl, Nabû, Sin, and [Šamaš] grant thee peace, life, and long days.

Of that which my lord did send, saying, "Send, that I may forward thee the money," see, I am sending Sin-nadin-aḫi unto my lord, that my lord may forward five mana of silver. If I can arrange as I should like, I will return the money to my lord in Marcheswan; but should it be impossible, then the money shall not change. By his seal will I send it to my lord.

No. **72**.—Letter from Bania unto Arad-Bêl, my brother. May Bêl and Nabû grant peace and life unto my brother . . .

Give fifteen (measures) of corn to Ardia. We have heard the former agreements; the workmen of Ardia shall give the flour (thereof) for (the) house. Speedily set him on his way.

NO. **73**—OBV : (1) *Duppi* ^{m}*Bur-šu-u a-na* ^{m} . . . (2) *abi-ia* ^{ilu}*Bêl u* ^{ilu}*Nabû šu-lum u balati* (3) *ša abi-ia likbu-u a-na-ku* (4) *ina ṭe-mi-ia u man-ma ul . . . -ka* (5) *ša it-ta-ḫu-u-a iz-zi-zu* (6) *u a-na* $^{m\,ilu}$*Za-ma-ma-iddin* $^{m\,ilu}$*Daîan-iddin* (7) ^{m}*Gu-ub-ba-a a-ḳab-bi-ma ša* ŠE-BAR (8) *ša ina pani-šu ul ib-ba-ku-nim-ma* (9) *ul i-nam-din-nu-nu en-na ši-pir-tum* (10) *a-na eli bêl liš-pu-ra-aš-šu-nu-tu* (11) *um-ma it-ta-ḫu* ^{m}*Bur-šu-u* (12) *iš-zi-za-ma ša man-ma ša* ŠE-BAR (13) *ina pani-šu ab-kan-nim ma a-na* (14) ^{m}*Bur-šu-u in-na-'* (15) [^{m}] ^{ilu}*Nabû-aḫi-šu u* ^{m}*Ri-mut* (16) *mârâni*^{pl} *ša* ^{m}*Etir-*^{ilu}*Marduk* REV : (17) *piš* (?)-*ki it-ti-ia* (?) . . . (18) *id-da-ab-bu-ub* . . . (19) *ul id-di-din-nu* . . . (20) *u mâr-šip-ri ki-i ša* ^{m}*Bar-zi-en-na* (21) *u ki-i ša* ^{am}*sukkalli bêl liš-ša-am-ma* (22) *a-na pani* ^{m}*Gu za-nu* ^{am}*pa-ḳu-du* (23) *u* ^{m}*Iddina-*^{ilu}*Nergal* ^{am}*u-pi-ṣa na-pa-ta* (24) *bêl lu-še-bi-lu a-mur kaspi te-ši* (25) ^{m}*Ša-*^{ilu}*Bêl-at-ta bêl liš-ši-ma a-na* (26) *eli ši-pir-tum u mar-šip-ri* (27) *bêl lid-din kap-du ṭe-e-mu* (28) *ša bêli-ia lu-uš-mu a-na êli* (29) *saluppi ša* $^{m\,ilu}$*Za-ma-ma-iddin* (30) *u* $^{m\,ilu}$*Daîan-iddin ša taḳ-ba-'* (31) *man-ma ul id-din-nu.*

[NO. 31,041]

NO. **74**. — OBV. : (1) *Duppi* ^{m}*Gu-za-nu a-na* ^{m}*Ši-ir-ku* (2) *aḫi-ia* ^{ilu}*Bêl u* ^{ilu}*Nabû šu-lum u balaṭi ša aḫi-ia* (3) *likbu-u ina* TIN-TIR-KI *ûmu(mu)-us-su* (4) *pi-ir-ṣa-tum it-ti-ia ta-dib-bu-ub* (5) *ta-ḳab-ba-a um-ma* ^{m}*Lib-lu-tu* (6) *mâr* ^{am}*si-si-i u* ^{am}*ur-li-šu*^{pl}*-ka* (7) *it-ti-ka ša-at-ru u* ^{am} *rab-dûri*

No. **73.**—Letter from Buršû unto . . . , my father. May Bêl and Nabû grant peace and life unto my father.

I am "in my own news" (*i.e.* know nothing of events elsewhere), and none hath told me (?) that my mill (?) hath stopped, and I spoke to Zamama-iddin, Daîan-iddin, and Gubbâ, but they have neither sent nor given the corn for it. Now let my lord write them a letter thereon, saying: "The mill (?) of Buršû hath stopped, and no one hath sent corn for it or delivered (it) to Buršû."

Nabû-aḫi-šû and Rimut, the sons of Eṭir-Marduk, have been devising wrong (?) against me; they have not given . . . ; but let my lord take a messenger, either Barzenna or my lord's servant, and send unto the presence of Guzanu, the magistrate, and Iddina-Nergàl, the . . . Let my lord send . . .

Behold, let my lord take money for the . . . of Ša-Bêl-atta and give it for a letter and messenger. Speedily let me hear news from my lord.

Concerning the dates for Zamama-iddin and Daîan-iddin, which thou hast stopped, no one has sent any.

No. **74.**—Letter from Guzanu unto Širku, my brother. May Bêl and Nabû grant peace and life unto my brother.

Thou dost perpetually tell lies about me in Babylon, for thou dost say that Libluṭu, the son of the horse-dealer, and thy . . . -men have written (for service) with thee; yet, when the commander of

(8) *ki-i il-li-ku ina ku-tal-li-ia* (9) ^{m}*Lib-lu-tu u mârâni*^{pl} ^{am}*si-si-i* (10) *gab-bi uḳ-ti-il um-ma at-tu-u-a* (11) *iš-šu-nu u* ^{am}*ur-li-šu*^{pl} *ša it-ti-ia* (12) *i-ta-bak at-ta pi-ia it-ti-šu* (13) *ša-ak-na-a-ta u ša-kas-su* (14) *a-na muḫ-ḫi-ia ina ḳatâ*^{II}*-šu kab-ta šu* (15) *en-na* ^{m}*Lib-lu-ṭu mâr* ^{am}*si-si i* (16) *ina ḳakḳad* ^{isu}*elippi*^{pl} *ša karani* . . . (17) *a-na* ^{alu}*Da-ni-pi-nu.* REV. · (18) *u* ^{am}*mârâni*^{pl} ^{am}*si-si-i* (19) ^{am}*ur-li-šu*^{pl} *u* ^{am}*sabi*^{pl} *mâr banûti*^{pl} (20) *ina katâ*^{II}*-šu la tu-maš-šir pi-ir-ki* (21) *a-na* ^{am}*rab-dûri it-ti* ^{am}*sabi*^{pl}*-ia* (22) *la i-dib-bu-ub at-ta a-na* (23) ^{m}*Ad-gal-a-na-mâr-E-sag-gil a-na muḫ-ḫi* (24) *ki-bi* ^{am}*sabi*^{pl} *ku-um* ^{am}*ṣabi*^{pl} *in-na-aš-šu* (25) *ba-ga-ni-'* ^{m}*Da-ri-ia-a-muš šarri* (26) *ina muḫ-ḫi-ka* ^{am}*sabi*^{pl} *ša ga-ar-du* (27) *ša te-e-me aš-ku-nu-ka pu-uṭ-ti-ir-šu-nu-tu* (28) *a-mur* ^{am}*maṣṣarti abulli*^{pl} ^{am}*mârâni*^{pl} *si-si-i* (29) *gab-bi ina pa-ni-ka u* ^{am}*ṣabi*^{pl} (30) *ša Bit-Da-ku-ru ša ina* TIN-TIR-KI *aš-bu-'* (31) *ina pa-ni-ka it-ti* ^{am}*sabi*^{pl} (32) *ša bît* ^{isu}*narkabti-ia la ta-dib-bu-ub*

[No 33,077]

NO **75**.—OBV (1) *Duppi* $^{m\,ilu}$*Gu-la-balat-su-iḳ-bi* (2) *a-na* ^{m}*Kur-ban-ni-*^{ilu}*Marduk* (3) *aḫi-ia* ^{ilu}*Nabû u* ^{ilu}*Marduk* (4) *a-na aḫi-ia lik-bu-ru* (5) ŠE-BAR *a-na* ŠE-KUL *ina pa-ni* (6) ^{m}*Šad-din-nu ia-a-nu* (7) *I gur* ŠE-BAR *bêl lid-din-šu* (8) *u u-il-tim ina muḫ-ḫi-šu* (9) *bêl li-'-il* (10) *ki-i na-ḳut-ti* (11) *a-na aḫi-ia.* REV (12) *al-tap-par* (13) *bêl la u-še-ti-iḳ-šu* (14) ŠE-BAR *a-na* ŠE-KUL (15) *bêl lid-din-šu.*

[No. 79,446.]

NO **76**—OBV. · (1) *Duppi* ^{m}*Gi-mil-lu a-na* (2) [^{m}*Arad*]-^{ilu}*Bêl aḫi-ia* (3) ^{ilu}*Bêl u* ^{ilu}*Nabû šu-lum u balaṭi* (4) *ša aḫi-ia lik-*[*bu-u*] (5) *a-mur* ^{am}*šangi* . . . *-ri* (?) (6) *ina* ^{alu}*Sip-par*[^{ki}] . . . (7) ^{am}[*rab*]*-ešritim*(*tim*) . . . *ma-'-du* (8) *ina* ^{alu} . *a-ka-* . . . *at* (9) *ta* . . . *a* . . (10) . . . *ud* . . (11) . (12) .

the fortress had come, Libluṭu and the sons of the horse-dealer all spake behind my back that they had accepted me, and he took the . . . -men that were with me. Thou art set as my mouth with him, and the punishment on me at his hands will be grievous. Now Libluṭu, the son of the horse-dealer, is in charge of the wine (?)-boats for the city Danipinu; leave thou not the sons of the horse-dealer, the . . . -men, or the better-class workmen with him, so that he shall not speak violently unto the commander of the fortress against my men. Do thou speak to Adgal-ana-mâr-Esaggil about it (that other) men be ṭaken instead of the men . . . Darius, the king, against thee; the men that are strong, about whom I commanded thee, disband them. Behold, the wardens of the city gates and the sons of the horse-dealer are all with thee, and the men of Bît-Dakkuri are with thee; meddle not with the men of my stables.

No. **75.**—Letter from Gula-balaṭsu-ikbi unto Kurbanni-Marduk, my brother. May Nabû and Marduk bless my brother.

Šaddinnu has no corn for sowing, so let my lord give him one *gur* of corn, and let my lord reckon it as a debt against him. Though I am importuning my brother, let not my lord forget it, but let my lord give him the corn for sowing.

No. **76.**—Letter from Gimillu unto [Arad]-Bêl, my brother. May Bêl and Nabû grant peace and life unto my brother.

(13) *man-nu* . . . (14) *ba-ab-ti.* REV.: (15) *ina alu* [erasure] (16) *i-te-nu-'* (17) ŠE-BAR *a-na ki-na-al-tum* (18) *at-ta-di-in* (19) ŠE-BAR (?) *mal*(?)*-ma-liš a-na* (20) [am] *ṣab-bi-zu mi-nam* (21) ŠE-BAR *ša* [m] *Šul-lu-ma-a* (22) *lu-u-ti-i-di a-na muḫ-ḫi* (23) [m] *Kal-ba-a* [m] *Kaš-ba-nu* (24) *u* [m] *Ḫa-aš-ša-da-a-a* (25) *šu-tur-ru* [am] *ku-um-mu* (26) *a-na muḫ-ḫi* [m] *Šul-lu-ma-a* (27) [*a*]*-na* [am] *šangi Sip-par* [ki] (28) . . . *ku kap-du* (29) . . . (Left-hand edge) (30) *a-mur* [am] *piḫatu* . . . *Sip-par* [ki] *iḳ-ta-ba-' um-ma* (31) ŠE-BAR[a an] *ša ina ši-pir-tum na-da-tum III C* . . .

[No. 75,764]

NO. **77**.—OBV.: (1) *Duppi* [m] *Gi-mil-lu* (2) *a-na* [m] *Arad-* [ilu] *Bêl* (3) *aḫi-ia* [ilu] *Nabû u* [ilu] *Marduk* (4) *a-na aḫi-ia lik-ru-bu* (5) *a-mur* [m] *Gi-mil-lu* (6) *a-na pa-ni-ka* (7) *it-tal-ku* [m] *Gi-mil-lu* (8) *it-ti-ka a-mur* (9) *at-ta ti-i-di* (10) *ki-i te-du-tum* (11) *ša* [m] *Gi-mil-lu* (12) *sa-ba-a-tum* REV: (13) *ina lib-bi-ia* . . . (14) *at-tu-u-a* (15) *ma-la al-la-*[*ka*] (16) [am] *niše* . . . *-pi-* . . .

[No. 75,919.]

NO. **78**—OBV.. (1) *Duppi* [m ilu] *Daîan-bêli-*[*usur*] (2) *a-na* [m] *Iddina-* [ilu] *Marduk bêli-ia* (3) *ûmu*(*mu*)*-us-su* [ilu] *Bêl u* [ilu] *Nabû* (4) *a-na balat napšâti* [pl] *ša bêli-ia* (5) *u-ṣal-la a-mur I CLXXX gur* (6) *saluppi a-na bêli-ia* (7) *ul-te-bi-lu ina lib-bi* (8) *XXVII ša* [m] *Na-din saluppi* (9) *ki-i u-kal-lim-an-ni a-ḫi* (10) *nu-ku-su u a-ḫi ša it-bu-ku* (11) *Bêl u* [ilu] *Nabû lu-u* (12) *i-du-u ki-i II gur* (13) *106 ḳa nu-ku-su u la ina lib-bi* (14) [*a*]*-mur 24 ka saluppi* (15) [*ina*] [iṣu] *elippi a na.* REV.: (16) [*pani bêli*]*-ia ul-te-bi-*[*la*] (17) *eš-ru-u ša šadi*(*i*) *ša* [ilu] *Nergal* (18) *pi-ḫa-tum bêl liš-ša-'* (19) *u ši-ba-šu ša bêl eḳli* [pl]

Behold, the priest . . . in Sippar . . . . . . in the city it hath been despatched. I am giving corn to Kinaltum (?); the corn (?) hath been apportioned in two equal parts to the *ṣabbizu*. (As for) the corn of Šullumâ, be thou advised (of this); write unto Kalbâ, Kašbanu, and Ḫaššadaî, the *kummu* (?)-officer, unto Šullumâ, to the Priest of Sippar . . . Behold, the Governor of Sippar hath spoken thus: "The corn which was mentioned in the letter, three hundred . . . ."

No. **77.**—Letter from Gimillu unto Arad-Bêl, my brother. May Nabû and Marduk bless my brother.

Behold, Gimillu is come into thy presence, look upon Gimillu before thee. Thou knowest that the *tedutum* of Gimillu is . . . in my own heart . . .

No. **78.**—Letter from Daîan-bêl-[uṣur] unto Iddina-Marduk, my lord. Daily I pray Bêl and Nabû for the life of my lord.

Behold, I am sending unto my lord one hundred and eighty *gur* of dates. Among them are twenty-seven (*gur*) belonging to Nadin. When he shewed me the dates, some had been cut off and the others were those which were sent. I call Bêl and Nabû to witness that two *gur*, a hundred and six *ḳa* had been cut off and were not amongst them. Behold, I am sending by boat unto my lord twenty-four *ḳa* of dates as the "tithe of the mountains" for Nergal. May my lord accept the exchange, and may my lord accept the tax-

(20) *lib-bu-u ša šad-da-giš* (21) *bêl liš-ša-' a-mur IX šiḳli kaspi* (22) *eš-ru-u ša* [ilu] *Nergal ša immeri* [pl] (23) *a-na ekurri nadnu(nu) ina muḫ-ḫi* (24) *bêl la i-sil-li kap-du* (25) *te-e-me ša bêli-ia ina ḳatâ* [II] (26) [m] *Še-el-li-bi lu-uš-me* (27) [am] *mar-šip-ri-ia u ši-pir-ta-a* (28) *bêl ul i-mur mi-na-a* (29) *XIII šiḳli kaspi a-na* [m] *Ḫa-ba-ṣi-[ri]* (30) *bêl id-din kap-du ši-kir-tum* (31) *ša pi-ḫa-tum a-na pani* [m] . . . (32) *apli-šu-ša* [m] *Ni-ḳu-du* . . . (33) *eš-ru-u bêl* . . .

[No. 30,763]

NO **79**—OBV (1) *Duppi* [m ilu] *Daîan-bêli-uṣur* (2) *a-na* [m] *Iddina-* [ilu] *Marduk* (3) *bêli-ia ûmu(mu)-us-su* (4) [ilu] *Bêl u* [ilu] *Nabû a-na balaṭ napišti(ti)* (5) *ša bêli u-ṣal-la* (6) [m ilu] *Ḳu-mur-pu-tu il-lik-[kam]-ma* (7) . . [[m]] [ilu] *Bêl aḫi-iddin* (8) . . *a* [subatu] *ṣa-pi-tum* (9) . . . *ul-tu* (10) . . . *ka-tum* (11) . . . (Remainder of obv. and top of rev broken off) REV. (12) . . (13) . . . (14) . . *-as-sa-ḫu* (15) . . . *ki-i* (16) . . . *nâri* [pl] (17) . . *al-la* (18) *[at]-tu-nu* [m] *Suḳâ-a-a* (19) *ki-i i-te-ku* (20) [am] *ṣabi* [pl] *a-na ši-kit-tum* (21) *ki-i iš-pu-ru* (22) *um-ma pu-gul* [1] ŠE-BAR-*šu ḫa-* . (23) *al-la ša iš-mu-u* (24) *um-ma* [m] *Iddina* [ilu] *Marduk* (25) *un-da-aš-šir*.

[No 41,595]

No **80**—OBV. (1) *Duppi* [m ilu] *Daîan-bêli-uṣur* (2) *a-na* [m] *Iddina-* [ilu] *Marduk* (3) *bêli-ia* [ilu] *Bêl u* [ilu] *Nabû* (4) *šu-lum u balaṭi ša bêli-ia* (5) *liḳ-bu-u a-mur* (6) *IV C gi-di-im ša ḫu-ṣa-bi e-lat ḫa-ru-ut-tum* (7) *IMVCLXX gid-dil* (8) *ša šûmi I gur 30 ḳa* (9) *gi-di-pi(?) ša šûmi* (10) *IV pi an-* . . . *-li* (11) *ina katâ* [II] [m] *Bêli-šu-nu* (12) *a-na bêli-ia*. REV.

[1] Possibly a scribal error for ŠE-KUL.

corn for my lord from the fields according to former arrangement. Behold, nine shekels of silver as the tithe for Nergal, for the sheep for the temple have been paid. Let my lord not be neglectful; speedily let me hear news of my lord by the hand of Šellibi. My lord did not see my messenger or my letter. Why hath my lord given thirteen shekels of silver to Ḫabaṣi[ru]? Speedily [send] the . . . for the exchange to . . . , the son of Niḳudu; the tithe of my lord . . .

No. **79.**—Letter from Daîan-bêl-uṣur unto Iddina-Marduk, my lord. Daily I pray unto Bêl and Nabû for the life of my lord.

Ḳumurputu (?) hath gone and [unto?] Bêl-aḫi-iddin . . .

. . . Sukâ after the workmen had departed unto the building, when he sent thus . . . according to what he heard that Iddina-Marduk hath left.

No. **80.**—Letter from Daîan-bêl-uṣur unto Iddina-Marduk, my lord. May Bêl and Nabû grant peace and life unto my lord.

Behold, I am sending by the hand of Belišunu unto my lord four hundred branches[2] of palms besides the cutting thereof, one thousand five hundred and seventy strings of garlic, one *gur*, thirty *ḳa* strings of garlic, four *pi* . . .

---

[2] *Gidim*, the Chaldee גִּדְמָא.

(13) *ul-te-bi-la* (14) ^{m}*Ku-sur-u-a* (15) *i-kab-ba-'* (16) *umma ši-pir-tum* (17) *ša* ^{am}*rab ṣip-ti* (18) *a-na-aš-ša-' a-na-ad-dan-ka* (19) *ša sip-ti ša bir-ri nâri*^{pl} (20) *ša man-ma it-ti-ka* (21) *la i-dib-bu-ub-'* (22) *a-na muḫ-ḫi bêli* (23) *la i-sil-li* (24) *ši-pir-tum* (25) *liš* (?)-*ša-aš-šu* (26) *ši-pir-tum a-na pani* (Left-hand edge) ^{am}*rab sip-tum ša ina pa-ni-ia liš-ša-'*.

[No. 30,751.]

No. **81**—Obv.: (1) *Duppi* $^{m\,ilu}$ *Daîan-bêli-usur* (2) *a-na* ^{m}*Iddina-*^{ilu}*Marduk* (3) *bêli-ia ûmu(mu)-us-su* (4) ^{ilu}*Bêl u* ^{ilu}*Nabû a-na balat* (5) *napšâti*^{pl} *ša bêli-ia* (6) *u-sal-la a-mur* (7) $^{m\,ilu}$*Nabû-šuma u-kin a-na* (8) TIN-TIR-KI *it-tal-lak* (9) *it-ti-šu be-ili* (10) *li-id-dib-dib šûmi-ia* (11) *maḫir mâti-ni li-pu-uš* (12) *šûmu-' lib-bu-u* (13) . . . *ina katâ*^{II}-*šu* (14) . . . *tu* (Remainder of obv. and top of rev broken off) Rev · (15) . . . *VI šikli kaspi* (16) . . . *li-id-da-aš* (17) *a-mur šûmu eš-še-tu* (18) *in-na-as-sa-ḫu-'* (19) *šûmi-ka bat-tuk* (20) *li-id-din u šûmu* (21) *a-ga-a a-na muḫ-ḫi* (22) *mi-ni-i ki-i la as-'* (23) *u* ^{isu} *elippi be-ili li-iš-par-ra-am-ma* (24) *šûmu saluppi* (25) *li-ul-lu-u kap-du* (26) *te-e-mu bêli-ia* (27) *ina muḫ-ḫi šûmi u saluppi* (28) *lu-uš-me*.

[No. 30,547]

No. **82**.—Obv.: (1) *Duppi* $^{m\,ilu}$ *Daîan-bêli-usur* (2) *a-na* $^{m\,ilu}$ *Marduk-na-ṣir-apli* (3) *bêli-ia ûmu(mu)-us-su* (4) ^{ilu} *Bêl u* ^{ilu} *Nabû a-na bul-lu-tu* (5) *napšâti*^{pl} *ša bêli-ia u-sal-la* (6) *ši-pir-tum ša* $^{m\,ilu}$ *Bêl-etir* (7) *ša a-na muḫ-ḫi immeri* (8) *a-na* ^{m} *Nûr-*^{ilu}*Šamši ta-aš-pur-ru* (9) *immeri ki-i id-din-nu* (10) *immeri ul at-tu-u-a* (11) *ul-te-pi-il* (12) *u id-dan-nu u* (13) *mârâni*^{pl}-*šu-nu it-ti* (14) . . . *šu-ṭur immeri* (15) . . *-rak-šu u* SUR-DU *šu* (?) *ku* (16) . . *di na* (?) *ša šat ḫu* (17) [*li*]-*bu-ku*. Rev. (18) . . . *ṣur-id-din-nu* (19) *ša il-lak-ku dib-bu-u* (20) ^{sal}*Amti-i-na-ad-an-ni*

Kuṣurua hath spoken thus: "I have received a letter from the tailor." I give it thee; concerning the clothes for the *birri* of the rivers, which none hath discussed with thee, let not my lord be neglectful in this matter. As for the letter, let him take it, let him bring a letter to the tailor who is with me.

No. **81.**—Letter from Daîan-bêl-uṣur unto Iddina-Marduk, my brother. Daily I pray unto Bêl and Nabû for the life of my brother.

Behold, Nabû-šuma-ukin hath come into Babylon, (so) let my lord discuss with him (and) let him make up the garlic according to the markets of our land. Is there garlic . . . ? Let him pay six shekels of silver. Behold, fresh garlic hath been gathered; let him give thy cut garlic, and if this garlic reach not the required amount, let my lord send a boat, that I may send up garlic (and) dates. Speedily let me hear news from my lord about the garlic and dates.

No. **82.**—Letter from Daîan-bêl-uṣur unto Marduk-naṣir-apli, my lord. Daily I pray Bêl and Nabû for the life of my lord.

As for the letter of Bêl-eṭir, which thou didst send about a sheep to Nûr-Šamši; when he had sold the sheep he annulled the contract (?) (saying), "the sheep is not mine," and he had (already) sold it; and their offspring with . . .

. . . -iddinnu, who has arrived, hath ended the matter of the lady Amtu-inadanni and my judge. He

(21) *u* ^am^ *dı-ı-nı-a* (22) *ul-te-pu-uš* (23) *II-ta enzı* ^pl^ *u* (24) *I-ta im-mır-tum* (25) *ı-ta-bak-ku ku-ru-bı-e-tum* (26) *im-mır-tum u mârı-šu* . . . (27) *ul ı-nam-dın-nu ı-ti-* . . (28) *u at-tu-šu a-na ku-* . . . (29) *ıl-ta-par-ri* (30) *kap-du te-en ša bêlı-ıa* (31) *a-na muḫ-ḫı lu-šım-me*

[No. 30,717]

No **83**—Obv : (1) *Duppi* ^m ilu^ *Daîan-bêlı-[usur]* (2) *a-na* ^m ilu^ *Marduk-na (naṣır)-aplı [bêlı-ıa]* (3) *ûmu(mu)-us-su* ^ilu^ *Bêl u* ^ilu^ *Nabû* (4) *a-na balat napšâtım(tım)* ^pl^ *ša bêlı-ıa* (5) *u-sal-la bêli lu-u-ı-dı* (6) *ultu ûmu V* ^kam^ *ša* ^arḫu^ *Nısanni* (7) *ına muḫ-ḫi ı-ni-ıa* (8) *na-kıs ka-ak-kıb* (9) *ul u-su kap-du* (10) *kap-du nu-bat-tum* (11) *lá ta-ba-ta-ıa* (12) ^am^ *sabı* ^pl^ *[šu]-pur-ra* (13) *ına pani-* . . . (14) *nârı* . . (15) . . ^pl^ . . . (16) *kap-du* ^m ilu^ *Nabû* (?) . . . (17) *šu-pur nu-bat-tı* . . (18) *la ı-ba-ta-a* . . . (19) *ûmu(mu)-ma* (?)*-am šûmu* (?) (20) *ul ıs-su-uḫ u* (?) *[dul-lu]* (21) *ra-bu-u a-[gan-na* . . .]*-gı* (22) *kaspı ša aš-pur-rak-ka mı-nam-ma* (23) *kaspı ul tu-še-bı-lu.*

[No. 42,448]

No **84**—Obv. : (1) *Duppı* ^m ilu^ *Daîan-šuma-[usur ?]* (2) *a-na* ^m ilu^ *Nabû-na-dın-aḫı* (3) *aḫı-ıa* ^ilu^ *Nabû u* ^ilu^ *[Marduk]* (4) *a-na aḫı-ıa lık-ru-bu* (5) ^m ilu^ *Bêl-usur ša a-gan-na-ka* (6) *mımma ma-la* (7) *ı-rıš-šu-ka* (8) *lu-u ku-up-ru* (9) *lu-u ıt-tu-u* (10) *lu-u* ^isu^ *elıppı* . . . (11) *lu-u* ^isu^ . . (12) . . . Rev : (13) ^m(?)^ *Kı* (?) . . . (14) BAR *ma-na kaspı* . . (15) *bêlı lıd-da-aš-šu* (16) *a-na-ku ul-tu a-gan-na* (17) *saluppu eš-šu-tu* (18) *u saluppu* (19) *la-bı-ru-tu* (20) *ša a-na ša-tı-kı* (21) *ta-a-bı a-na* (22) *aḫı-ıa u-še-bı-la* (23) *šı-pır-ta-a* (24) *lu-u mu-kın-nı-ıa*

[No. 30,226]

No. **85**—Obv (1) *Duppı* ^m ilu^ *Daîan-šarrı-usur* (2) *a-na* ^m^ *Mu-še-zıb-* ^ilu^ *Marduk* (3) *aḫı-ıa* ^ilu^ *Nabû u* ^ilu^ *Marduk*

has delivered two goats and one lamb ; the *ḳurubîtu* of the lamb and . . . he will not give . . . and he hath sent unto . . . Speedily let me hear news of my lord.

No. **83**.—Letter from Daîan-bêl-[usur] unto Marduk-nasir-apli, [my lord]. Daily I pray Bêl and Nabû for the life of my lord.

May my lord be advised that, to my knowledge, since the fifth of Nisan no cutter of *kakkib*(?) hath come out. Speedily, speedily end thy holiday ; send me workmen . . . Speedily send Nabû (?)- . . . (and) let him not keep holiday. The day . . . he hath not gathered the garlic (?), and there is much [work] here. As for the money about which I sent thee, why hast thou not sent the money ?

No. **84**.—Letter from Daîan - šuma - usur (?) unto Nabû - nadin - aḫi, my brother. May Nabû and [Marduk] bless my brother

Bêl-usur, who is over yonder (with thee), whatever he desireth thee [do thou give him], be it bitumen, pitch, a boat, or . . .

. . . Let my lord give him half a mana of silver. As for me, I am sending hence unto my lord dates, both new and old, such as are good for *šatiki* ; let my letter be my witness.

No. **85**. — Letter from Daîan - šarri - usur unto Mušezib - Marduk, my brother. May Nabû and Marduk bless my brother.

(4) *a-na aḫi-ia* (5) *lik-ru-bu* (6) *a-mur* [m ilu] *Bêl-mušallim* (7) [am] . . . *a-na* (8) *aḫi-ia al-tap-par* (9) [isu] *dalâti* [pl] *ša abullu(u)* (10) *ša pa-ni* (11) *daîanu* . . . REV.: (12) *šu-ul-li-in-nim-ma* (13) *mi iš-ḫa-tum-si-na* (14) *liš-ša-am-ma* (15) [urudu] *su-ni-e* (16) *a-gan-na* (17) *li-zi-ib.*

[No 67,368]

NO **86** — OBV.: (1) *Duppi* [m ilu] *Daîan-[šarri-usur]* (2) *a-na* [m] *Mu-še-zib-* [ilu] *[Marduk]* (3) [ilu] *Bêl u* [ilu] *Nabû šu-lum u [balaṭi]* (4) *ša aḫi-ia lik-bu-u* (5) *en-na šipâti ma-la a-gan-na-ka i-ba-aš-[šu]-u* (6) *a-na* [m] *Ab-du-'* (7) [am] *ar-ba-a-a i-din* (8) *u ṭe-e-mu* (9) *ša aḫi-ia lu-uš-me* (10) . . . (11) . . . *šu* (?).

[No 56,012]

NO. **87** —OBV.: (1) *Duppi* [m] *Du-muk a-na* (2) [m] *Suka-a-a aḫi-ia* [ilu] *Bêl u* [ilu] *Nabû* (3) *šu-lum u balaṭi ša aḫi-ia lik-bu-u* (4) *ši-pir-tum ši-i maḫ-ru-u* (5) [m] *Ka-su-su il-tap-ra* (6) *ši-pir-tum-šu* [a an] *ul šu-ud-gu-lat* (7) *il-tap-ra um-ma ni-si-iḫ-tum* (8) *ša šimâti* (?) [pl] *a-na* [am] *ṣabi* [pl] (9) *kul-lim-ma* ŠE-BAR *lid-ku-u-ni* (10) *duppi* [pl] *ina bîti šak-nu u bâbi* (11) *a-na muḫ-ḫi ka-nik-u šu-u* (12) *ul iš pu-ru um-ma bâbu pi-tu* (13) *nišê* [pl] *i-kab-bu-ni um-ma pi-tu* (14) . . . *-man-ni u ši-pir-tum* [pl] (15) *a* . . . (16) *u a-na muḫ-ḫi* . . . *ša* . . . (17) *ṣi-bu-ti-šu šak-nu ki-i* (18) *aš-pu-raš-šu gab-ri ši-pir-tum* [pl] (19) *ul iš-pu-ru en-na-'* . . . (20) *[a]-na bîtâte* [pl] *(te) te-ru-[ub?]* (21) *[a]-na ši-pir-tum a-[ga a]* (22) . . . *[ši]-pir-tum* [a an] . . . (23) . . . *ri-e-tum ina eli* (?) . . . (24) . . *su u ta* . . . REV.: (25) . . . *-mur bêl liš-[al]* . . . (26) *[lu]-še-bi-lu* . . . (27) *[en] na ti-i-di ša* (28) *gab-bi ši-i-tu a-na[eli]* (29) *ṣi-bu-ti-ka* (30) *bêli lu-te-ir-šu u kap-du* (31) *ḫarrana* [II] *a-na šepâ* [II] *-šu ša* [am] BUR-LA (32) *bêl liš-kun u te-e-[mu]* (33) *ša bêli-ia ša šu-lum* . . . (34) *lu-uš-mu u mi-nu-u* (35) *ṭe-en-ka at-tu-ku* (36) *bêl liš-pu-ru maḫ-ru-u* (37) [m] *Mu-še-zib ki-i aš-pu-ru* (38) *ki-i u-ba-'-u-ka* (39) *ul*

Behold, I send Bêl-mušallim, the . . . , unto my brother. Have raised for me the doors of the Great Gate which is in front of the judgment-seat (?), and let him take their measurements. He can leave the copper fastenings here.

No. **86.**—Letter from Daîan-[šarri-usur] unto Mušezib-[Marduk, my brother]. May Bêl and Nabû grant peace and [life] unto my brother.

Now, give all the wool which is over yonder (with thee) unto Abdu', the *arbâ*, and let me hear news from my lord.

No. **87.** — Letter from Dumuk unto Sukâ, my brother. May Bêl and Nabû grant peace and life unto my brother.

There was a first letter which Kasusu sent, but this particular letter was not seen. He sent thus: "Shew the copy of the arrangements (?) to the workmen, and let them gather the corn for me."

The tablets were put away in the house (*or* in a box), and the door was sealed thereon, but he did not report that the door was opened. The people were saying that it was open . . . letters . . .

. . . and according to all his desire. When I sent it, he sent back no answer . . .

. . . Now, thou knowest that they are all despised. According to thy wish let my lord return him, and speedily let my lord set the *burla* on his way, and let me hear news of my lord's well-being, and what thine own news is let my lord send. When I sent the former (letter) to Mušezib, although he

i-mur-ka a-mur (40) *ši-pir-tum*^{pl} *maḫ-ri-e-tum* (41) *ša a-na* ^{m}*Ka-su-su aš-pur* (42) *ina pani* $^{m\ ilu}$LUGAL-MARADA(DA)-*ibni* (43) ^{am}*ša-ku-u šak-na-'* (44) *ina pani-šu ši si ši-ni-* . . . (45) *ki-i ta-am-ma-ru* . . . (46) *lib-bu-u ši-ik-ni-šu*$^{a\ an}$ (47) *ab-bu-ut-ta-šu* (48) *na-as-ka-ta.* (Left-hand edge) (49) [*ki-i*] *la ta*-[*am-mar*] *al-la a-na muḫ-ḫi mi-ni-i* (50) . . . *ab-bu ut*-[*ta*]-*šu na-as-ka-ta ḫu ur-ṣu* (51) *u* [*šu*]-*pur*

[No. 38,713]

No **88**.—Obv.: (1) *Duppi* ^{m}*Ḫa-ba-ṣi-ru* (2) *u* ^{m}*Ni-din-it-tum a-na* (3) $^{m\ ilu}$*Šamšu bêl-ilâni*^{pl} *aḫi-i-ni* (4) ^{ilu}*Nabû u* ^{ilu}*Marduk a-na aḫi-i-ni* (5) *lik-ru-bu II C saluppi* (6) *a-na* ^{m}*Bêli-šu-nu u* $^{m\ ilu}$*Nabû-šuma-uṣur* (7) *i-din e-lat* (8) *L gur saluppi maḫru-u-tu* . . . (9) *ša a-na* ^{m}*Bêli-šu-nu ni-ip-ḳi-du* (10) *XXXIV gur saluppi* (11) *a-na* ^{m}*Arad-*^{ilu}*Bêl* (12) *aḫi ša* $^{m\ ilu}$*Bêl-ri-man-an-ni* (13) ^{am} . . . *ša* ^{ilu}*A-nu-ni-tum i-din* (14) [^{arḫu}] *Addaru ûmu XIII*^{kam} *šattu VI*^{kam} (15) [^{m}*Kam*]-*bu-zi-ya šar Babili šar mâtâti* (Left-hand edge) (16) *kurummati ša ni-* . . . (17) *la ta-maḫ-ḫar-šu.*

[No 75,492]

No **89**—Obv · (1) *Duppi* ^{m}*Tâbi-ia* (2) *a-na* $^{m\ ilu}$*Bêl-uballiṭ(iṭ) aḫi-ia* (3) ^{ilu}*Bêl u* ^{ilu}*Nabû a-na* (4) *aḫi-ia lik-ru-bu* (5) [*al-ta*]-*par-ru* (6) *a-na* $^{m\ ilu}$*Šamšu-uballiṭ* (7) *um-ma* (8) ^{sal}*Nu-ub-ta-a* (9) *a-di pa-ni*-[*ia*] (10) *ina lib-bi* . . Rev. (11) *tal-li-ku* (12) *nu-bat-tum* (13) *ina pani-ia* (14) *ul ta-ba-at* (15) *a-na aḫi-ia* (16) *a-šap-par-ra-aš*

[No 74,958]

No **90**.—Obv. · (1) *Duppi* ^{m} *Ta-bi-ia* (2) *a-na* $^{m\ ilu}$*Šamšu-rabû-šarri-uṣur* (3) *bêli-ia* ^{sal}*Bi-is-sa-a* (4) *bêlti-ia ûmu(mu)-ut-su* ^{ilu}*Bêl* (5) *u* ^{ilu}*Nabû* ^{ilu}*E-a u* ^{ilu}*Dam-ki-na* (6) *a-na balat napšâti*^{pl} *ša bêli*-[*ia*] (7) *u-ṣal-lum ina ṣilli* (8) *ša ilâni*^{pl} *šu-lum* (9) *ša-kin šu-lum* . . . (Remainder of obv broken off: what remains of the rev is blank)

[No. 55,900.]

sought thee, he could not find thee. Behold, the first letters which I sent to Kasusu were entrusted to Lugalmarada-ibni, an officer; read it in his presence, if thou seest him. Prison is ready for him for what he has done; [if] thou canst not [see] the reason why prison is ready (for him), ask and send.

No. **88.**—Letter from Ḫabasiru and Nidinittum unto Šamaš-bêl-ilâni, our brother. May Nabû and Marduk bless our brother.

Give two hundred (measures) of dates to Bêlišunu and Nabû-šuma-usur in addition to the former fifty *gur* of dates which we ordered for Bêlišunu. Give thirty-four *gur* of dates to Arad-Bêl, the brother of Bêl-rimanni, the . . . of Anunitum.

[Month] Adar, thirteenth day, sixth year of Kambyses, King of Babylon, king of countries.

The food for . . . buy it not for them.

No. **89.**—Letter from Ṭâbia unto Bêl-uballiṭ, my brother. May Bêl and Nabû be gracious unto my brother.

I have sent unto Šamaš-uballiṭ thus: "Nubtâ has come to me in . . . (but) she will keep no holiday with me, (for) I shall send her unto my brother."

No. **90.**—Letter from Ṭâbia unto Šamaš-rabû-šarri-uṣur, my lord, (and) Bissâ, my lady. Daily I pray unto Bêl and Nabû, Ea and Damkina, for the life of my lord [and lady]. I myself am under the protection of the gods . . .

No. **91**—Obv. (1) *Duppi* ^m^ *Kudur-* . . . (2) ^m^ *Ku-na-a* . . . (3) *lu-u šu-lum* . . . (4) *abi-ia* . . . (5) ^ilu^ *Bêl u* ^ilu^ *Nabû* . . . (6) *balat napšâti*^pl^ *ša abi-[ia]* . . . (7) *u-sal-lu* . (8) *dib-bi* . . . (9) *šu* . . (Remainder of obv and top of rev broken off) Rev: (10–13 broken) (14) . *su* . . . (15) *u pa-ni* . . (16) . . . (17) *ina muḫ-[ḫi]* . . (18) *pa-ni* . . (19) *ba* . . . *ni* . . . (20) *gab-ri ši-[pir-ta ša]* (21) *bêli-ia lu-[mur].* [No. 49,111]

No **92**—Obv: (1) *Duppi* ^m^ *Ki-i-* ^ilu^ *Bêl* (2) *a-na* ^m^ *Ib-gi-* ^ilu^ *Bêl* (3) *aḫi-ia* ^ilu^ *Nabû u* ^ilu^ *Marduk* (4) *a-na aḫi-ia lik-ru-bu* (5) *a-ki-i II al-la-nu* (6) *nûni a-na* ^m^ *Suka-a* (7) *i-din a-ki-i II* (8) *al-la-nu* (9) *nûni a-na* (10) ^m^ ^ilu^ *Nabû-šuma-* . . . (11) *i-din.* [No 31,292.]

No. **93**.—Obv.: (1) *Duppi* ^m^ *Ki-i-* ^ilu^ *Nabû a-[na]* (2) ^m^ ^ilu^ *Bu-ne-ne-ibni aḫi-[ia]* (3) ^ilu^ *Bêl u* ^ilu^ *Nabû šu-lum-ka* . . . (4) I BAR *ḳi-me a-na* ^am^ *um-man-nu i-din* (5) *u mi-nam-ma ul tal-kam-ma* (6) ŠE-BAR *ul ta-aš-ši.* Rev.: (7) ^arḫu^ *Simanu ûmu VI*^kam^ (8) *šattu VIII*^kam^ ^m^ *Ku-raš šar* TIN-TIR-KI (9) *šar mâtâti ḳi-me kurummati* (10) *ûmu V*^kam^ *ša* ^arḫu^ *Simani i-tir-šu-nu.* [No 60,582.]

No. **94**.—Obv.: (1) *Duppi* ^m^ *Ki-i-* ^ilu^ *Nabû* (?) (2) *a-na* ^m^ *Eṭir-* ^ilu^ *Marduk* (3) *abi-ia* ^ilu^ *Nabû u* ^ilu^ *Marduk* (4) . *ia.* (Remainder of obv. obliterated.) Rev: (9) . . . *ip* (?)*-te* (?)-' (10) *[ši]-pir-ta-a* (11) *šu-u* ^am^ *mu-u-tu* (12) *ki-i kaspi* (13) *a-na na-da-nu* (14) *si-ba-a-tu* (15) *man-ma at-ta* (16) *la'i-mur* (17) . . . *[i]-ru-ub* (Left-hand edge) (18) . . . ^am^ *mâr-šip-ri-ia* . . . [No. 84,921.]

No. **95**—Obv.: (1) *Duppi* ^m^ *Kal-ba-a a-na* (2) ^m^ *Iddina(na)-apli bêli-ia* (3) ^ilu^ *Bêl u* ^ilu^ *Nabû šu-lum u balati* (4) *ša bêli-ia*

No. **91**. — Letter from Kudur- . . . [unto] Kunâ . . .

No. **92**.—Letter from Kî-Bêl unto Ibgi-Bêl, my brother. May Nabû and Marduk bless my brother.

Now give two strings of fish to Suḳâ, and give two strings of fish to Nabû-šuma- . . .

No. **93**.—Letter from Kî-Nabû unto Bunene-ibni, my brother. May Bêl and Nabû grant thee peace.

Give one and a half (measures) of flour to the workmen; and why dost thou not come and take the corn?

Month Siwan, sixth day, eighth year of Cyrus, King of Babylon, king of countries. Pay the flour as the food allowance for the fifth day of Siwan.

No. **94**.—Letter from Kî-Nabû (?) unto Eṭir-Marduk, my father. May Nabû and Marduk [bless my father] . . .

. . . he hath opened my letter, he is the *mûtu*-official. When thou didst desire to give the money no one saw thee . . .

No **95**.—Letter from Kalbâ unto Iddina-apli, my lord. May Bêl and Nabû grant peace and life unto my lord.

lik-bu-u (5) *ša ta-aš-pu-ur um-ma ki-i* (6) *ri-ka-a-ta ni-ba-am-ma* (7) *ina du- . . . -ia ša* (?)*-al* (8) *itti* ^{m}*Ri-mut-*^{ilu}*Ba-u* (9) *e-pu-uš bêl mâr banu-tu* (10) *liš-pur-am-ma mi-nu-u* (11) *i-pu-uš li-mur* (12) *u a-na-ku u* ^{m}*Ri-mut-*^{ilu}*Ba-u* (13) *it-ti-šu a-*[*na*] (14) *pa-ni bêli.* REV.: (15) *ni-ru-bu* (16) *ina eli* ^{m}*Kal-ba-a* (17) *apil* ^{m}*Na-ba-a-a* (18) *ša bêl iš-pu-ru a-di eli* . (19) *en-na Kiš*^{ki} *ul il-li-ku* (20) *a-mur ûmu*(*mu*) *ša il-la-ku* (21) *bêli-ia a-šap-pa-ru.*

[No. 30,562.]

NO. **96**—OBV.: (1) *Duppi* ^{m}*Kal-ba-a* [*a-na*] (2) ^{m}*Iddina*(*na*)*-apli bêli-ia* ^{ilu}*Bêl u* ^{ilu}*Nabû* (3) *šu-lum u balati ša bêli-ia lik-bu-u* (4) *XLI dan-nu šikari mâr šatti* (5) *XII dan-nu šikari la-bi-ru* (6) *ina IV arḫâni*^{pl} *ina bît ka-ti* (7) *ša šid-di* ^{m}*Ri-mut-*^{ilu}*Ba'u* (8) *ki-i e-pu-šu I ma-na kaspi* (9) *ma-ṭu ak-ta-bi* (10) *um-ma kaspi* . . . (11) . . . (One or two lines wanting.) REV.: (13) *ul e-pu-*[*uš*] . . . (14) *ki-i u-ṣu-u* (15) *ultu ûmu IV*^{kam} *ul a-mur-šu* (16) *bêl* ^{am}*gal-la bêli* (17) *liš-pur-am-ma immeri-šu-u* (18) *u ši-kit-tum ša bêli* (19) *ik-ba-' ina katâ*^{II}*-šu* (20) *a-na bêli lu-še-bi-lu* (21) *man-ma ina pani-ia* . . . (22) *ina lib-bi ki-i* . . .

[No 31,286]

NO. **97**.—OBV.: (1) *Duppi* ^{m}*Kal-ba-a* (2) *a-na* ^{m}*Iddina*(*na*)*-apli aḫi-ia* (3) ^{ilu}*Bêl u* ^{ilu}*Nabû šu-lum balaṭi* (4) *ša aḫi-ia lik-bu-u* (5) *ki-i ik-bu-nu* (6) ^{m}*Šad-din-nu ul-tu* (7) ^{alu}*Ḫar-ra-nu it-te-ru-bu* (8) *man-ma bêl liš-pu-ru-'-ma* (9) *li-bu-ku-ma* REV.: (10) *a-na bêli-ia* (11) *lid-din id-su* (12) *pa-ni-šu ba-nu* (13) *šipâti it-ti-šu* (14) *it-ta-ša-'* (15) *ûmu IV*^{kam} *a-na* (16) TIN-TIR-KI *ir-ru-ub.*

[No. 30,997]

Of that which thou didst send, saying, "Count how (many) are empty, and . . . work with Rimut-Bau." Let my lord send a man of good standing that he may see what hath been done, and I and Rimut-Bau will come to my lord's presence with him.

Concerning Kalbâ, the son of Nabâ, about whom my lord sent, up to this present time he has not reached Kiš. Behold, the day that he arrives I will send word to my lord.

No. **96**.—Letter from Kalbâ unto Iddina-apli, my lord. May Bêl and Nabû grant peace and life unto my lord.

After I have made forty-one casks of one-year-old beer (and) twelve casks of old beer in four months in the cellar adjoining Rimut-Bau, one mana of silver is too little. I agreed thus: "The money . . . " . . . he did not do it. After he went forth, from the fourth day I saw him not Let my lord send one of my lord's servants, that I may send with him to my lord his sheep, and the work of which my lord spoke. No one in my presence with regard to it . . .

No. **97**.—Letter from Kalbâ unto Iddina-apli, my brother. May Bêl and Nabû grant peace and life unto my brother.

According to what people are saying, Šaddinnu has arrived from the city of Harran. Let my lord send some one to fetch him that he may give his hand (?) to my lord. If it seem good, he shall bring the wool with him; he will arrive at Babylon on the fourth day.

NO. **98.**—OBV.: (1) *Duppi* ^m *Ka-ṣir* (2) *a-na* ^m ^ilu *Bêl-ri-ṣu-u-a* (3) *aḫi-ia* ^ilu *Bêl u* ^ilu *Nabû* (4) *šu-lum u balaṭi šu aḫi-ia* (5) *lik-bu-u a-mur* (6) ^m *Bur-šu-u a-na* (7) *pani-ka it-tal-ku* (8) *u-il-tim* (9) *ša I gur III pi* ŠE-BAR (10) *ša ina muḫ-ḫi-ia* (11) *mu-ḫur-šu.* REV.: (12) *u* ŠE-BAR ^a-an (13) *I gur III pi* (14) *in-na-aš-ši* (15) *la tu-še-ti-ik-šu* (16) *ia-a-nu-u* ŠE-BAR (17) *ina* TIN-TIR-KI *i-maḫ-ḫar-an-ni* (18) *lu-u i-da-tum* (19) *ša tak-ba-'* (20) *um-ma in-za-ḫu-ri-tum* (21) *u abnu gab-bu-u* (22) *i-ša-'*

[No. 31,195.]

NO. **99**—OBV.: (1) *Duppi* ^m *Ki-rib-tum-* ^ilu *Marduk* (2) *a-na* ^m *Arad-* ^ilu *Gu-la* (3) *aḫi-ia* ^ilu *Nabû u* ^ilu [*Marduk*] (4) *a-na aḫi-ia lik-*[*ru-bu*] (5) ^am *u-ra-ši-ka ša* . . . (Remainder of obv. broken off: what remains of rev is blank.)

[No 54,006]

NO. **100**—OBV.: (1) *Duppi* ^m *Ki-rib-tum-* ^ilu *Marduk* (2) *a-na* ^m *Su-ka-a-a u* (3) ^m ^ilu *Bêl-iddin aḫi* ^pl *-e-a* (4) ^ilu *Bêl u* ^ilu *Nabû šu-lum u balaṭi* (5) *ša aḫi* ^pl *-e-a lik-bu-u* (6) ^m *It-ti-* ^ilu *Bêl-li-im-ḫir* (7) *ša a-na pani-ku-nu aš-pur-ru* (8) ^m *Ri-mut-* ^ilu *Bêl apil-šu ša* (9) ^m *Kur-ban-ni-* ^ilu *Marduk* (10) *apil* ^am *ri'i-* ^imeru *sisi* ^pl (11) *a-ki u-il-tim* (12) *ša* ^m *Itti-* ^ilu *Bêl-lim-ḫir.* REV.: (13) *ša ina muḫ-ḫi-šu harrana* ^II (14) *a-na šepi-šu ina pani-ku-nu* (15) *liš-kun ia-a-nu-u* (16) ^m *Ri-mut-* ^ilu *Bêl it-ti* (17) ^m *Itti-* ^ilu *Bêl-li-im-ḫir* (18) *a-na pani-ia* (19) *šu-up-ra-a-nu.*

[No. 65,242]

NO. **101**—OBV.: (1) *Duppi* ^m *Kur-ban-ni-* ^ilu *Marduk* (2) *a-na* ^m ^ilu *Nabû-ga-mil abi-ia* (3) ^ilu *Nabû u* ^ilu *Marduk a-na* (4) *abi-ia lik-ru-bu* (5) *ûmu(mu)-us-su* ^ilu *Bêl u* ^ilu *Nabû* (6) *a-na*

No. **98**. — Letter from Kaṣir unto Bêl-riṣûa, my brother. May Bêl and Nabû grant peace and life unto my brother.

Behold, Buršû comes into thy presence; obtain from him a receipt for a debt to me for one *gur*, three *pi* of corn, and he shall take the one *gur*, three *pi* of corn. Neglect it not. Is there no corn in Babylon that he should buy from me? Let there be a contract (?) for that which thou didst say, thus. "Take the *inzaḫuritum* stones and all the stones."

No. **99**.—Letter from Kiribtum-Marduk unto Arad-gula, my brother. May Nabû and Marduk bless my brother . . .

No. **100**. — Letter from Kiribtum unto Sukâ and Bêl-iddin, my brothers. May Bêl and Nabû grant peace and life unto my brothers.

As for Itti-Bêl-limḫir whom I sent unto your presence, let Rimut-Bêl, the son of Kurbanni-Marduk, the son of the horse-dealer (according to the debt of Itti-Bêl-limḫir which is outstanding against him), set him on his way to you. Is not Rimut-Bêl with Itti-Bêl-limḫir? Send unto my presence.

No. **101**. — Letter from Kurbanni-Marduk unto Nabû-gamil, my father. May Nabû and Marduk bless my father. Daily I pray unto Bêl and Nabû for the life of my father.

balaṭ napšâti ^{pl} *ša bêli-ia* (7) *u-ṣal-lu* ^{am} *apil-šip-ri* (8) *ša a-na* ^{alu} *Ša- . . . -ri* (9) *bêl iš-pur* ^{ilu} *Bêl u* ^{ilu} *Nabû* (10) *lu-u-i-du-[u]* (11) *ki-i ina* ^{alu} . . . (12) *a-na-ku a-[mur-ši]-im-ma* (13) . . . *-ša* REV.: (14) *ša ina bâb šarri iḳli-šu* (15) I BAR *ma-na kaspi-šu* (16) *aš-ta-bi u aḳ-ḳi* (?) (17) *u a-di ra-šu-ti-ia* (18) *ap-te-kid liš-ši-ma* (19) *ši-pir-tum a-na eli* (20) *bêli liš-pur-am-ma kaspi* (21) *ša la* ^{am} ŠA-KU *a-na* (22) *man-ma la in-nam-din* (23) *ki-i na-kut-tum* (24) *a-na bêli-ia al-tap-ra* (25) *ṭâbti-ka ina muḫ-ḫi-ia* (26) *bêl liš-kun IV ma-na* (27) *kaspa-a ina muḫ-ḫi-šu* . . . (28) . . . (Left-hand edge) (29) *bêli-ia a-na* ^{am} ŠA-KU *a-na eli kaspi-ia* (30) . . . *ša ina tar* . . .

[No 47,584]

NO. **102**—OBV.: (1) [*Duppi* ^{m} *La*]*-ba-a-ši* (2) *a-na* $^{m\ ilu}$ *Nabû-zira-ešir* (3) *abi-ia* ^{ilu} *Bêl u* ^{ilu} *Nabû* (4) *šu-lum ša abi-ia* (5) *liḳ-bu-u* (6) *ûmu(mu)-us-su* (7) ^{ilu} *Šamšu a-na balat napšâti* ^{pl} (8) *ša abi-ia* (9) *u-ṣal-la* (10) *a-mur ICVI ma-ši-ḫu.* (Reverse too mutilated for insertion)

[No. 69,856]

NO **103**.—OBV.: (1) *Duppi* ^{m} *La-a-ba-ši* (2) *a-na* ^{m} *Arad-* ^{ilu} *Marduk* (3) *aḫi-ia u* ^{ilu} *Marduk* (4) *a-na [aḫi-ia]* (5) *liḳ-[ru-bu]* REV.: (6) *kal-la-nu* (?) . . . (7) *ša taḳ-ba-[a]* (8) *man-ma ul id-di-nu* (9) *bêl lu-u-i-di.*

[No. 54,160]

NO **104**.—OBV: (1) *Duppi* ^{m} *La-ba-a-ši* (2) *a-na* $^{m\ ilu}$ *Adad-ri-ṣu-u* (3) *aḫi* ^{ilu} *Bêl u* ^{ilu} *Nabû* (4) *šu-lum aḫi liḳ-bu-u* (5) *ši-pir-ta al-tap-par-ra* (6) *um-ma XL gur saluppi* (7) *bat- . . . -tu a-na* (8) . . . (9) *mi-na-am* (10) *tu-še-ti-iḳ-šu* (11) . . . *en* . . . REV.: (12) *man-ma*

As for the messenger whom my lord sent to the city of Ša . . âri, by Bêl and Nabû, I have not seen him in the city of . . . , which is in the King's gate. His land (and) one and a half mana of his money I have distrained on and . . . (?) and added to my debt. Let him take and send a letter to my lord, and then the money, without the authority of the *šaku*, shall not be paid to anyone. Though I am laying a care on my lord, yet let my lord shew kindness to me ; send four manas of my money unto him . . . let my lord . . . unto the *šaku* about my money which . . .

No. **102**.—[Letter from Lâ]baši unto Nabû-zira-ešir, my father. May Bêl and Nabû grant peace and life unto my father. Daily I pray unto Šamaš for the life of my father.

Behold, one hundred and six measures . . .

No. **103**.—Letter from Lâbaši unto Arad-Marduk, my brother. May (Nabû) and Marduk bless my brother.

The *kallanu* . . . (?) which thou didst order, no one hath given me. Let my lord mark this.

No. **104**.—Letter from Labâši unto Adad-risû, my brother. May Bêl and Nabû grant peace unto my brother.

I sent (thee) a letter saying, "Give forty *gur* of . . . dates to . . ." Why hast thou omitted to do this?

. . . (13) *a-dı* E-KI (14) *gu-um-* . . . (15) *ın-na-aš-šı* (16) *la tu-še-[tı-ık-šu]* (17) *šı-pır-ta-a* (18) *am mu-kın-nı-e* (19) *kaspi-šu-nu ına* E-KI (20) . . . *e* . . . (21) *lu-u* . . . (22) . . (23) . . .

[No 31,196]

No **105**—Obv : (1) *Duppi m Lib-lu-ṭu a-na* (2) *m Rı-mut aḫi-ia* (3) *ılu Nabû u ılu Marduk a-na* (4) *aḫı-ıa lık-ru-bu* (5) *XXV gur* ŠE-BAR *a-na* (6) *m Mu-ra-nu a-na elı-ka* (7) *e-te-taḳ II šıkli IV tu kaspi* (8) *man-da-at-tum ša gu-* . . . (9) *ına panı-ka bêlı subatu na-aṣ-ba-tı* (10) *at-ta-nak-ka u bu-ud-ka* (11) *ku-ut-mu VIII šıḳlı ina katâ II* (12) *m Ag-gı-ıa na-ša-a-ka* (13) *kaspı m Ag-gı-ıa* (14) *e-taḳ ia-a-nu-u* (15) *mi-nu-u kı-i* ŠE-BAR-*a* (16) *m Ag-gi-ıa ı-kıl-lu-u* (17) *a-maḫ-ḫar-ka a-na-ku* (18) *a-gan-nu m ılu Nabû-zıra-ešır* (19) *a-na muḫ-ḫi* ŠE-BAR-*šu*. Rev.: (20) *u-ša-an-za-ḳa-an-nı* (21) *X šıklı kaspi kap-du* (22) *i-ša-am-ma ina arḫu Šabati.* (23) *šu-bı-lu ılu Bêl u ılu Nabû* (24) *kı-ı kaspı kap-du* (25) *ul tu-še-bı-lu* (26) *a-dı-'-šu bît dı-ı-ni* (27) *ša šar* TIN-TIR-KI (28) *u-še-rı-bu-ka* (29) *u* ŠE-BAR *ḫar-ra-na* (30) *ša m ılu Nabû-zıra-ešır* (31) *a-ma-aḫ-ru-ka* (32) *ılu Bêl u ılu Nabû lu-u* (33) *ı-du-u ki-ı* (34) *I šıklı kaspı ina* TIN-TIR-KI (35) *dag-la-ka* (36) *a-na bêl da-ba-ba-ıa* (37) *la ta-ta-bak* (38) *a-na m Ba-nı-ıa* (Left-hand edge) (39) *apıl-šu ša m Du-muḳ ḳı-bı um-ma bıt-lı-ıa ru-ku-us* (40) *ku-nu-uk-ma ına ḳatâ II man-ma al-la-ka kap-du kap-du* (41) *šu-bı-lu su bıt-lı gı-mı-ru-tum ıt-tı-ı šu-bi-la.*

[No. 74,334]

No. **106**—Obv. · (1) *Duppı m Lıb-lut* . . . (2) *a-na m Mu-še-zıb-ılu Marduk* (3) *am* E-BAR UD-KIB-NUN-KI (4) *abı-ıa ılu Bêl u ılu Nabû* (5) *šu-lum u balatı ša abı-ıa* (6) *lıḳ-bu-u šıkaru* LID(?) (7) *a-gan-nı ıa-a-nu* (8) *ba-aṭ-[lu]* . .
(Remainder of obv. broken off: reverse too mutılated for insertion)

[No 84,955]

. . . no one hath taken . . . unto Babylon. Do not fail in this ; let my letter be my witness. Their money in Babylon . . .

No. **105**.—Letter from Liblutu to Rimut, my brother. May Nabû and Marduk bless my brother.

Twenty-five *gur* of corn for Muranu is being transported unto thee ; two shekels four *tu* of silver is the price for . . . I am giving thee the bags (?), and I am thy secret (?) guarantee for eight shekels in the hands of Aggiya. Forward the money for Aggiya, for if it is not forthcoming, what if Aggiya withholds my corn ? Am I here to buy it for thee ?

Nabû-zira-ešir is importuning me for his corn, so obtain ten shekels of silver speedily and send it in Sebat. By Bêl and Nabû, if thou dost not send the money quickly according to (?) its contract, I will summon thee at the tribunal of the King of Babylon ; and as for the corn for the journey for Nabû-zira-ešir, I have bought it for thee (already). I call Bêl and Nabû to witness that I have not set eyes on a single shekel of silver in Babylon. Send it not unto my rival.

Tell Bania, the son of Dumuk, to bind up and seal my *bitlî* and send it speedily and at once by the hand of some traveller, and send the whole of the *bitlî* therewith.

No. **106**.—Letter from Liblutṭ unto Mušezib-Marduk, the Priest of Sippar, my father. May Bêl and Nabû grant peace and life unto my father.

There is no . . . -beer here, it is wanting . . .

No. **107**. — Obv.: (1) *Duppi* ^{m}*Li-ši* . . . *a*-[*na*] (2) ^{am}*šangi* UD-KIB-NUN-KI *bêli-ia* (3) ^{ilu}*Bêl u* ^{ilu}*Nabû šu-lum ṭu-ub lib-bi* (4) *tu-ub šeri*^{pl} *u a-ra-ku* (5) *ûmi*^{pl} *ša bêli-ia lik-bu-u* (6) *man-zal-ta-a uk-ku-pat* (7) *u šikaru u-sa-a ia-a-nu* (8) *a-na-ku a-gan-na ma-as-sar-tum* (9) *ša bêli-ia a-nam-ṣar a-na* (10) . . . *bêli liš*-[*pur*] (Remainder of obv and top of rev. broken off.) Rev.: (11) [*a-na*] ${}^{m\ ilu}$*Šamšu-šarri-uṣur* (12) *at-ta-din.*

[No. 84,945.]

No. **108** — Obv.: (1) *Duppi* ${}^{m\ ilu}$*Marduk-ukin-apli* (2) *u* ${}^{m\ ilu}$*Marduk-bêli-šu-usur* ^{am}*šangi*^{pl} (3) *a-na* ^{m}*Ni-din-tum u* ${}^{m\ ilu}$*Šamšu-* . . . (4) *aḫi*^{pl}*-e-a* ^{ilu}*Bêl u* ^{ilu}*Nabû* (5) [*šu-lum u balaṭi*] *ša aḫi*^{pl}*-e-a* (6) [*lik-bu-u*] . . . *ru* . . . (Remainder of obv. and top of rev. broken off) Rev.: (7) . . . *šattu V*^{kam} ^{m}*Da-ri-muš* (8) *šar mâtâti*^{pl}.

[No. 76,701]

No. **109**. — Obv.: (1) [*Duppi* ^{m}] ^{ilu}*Marduk-eriba u* (2) [^{m}] . . . *-nu a-na* ^{m}*Arad-*^{ilu}*Marduk* (3) [*abi*]*-i-ni* ^{ilu}*Nabû u* ^{ilu}*Marduk* (4) [*a-na*] *abi-i-ni lik-ru-bu* (5) . . . *a-na* (6) . . . *-nu ki-i* (7) . . . *-ri-šu pa-ni bêli-ia* (8) *ul* (?) *ta-ad-gi-la-an-na-a-šu* (9) . . . *ni-is-ḫu ša-nam-ma* (10) . . . *-nu-ba-' ḫarrana*^{II} (11) . . . *-de kap-sa-nu* Rev: (12) [*te*]*-e-mu* (13) [*ša*] *bêli-ia a-na eli* (14) *ni-iš-me* (15) . . . *II* . . . ^{pl} (16) . . . ${}^{m\ ilu}$*Nergal-iddin* (17) . . . *bêli-ia nu-ul-te-bi-la* (18) [${}^{m\ ilu}$]*Nergal-iddin ina pani-ka* (19) [*ul* ?] *i-ka-šu gab-ri* (20) [*ši*]*-pir-ti ša bêli-ia* (21) [*lu*]*-mu-ur.*

[No 31,936.]

No. **110**. — Obv.: (1) [*Duppi*] ^{m}*Itti-*^{ilu}*Marduk-balatu* (2) [*a-na*] ^{m}*Iddina-*^{ilu}*Marduk abi-ia* (3) [^{ilu}*Nabû*] *u* ^{ilu}*Marduk a-na* (4) [*abi-ia*] *lik-ru-bu* (5) ^{sal}*Nu-ub-ta-a* (6) *u La-mu-ta-nu* (7) *it-ti ka-a-ti-ka* (8) *ina muḫ-ḫi bîti la ta-* . . .

No. **107**.—Letter from Liši (?) . . . [unto . . .] the Priest of Sippar, my lord. May Bêl and Nabû grant peace, happiness, health, and long days unto my lord.

My position (?) is straitened (?), and there is no *usâ*-beer. I am here guarding my lord's interests, (so) let my lord send . . .

. . . [unto] Šamaš-šarri-uṣur I will give.

No. **108**.—Letter from Marduk-ukin-apli and Marduk-bêlišu-uṣur, the Priests, unto Nidintum and Šamaš- . . , my brothers. May Bêl and Nabû grant [peace and life] unto my brothers.

. . . fifth year, Darius, king of countries.

No. **109**.—[Letter from] Marduk-eriba and . . . -nu unto Arad-Marduk, our [father]. May Nabû and Marduk bless our father. (*Remainder too mutilated for connected sense.*)

No. **110**.—Letter from Itti-Marduk-balaṭu [unto] Iddina-Marduk, my father. May [Nabû] and Marduk bless [my father].

Do not . . . the lady Nubtâ or Lamutanu with thy . . . about the house. Behold, after I had

(9) *a-mur duppi ša bîti* (10) ^{m}*Šu*(?)*-ut-nu ki-i aš-pur-'* (11) *a-na* ^{sal}*Nu-ub-ta-a* (12) *ša bêl* $\frac{1}{3}$ *ma-na V šiḳli kaspi* (13) *ina bîti ina pâni* ^{sal}*Nu-ub-*[*ta-a*] (14) $\frac{2}{3}$ *ma-na VI šiḳli* . . . (15) . . . REV: (16) *la*(?) *id*(?)*-di-bu-ub* . . . (17) *a-mur* $^{m\ ilu}$*Nabû-a-a* (18) *it-ti-ia id-* . . . (19) *ki-i pa-ni bêli-ia maḫ-ru* (20) $^{m\ ilu}$*Nabû-di-i-ni-epuš*(*uš*) (21) *bêl li-bu-uk-ma* (22) *ku-um na-aš aš-* . . . (23) *ša bêli-ia lil-li-ik* (24) *a-na* ^{m} . . . *-ga a-na* (25) . . . (26) . . . *-te-it-* . . . *-ka* (27) . . . *lil-lik* (28) . . . *-lum-* . . . (29) . . . *pani* ^{ilu} . . .

[No. 31,457.]

No. **111**—OBV.: (1) *Duppi* $^{m\ ilu}$*Marduk-epuš* (2) *a-na* ^{m}*Ši-iš-di* (3) *aḫi-ia* ^{ilu}*Marduk* (4) *u* ^{ilu}*Ṣar-pa-ni-tum* (5) *šu-lum balaṭi ša aḫi-ia* (6) *liḳ-bu-u a-mur* (7) ^{m}*Iddina-*^{ilu}*Bêl it-ti-ia* (8) *a-na* ^{alu}*Šu-u-nu* (9) *it-ta-el-li* (10) *kur-ba-nu it-ti.* REV.: (11) $^{m\ ilu}$*Nergal-iddin aḫi-šu* (12) *aš*(?)*-šu la lib-bu-u* (13) *a-na eli ma-ṣar-aṣ-tum* (14) *ša aḫi-ia a-na-as-ṣar.*

[No. 31,279]

No. **112**—OBV: (1) *Duppi* $^{m\ ilu}$*Marduk-zira-ukin* (2) *a-na* ^{m}*Ri-mut* (3) $^{m\ ilu}$*Bêli-šu-nu* $^{m\ ilu}$*Marduk-etir* (4) *aḫi*^{pl}*-ia* ^{ilu}*Bêl u* ^{ilu}*Nabû* (5) *šu-lum ša aḫi*^{pl}*-ia* (6) *liḳ-bu-u* (7) *al-ka-nim-ma* (8) *ša-nam-ma* (9) . . . (10) ^{am}*rab-* . . . *ku-nu* (11) *e-pu-uš-ma* (12) *mimma*(*ma*) (13) ^{m}*Pir-ki* REV.: (14) *na-šu-u lu-ša-am-ma* (15) *bilti*(?)*-ku-nu-ši* (16) *ia-a-nu-um-ma* (17) *mi-di-tu* (18) UŠ *šaplitu*(*tu*) (19) *ina muḫ-ḫi-ku-nu* (20) *id-dan-nin* (21) *na-di a-ḫi* (22) *la ta-raš-šu* (23) ^{ilu}*Nabû lu-u* (24) *ki-i ḫi-tu* (Left-hand edge) (25) *a-na bêli ina lib-bi-šu-nu* (26) [*ul*] *aḫ-ta-tu-u.*

[No. 47,410]

No. **113**.—OBV: (1) *Duppi* $^{m\ ilu}$*Marduk-zira-ibni* (2) *a-na* ^{m}*Šu-la-a* (3) *aḫi-šu* ^{ilu}*Bêl u* ^{ilu}*Nabû* (4) *šu-lum ša aḫi-ia*

sent the agreement for the house of Šutnu (?), [I paid] unto Nubtâ for my lord one-third of a mana and five shekels of silver in the house before Nubtâ's eyes. Two-thirds of a mana, six shekels . . .

. . . Behold, Nabûâ hath agreed (?) with me. If it be pleasing to my lord, let my lord send Nabû-dîni-epuš, and let him come instead of taking the . . . of my lord . . .

No. **111**.—Letter from Marduk-epuš unto Šišdi, my brother. May Marduk and Sarpanitum grant peace and life unto my brother.

Behold, Iddina-Bêl is going up with me to the town of Sûnu; I am taking (?) a present for his brother Nergal-iddin.

. . . I will watch my brother's interests.

No. **112**.—Letter from Marduk-zira-ukin unto Rimut, Bêlišunu, and Marduk-eṭir, my brothers. May Bêl and Nabû grant peace unto my brothers.

Come and make another as the head man of your . . . , and let him receive all that Pirki hath received; and as for your . . . there is none, and the lower boundary (?) hath been strengthened because of you. Ye have no other means (?). I call Nabû to witness that I am not wronging my lord in this.

No. **113**.—Letter from Marduk-zira-ibni unto Šulâ, his brother. May Bêl and Nabû grant peace unto my brother.

(5) *lik-bu-u am-me-nı* (6) *bîti-a ta-ḫı-ıp-pu* (7) *ına pa-nı ḫa-pi-e bîtı-ka* (8) *ta-al-lak nar*(?)*-tu* (9) *e-te-ru ša ıḳli* (10) *ki-i ta-aš-šu-u* (11) *iḳli-a ın-na-dan* (12) . . . *ši* (13) *u* *isu**gıšimmari ša* (14) *u-rab-bu-u* (15) *id-di-ku-'*. REV.: (16) *u at-ta ına bîtı-ka* (17) *lib-ba-ka ṭa-ab-ka* (18) *en-na* ŠE-BAR *ša ina lib-bi* (19) *e-ri-šu gab-bi* (20) *na-ša-a-ta* (21) *en-na a-na bêlı-ıa* (22) *al-tap-ra* (23) *al kam-ma iḳli-a* (24) *e-ṭir-šu eburi* *pl**-ia* (25) *i-bi-ın-ni* (26) *a-mur* ŠE-BAR *ša* (27) *paḳ-da ma-na-a-ta* (28) *m* *Iḳıša*(*ša*)*-apli* (29) *u* *m ilu* *Nabû-aḫi-iddin* (30) *ki-i i-li-u* (Left-hand edge) (31) *ıt-ta-šu-u a-na* *am* *daîani* *pl* (32) *a-na muḫ-ḫi ḳı-bi.*

[No. 47,570.]

NO. **114** — OBV. · (1) *Duppi* *m ilu* *Marduk - naṣir a - na* (2) *m* *Šuma-ıddın* *m* *Bêli-šu-nu u* *m ilu* . . . (3) *aḫi* *pl* *- e - a* *ilu* *Bêl u* *ilu* *Nabû* (4) *šu-lum u balaṭı ša aḫi* *pl* *lıḳ-bu-u* (5) *ın-nı-ta-a at-tu-nu* (6) *ana muḫ-ḫı* *am* *mâr-banûti* *pl* (7) *ša* TIN - TIR - KI . . . (8) *ına kab - lu* (?) *aš - mu - u* (9) *ša* *m* . . . *mâr - banı* (?) (10) *iḫ - ta - šal* . . . (11) *ina mı-iḫ-ṣi-šu* (12) *mur-ṣi mit-kur.* REV.: (13) *in-da-ru-uṣ* (14) *ul i-di ina lıb-bi* (15) *i-pat-ta-ma ı-pal-la-tu* (16) *ki-i ina lıb-bi mi-i-tum* (17) *m ilu* *Bêl-balaṭ-su-iḳbı i-ḳab* (?)-[*bi*] (18) *la ta-sıl-la-'* (19) *ap-pi-it-*[*ti-ma*] . . . (20) *kı-ı ap-pi-*[*it-ti*] (21) *ıp* (?) . . . *man-ma lib-ba-ti* (22) *la i-kal-lu uz-*[*nı*] (?) (23) *ša* *am* *ṣabi* *pl* *ana muḫ-ḫı pi-*[*tı*].

[No. 59,610.]

NO. **115**. — OBV : (1) *Duppi* *m ilu* *Marduk - šuma - iddın* (2) *a-na* *m ilu* *Nabû-šuma-ešir* (3) *m ilu* *Bêl-apli-iddin u* *m* *Ki-i-* *ilu* *Nabû* (4) *aḫi* *pl* *-e-a* *ilu* *Nabû u* *ilu* *Marduk* (5) *ana aḫı* *pl* *-e-a*

Why art thou pulling down my house before thou pullest down thine own? Thou shalt come, and when thou hast received the . . . for the payment of the field, my field shall be sold . . . and the palms which I have increased shall be gathered together and thou shalt rest happy in thy house. Now I send unto my lord. Come, and as for my field, the payment thereof shall cause my crops to grow (?). Behold, the corn which hath been assigned (thereto) hath been weighed out; Ikiša-apli and Nabû-aḫi-iddin, if they wish, can take it. Inform the judges on this matter.

No. **114**.—Letter from Marduk-naṣir unto Šuma-iddina, Bêlišunu, and . . . my brothers. May Bêl and Nabû grant peace and life unto (my) brothers.

Ye stand as my protection towards the gentlefolk of Babylon . . . In the fight (?) I heard that [so-and-so, whom] the noble (?) smote, when he was smitten, fell sick of a suppuration.[1] He did not understand it (and) it enlarged and spread, so that he died therefrom. Bêl-balaṭsu-iḳbi told me (?) Be not neglectful, quickly . . . for if [it be not done (?)] quickly, no one will restrain their anger. Inform the workmen of this matter.

No. **115**.—Letter from Marduk-šuma-iddin unto Nabû-šuma-ešir, Bêl-apli-iddin, and Kî-Nabû, my brothers. May Nabû and Marduk bless my brothers.

[1] *Mursi mitkur, mitkur* possibly being from the root *makâru*, "to pour profusely."

lik-ru-bu (6) *pap-pa-su ša maš-šir-ti* (7) *ša* ^arḫu^ *Âbi ša* ^am^ *mu-u-tu* (8) *ša ina bît ka-ri-e* (9) *ša* ^m ilu^ *Nabû-apli-iddin apil-šu ša* (10) . . *a-na* . . . (11) . (12) . Rev.: (13) . (14) . (15) *la* . (16) *i ḳab-ba-a um-ma* (17) *sa-ma-ku pap-pa-si-šu* (18) *in-na-niš-šim-ma* (19) *dul la-šu ina lib-bi* (20) *li-pu-uš*.

[No 75,640]

No. **116** — Obv (1) *Duppi* ^m ilu^ *Marduk - šuma - iddin* (2) *a-na* ^m ilu^ *Nabû-šuma-ešir* (3) ^m ilu^ *Bêl-apli-iddin* ^m ilu^ *Bêl-uballit(it)* (4) ^m^ *Ki-i-*^ilu^ *Nabû u* (5) ^m^ *Arad-*^ilu^ *Marduk aḫi*^pl^*-e-a* (6) ^ilu^ *Nabû u* ^ilu^ *Marduk a-na* (7) *aḫi*^pl^ *-e-a lik-ru-bu* (8) *mi-nam-ma* ^am^ *irriši* [^pl^] (9) *il lik-ku-nim* [*ma*] (10) *it-ti dul-li-ia* (11) *u-ša-* . (Remainder of obv. and top of rev. broken off) Rev · (12) *eli* (?) . (13) *a-mur-'* . . (14) *mit-ḳa ša* ^am^ *irriši-šu-nu* (15) *sab-ta-'* (16) *u mârâni*^p^ ^am^ *irriši* (17) *ša* ^m^ *Mu-ra-nu* (18) *u - kul - lim - ku - nu - šu* (19) *in-na niš-šu-nu-tu* (20) *kurummati ša* ^am^ *irriši*^pl^ (21) *ša ina pani* ^m^ *Šuma-ukin dul-lu* (22) *ip-pu-uš-' lib-bu-u* (23) *šad-da-giš* (24) *ma-nu* (25) *-šu-nu-tu*.

[No 79,588]

No. **117**. — Obv.: (1) *Duppi* ^m ilu^ *Marduk - šuma - iddin* (2) *a-na* ^m ilu^ *Nabû-šuma-ešir* (3) ^m ilu^ *Bêl-apli iddin u* (4) ^m^ *Ki-i-*^ilu^ *Nabû aḫi - e - a* (5) ^ilu^ *Nabû u* ^ilu^ *Marduk a - na aḫi*^pl^ (6) *lik-ru-bu dul-lu* (7) *ina muḫ-ḫi-ia ia-a-nu* (8) *kap-du XX mar-ri* (9) *L sab-bil-lum* (10) *šu-bi-la-nu* (11) *dul-la-a la i-bat-til* (12) *II ma-na kaspi* (13) *XX gur* . (A few lines broken off from bottom of obv and top of rev) Rev: (14) *liš-ša-' u* (15) *li-il-lik*

[No 75,695]

No. **118**. — Obv. · (1) *Duppi* ^m ilu^ *Marduk - šuma - iddin* (2) *a-na* ^m ilu^ *Nabû šuma-ešir* (3) ^m ilu^ *Bêl-apli-iddin* ^m^ *Na-sir* (4) ^m^ *Ki-i-* ^ilu^ *Nabû u* ^m^ *Ki-Bêl* (?) (5) *aḫi*^pl^ [*-ia*] ^ilu^ *Nabû u*

The payment of the interest for the month Ab of the *mûtu*-official, who is in the granary, whom Nabû-apli-iddin, the son of . . .

. He hath spoken, saying, "I am blind." His pay shall be taken, that I may get his work done therewith.

No. **116**—Letter from Marduk-šuma-iddin unto Nabû-šuma-ešir, Bêl-apli-iddin, Bêl-uballiṭ, Kî-Nabû, and Arad-Marduk, my brothers. May Nabû and Marduk bless my brothers.

Why have gardeners come, and with my work . . . ? . . . Lo, the . . . sent by their gardener hath been taken away, and the gardener's sons, whom Muranu shewed you, shall be accepted. The maintenance of the gardeners who are doing their work under Šuma-ukin hath hitherto therein been counted.

No **117**.—Letter from Marduk-šuma-iddin unto Nabû-šuma-ešir, Bêl-apli-iddin, and Kî-Nabû, my brothers. May Nabû and Marduk bless my brothers.

There is no work going on under me; send speedily twenty hoes and fifty baskets, that my work shall not cease. Two mana of silver, twenty *gur* . . . . . . let him take and come.

No. **118**.—Letter from Marduk-šuma-iddin unto Nabû-šuma-ešir, Bêl-apli-iddin, Nasir, Kî-Nabû, and Kî-Bêl (?), my brothers. May Nabû and Marduķ bless my brothers.

ilu Marduk (6) *a-na aḫi^pl-ia lik-ru-bu* (7) *a-na muḫ-ḫi m ilu Nabû-šuma-usur* (8) *ša bêli^pl iš pu-ru-nu* (9) *ina pa-ni-šu ki-i nar-bu-u* (10) *ša ti-ik-tum ša bu-ul* (?)-*tu* (11) *um-ma šipâtu* . . (12) *a - di* . . . (13) . . REV.: (14) *a-gur-ru* . . (15) *it-ti-šu bêli^pl* . (16) *ip-pu-šu ḳi-ba-'* (17) *ki-i a-gur-ru* (18) *ina maḫ-ra-ka* (19) *su ṭu-ra ma* (20) *it-ti-šu ḳub-ba-'* (21) *II ma na kaspi* (22) *bêli^pl lid-din-nu-ni-šu.*

[No. 73,331]

NO. **119**. — OBV: (1) *Duppi m ilu Marduk - šuma - iddin* (2) *a-na m ilu Nabû-šuma-ešir* (3) *m ilu Bêl-apli-iddin m ilu Bêl-uballiṭ(iṭ)* (4) *m Na - ṣir m Ki - i - ilu Nabû* (5) *aḫi^pl - e - a* (6) *ilu* . . (?) *ilu* . . (Remainder of obv. and top of rev. broken off.) REV.: (9) *I ka* ŠE-BAR *I ḳa saluppi* (10) *e - lat maḫ-ri* (?)- . . . (11) *man-ma la i-nam-din* (12) *ši-pir-ta-a* (13) *lu-u am mu-kin-ni* (14) *kap-du ḫarrana^II a-na* (Left-hand edge) (15) [*šepi-šu šu*]-*kun-na-'*.

[No. 84,950]

NO. **120**. — OBV.: (1) *Duppi m ilu Marduk - šuma - iddin* (2) *a-na m ilu Bêl-apli-iddin m Na ṣir* (3) *m Ki-i-ilu Nabû aḫi^pl-e-*[*a*] (4) *ilu Nabû u ilu Marduk a-na aḫi^pl-e-*[*a*] (5) *lik-ru-bu am sabi^pl a-na* (6) *a la-ku it-ti m Arad-ilu Bêl* (7) *ḫi-bi* (?)-*u su-tir-ma ma-sar-tum* (8) [*i-na*]-*as-sa-ru u mimmu*(*mu*) (9) [*ma-la*] *la ip-pu-uš-šu-'* (10) . *- lak* (?) *- ka - a - ma* (11) . *-nim-ma it-ti* (12) *-ša-tu ḫa-bur-ru.* (Remainder broken off: what remains of rev. is blank)

[No. 84,930.]

NO. **121** — OBV.: (1) *Duppi m ilu Marduk-*[*šuma-iddin*] (2) *a-na m ilu Nabû-šuma-ešir* (3) *m ilu Bêl-apli-iddin m Na-ṣir* (4) *u m Ki-i-ilu Nabû aḫi^pl-e* (5) *ilu Nabû u ilu Marduk a-na* (6) *aḫi^pl-e-ia lik-ru-bu* (7) *ša taš-pur-a-ni* (8) *um-ma am irriši^pl* (9) *ša ilu Šamši ab ka* (10) *u* ŠE-KUL *ša ilu Šamši* (11) *ina eli lib-bi-šu*

Concerning Nabû-šuma-usur, about whom my lords sent unto me, if in his presence the increase(?) of the end of the . . . thus: "The wool . " . . with him my lords shall make [a contract(?) about] the burnt brick. Say (to him) that the burnt bricks are with you. Write and discuss with him Let my lords give him two manas of silver.

No. **119.**—Letter from Marduk-šuma-iddin unto Nabû-šuma-ešir, Bêl-apli-iddin, Bêl-uballiṭ, Naṣir, Kî-Nabû, my brothers . . .

1 *ḳa* of corn, 1 *ka* of dates, in addition to the former . . . no one hath given. May my letter be my witness. Speedily set it on its way.

No. **120.**—Letter from Marduk-šuma-iddin unto Bêl-apli-iddin, Nasir, Kî-Nabû, my brothers May Nabû and Marduk bless my brothers.

Write for soldiers to go with Arad-Bêl . . . and they may guard him and [do] whatever hath not been done . . .

No. **121.**—Letter from Marduk-[šuma-iddin] unto Nabû-šuma-ešir, Bêl-apli-iddin, Nasir, and Kî-Nabû, my brothers. May Nabû and Marduk bless my brothers.

Of that which ye did send, saying, "Send the gardeners of Šamaš and the seed-corn for Šamaš."

(12) *ša* [m] *Še-bar-ra-nu* (13) *mi-it-la-ka-ma* (14) *mimma(ma)* *ša* . . . (15) *e-pi-eš* REV.. (16) *ḫarrani* (?)-*šu* [pl] (17) *a-gur-ra* . (18) *a-na muḫ-ḫi* . (19) *šu-pur* *u* [am] [*irriši*] [pl] (20) *ab - ka - nim - ma* (21) *dul - la li*-[*pu-šu*] (22) ŠE-KUL *ša* [ilu] *Šamši* [*in*]-*nam-din* (23) *a-na ti ik* [*ti* . . .]-*nu* (24) *a - na* (*libbi*) *a - šap - par - ak - ku - nu - šu* (25) *kurummati a-na* [am] *ṣabi* (26) *ša dul-lu u* [am] [pl] (27) *a-di* [arḫu]. . [*aš*]-*pur* (28) . . . -*šu al-ka-* . . (29) *dul-la* *ša šarri* (30) . . . *a-mu-ru* [No 56,010]

NO. **122**.—OBV : (1) *Duppi* [m ilu] *Marduk*-[*šuma-iddin a-na*] (2) [m ilu] *Nabû - šuma* - [*ešir*] (3) [m] . . (4) *aḫi* - . (5) *a-na* . . . (6) *lik* . (7) . . (Remainder of obv. and top of rev. broken off) REV.· (8) . . -*bu-* . . . (9) *maḫ-ru* . (10) *ša ta-ad-di*-[*nu*] (11) *ina* *ḫi-in-di* . . . (12) *u kurummati* . . . (13) . (14) .
[No 84,986]

NO. **123** —OBV. : (1) *Duppi* [m ilu] *Marduk - šuma - iddin* (2) *a-na* [m] *Mi-nu-u* [m] *U-da nu* (3) *bêli-ia* [ilu] *Bêl u* [ilu] *Bêlti-ia* (4) *šu-lum u balaṭi ša bêli-ia* (5) *lik-bu-u en-na* (6) *I* $\frac{5}{6}$ *ma na* *kaspi* (7) *ša* [isu] *elippi ša ka-si-ia* (8) *u* . . *ma-na kaspi*. (Remainder of obv. broken off: rev. mutilated.)
[No. 46,731.]

NO. **124**.—OBV. : (1) *Duppi* [m ilu] *Marduk-šuma-iddin* [*a-na*] (2) [m ilu] *Nabû-šuma-ešir* [m ilu] *Bêl-apli-iddin.* (Remainder of obv. and rev. mutilated) [No. 70,336]

NO. **125**.—OBV.. (1) *Duppi* [m ilu] *Marduk-* . . . (2) [am] *ki-na-at-* . . . (3) *a-na* [m] *Bi-ru-* . . (4) *ša* [ilu] *Šamši* *aḫi-i*[*a*] (5) *lik-bu-u ina* (?) . . (6) *ša šatti V* [kam] *ub-* . . . (7) *a-na* [m ilu] *Šamšu-* . (8) *ša* [m ilu] *Šamšu-šuma-* . . . (9) *šattu I* [kam] *ša* [m] . (Rev mutilated)
[No 84,954]

With regard to the matter of Šebarranu (?) it hath been agreed, so do whatever [is necessary] . With regard to your . . . , send and despatch [gardeners] to do the work. The seed-corn for Šamaš shall be given; at the end of their . . . I will send thereto unto you. Maintenance for the workmen on the work, and also the . . . -men until the month of . . . [I (?) have] sent . . .

No. **122.**—Letter from Marduk-[šuma-iddin] unto Nabû-šuma-[ešir] . . . (*Remainder mutilated.*)

No. **123.**—Letter from Marduk-šuma-iddin unto Minû and Udanu, my lord. May Bêl and Bêltis grant peace and life unto my lord

Now [pay] one mana and five-sixths in silver for the boat (-load) of cassia, and . . . of a mana of silver . . .

No. **124.**—Letter from Marduk-šuma-iddin [unto] Nabû-šuma-ešir, Bêl-apli-iddin . . .

No. **125**—Letter from Marduk- . . . , the servant . . . unto Biru . . . , the [priest (?)] of Šamaš, my brother . . .

NO. **126**.—OBV.: (1) *Duppi* ${}^{m\ ilu}$*Marduk-* . (2) *a-na* ${}^{m\ am}$*dupšarri*[^{pl}] (3) *aḫi*^{pl}*-e-a* ^{ilu}*Nabû u* ^{ilu}[*Marduk*] (4) *a-na aḫi*^{pl}*-e-a* (5) *lik-ru-bu* ${}^{m\ ilu}$*Bu-ne-ne-ibni* (6) *apil-šu ša* ${}^{m\ ilu}$*Marduk* (?)*-na'id* (7) [^{am}]*arad ekalli ša ina bâbi* (8) *u-šu-uz-zu* GIŠ-DA (9) *ša* ^{ilu}*Šamši pi-ta-'* (10) *a-ki-i* GIŠ-DA . . (11) [*kap*]*-du* [*ana*]. REV: (12) *šepâ*^{II}*-šu šu-*[*kun*] (13) *kurummati ša* . (14) . . GIŠ-DA . . (15) [*a*]*-mu-ur-ru ki-i* (16) *kurummati e-tir-ru-'* (17) [*ul* (?)] *ta-di-nu lu-mur* (18) [${}^{m\ ilu}$]*Bu-ne-ne-ibni* (19) *nu-bat-tum ina pa-ni-ku-nu* (20) *la i-ba-a-ta* (21) *lib-bu-u šattu* . . . (22) *kurummati in-na-*[*din*].

[No. 66,442]

NO. **127**.—OBV.: (1) *Duppi* ^{m}*Mar-duk* . . (2) *a-na* ^{m}*Ṣil-la-a* (3) *aḫi-ia* ^{ilu}*Bêl u* ^{ilu}*Nabû* (4) *šu-lum u balaṭi ša aḫi-ia* (5) *lik-bu-u en-na* ^{m}*Ši-iš-ki* (6) *apil-šu ša* ^{m}*Iddina-apli a-gan-na* (7) *iḳ-ta-ba-'* (8) *um-ma saluppi* (9) *ebur ikli ša* ŠE-KUL (10) *ša šatti XVIII*^{kam} (11) *ša li-ta-mu* (12) *um-ma* ^{m}*Ṣil-la-*[*a*] REV.: (13) *it-ta-ši* (14) *en-na ki-i* (15) *ab-bi-ti um-ma* (16) *šu-u ebur ša saluppi* (17) *taš-šu-u saluppi* (18) *te-ri-ma a-na* (19) ^{m}*Ši-iš-ki i-di-in.*

[No. 33,076.]

NO. **128**.—OBV.: (1) *Duppi* ${}^{m\ ilu}$*Marduk-* . . . (2) *a-na* ^{m}. . . *-su* (3) *u* ^{m}. . . *-ia* (4) *aḫi*^{pl}*-e-a* (5) ^{ilu}*Bêl u* ^{ilu}*Nabû šu-lum-ku-nu* (6) *liḳ-bu-u* . (7) ^{m}*Mu-še-ir* . . (Remainder of obv. and rev. blank as though left unfinished.)

NO. **129**.—OBV.: (1) *Duppi* ^{m}*Mu-ra-nu a-na* (2) ${}^{m\ sal}$*Bêlti-šu abi-ia* (3) ^{ilu}*Bêl u* ^{ilu}*Nabû šu-lum* (4) *u balaṭi ša abi-ia*

No. **126.**—Letter from Marduk . . . unto the scribes, my brothers. May Nabû and [Marduk] bless my brothers.

Bunene-ibni, the son of Marduk-na'id, the servant of the palace who standeth at the door, hath opened the tithe for Šamaš. Wherefore, do thou speedily despatch (another?) tithe on its way. The sustenance for . . . the tithe I have seen. If the sustenance hath been given, give [no more?]. I will see [it]. Let not Bunene-ibni take holiday with you; (it is) for this for one year sustenance hath been given [him]!

No. **127.**—Letter from Marduk . . . unto Sillâ, my brother. May Bêl and Nabû grant peace and life unto my brother.

Now Šiški, the son of Iddina-apli, hath spoken here, thus: "The dates which are the produce of the field of seed-corn for the eighteenth year . . . Sillâ hath received." Now when I opened (?) (the letter), and it was the date-harvest which thou hadst received, (if) thou likest the dates, give some to Šiški.

No. **128.**—Letter from Marduk . . . unto . . . and . . . my brothers. May Bêl and Nabû grant you peace . . .

No. **129.**—Letter from Muranu unto Bêltišu, my father. May Bêl and Nabû grant peace unto my father.

(5) *liḳ-bu-u šu-u* (6) *ṭâbti-ka li-bu-u* (7) *ša* $^{\text{m ilu}}$*Nabû-zira iddin abi-ia* (8) *ina muḫ-ḫi-ia ra-ba-a-ta* (9) *mimma(ma) gab-bi* (10) *a-na* ^{arḫu}*Tašriti* (11) *aḫ-te-ri ki-i* (12) *at-ta a-na* (13) *ka-pa-da* (?)*-ia* Rev: (14) *te-ir-bu* (15) *pa-ni abi-ia* (16) *lu-ul-gu-ul* (17) *ki-i si-bu-tu-ku* (18) *i-ba-aš-šu-u* (19) *a-na* ^{sal}*Amat-*^{ilu}*Ba'u* (20) *šu-pur-am-ma* (21) ^{sal}*Be-lit ta-aš-pu-ur* (22) *ḫa-aš-da* (23) *lu-uš-kun* (24) *ûmu VII*^{kam} ^{ilu}*Bêlit* (25) *i-rab-bi* (26) *ka-pa-ad* (Left-hand edge) (27) *ṭe-e-mu ša abi-ia lu-us-mu.*

[No 33,075]

No. **130**—Obv.: (1) *Duppi* ^{m}*Mu-ra-nu a-na* (2) . . . *bêli-ia* (3) *ša* ^{am}. . . ^{ilu}*Bêl* ^{ilu}*Nabû* (4) *u* ^{ilu}. . . ^{ilu}. . . (5) *ûmu(mu) ru-ḳu-tu* . . . (6) *u-ṣal-la i-na silli* (7) *ša ilâni*^{pl} *šu-lum i-na* [*dul-li*?] (8) *ša-ki-in lu-ma-du* (9) *na-kut-tum aš-ta-aš-ši* (10) [*mi*]*-nam-ma te-e-mu* (11) [*ša*] *bêli-ia i-ri-ig-*[*gam*] (12) . . . *ûmu III*^{kam} . . . (13) *ṭe* (?)*-e-mu* (?) (14) [*ša*] *bêli-*[*ia*] . . . Rev.: (15) . . . (16) . . . (17) . . . (18) . . . *-ia ul* . . . (19) . . . [*ki*]*-i-ma-'* ŠE-BAR . . . (20) [*a*]*-na pani* $^{\text{m ilu}}$*Nabû-it-* . . (21) *li-iš-ši u bêl liš-pu-ru* (22) *ICL gur* ŠE-BAR (23) *at-ta-na-aš* (?)-[*šu* ?] (24) *a-na* ^{m}*Kar-* . . (25) *a-*[*na*] *bêli-ia al-*[*tap-ra*] (26) *ḳap-du ṭe-e-mu ša* (27) *bêli-ia lu-uš-mu* (28) *a-mur* 30 *ḳa bit-li-e* (29) *ina ḳatâ*^{II} $^{\text{m ilu}}$*Itti-Nabû-* . . . (30) *ul-te-bi-la* (Left-hand edge) (31) [^{m}*Mu-ra-nu šu*]*-lum ša bîti gab-bi* (32) [*i-ša-a*]*-al.*

[No. 38,998]

No. **131** — Obv.: (1) *Duppi* ^{m}*Mu-šal-lim-*^{ilu}*Marduk* (2) *a-na* ^{m}*Šuma-uṣur* (3) *u* ^{m}*Kal-ba-a aḫi*^{pl}*-e-a* (4) ^{ilu}*Nabû u* ^{ilu}*Marduk a-na* (5) *aḫi*^{pl}*-e-a lik-ru-bu* (6) *ina muḫ-ḫi*

Thy bountiful kindness for Nabû-zira-iddin, my father, hath been very great towards me; I have dug all until the month Tisri If thou wilt enter into my ideas (?), then shall I see[1] my father's face.

If it be thy wish, send unto the lady Amat-Ba'u, and thou hast sent unto the lady Bêlit that I may set . . . The seventh day Bêltis increaseth. Speedily let me hear news of my father.

No. **130**.—Letter from Muranu unto . . . my lord. Daily unto Bêl, Nabû, and . . . for . . . lengthy days I pray.

The work is going on happily under the protection of the gods; I am taking much trouble. Why hath news from my lord been delayed? [Now] for three [or four] days (?) [I have heard no?] news from my lord . . .

. . . flour from the corn for Nabû-it- . . . let him obtain and let my lord send. I have received one hundred and fifty *gur* of corn; unto Kar . . . for my lord I have sent (it). Speedily let me hear news from my lord. Behold, I have sent 30 *ka* of *bitlî* by the hand of Nabû-it . . . Muranu sendeth greeting to all the household.

No. **131**.—Letter from Mušallim-Marduk unto Šuma-uṣur and Kalbâ, my brothers. May Nabû and Marduk bless my brothers.

---

[1] *Lulgul*, probably a scribe's mistake for *ludgul*.

ma-as-sar-tum (7) *ša ekurri la ta-sil-la-'* (8) *kaspi ša mâr šarri* (9) *kaspi ša* ${}^{m\,ilu}$*Šamšu-iddin* (10) *u kaspi ma-la ina ḳu-up-pu* (11) *pi-it-ḳa-nim-ma* (?) (12) *I ma-na* . (13) . . . REV.: (14) *liš-al* (15) ${}^{m\,ilu}$*Bêl-mušallim u* ${}^{m\,ilu}$*Bêl-* . . . (16) *in-na-ma immeri* (17) *ina muḫ-ḫi ti-tur-ru* (18) *li-in-ḫar-ru-nu* (19) *a-di muḫ-ḫi ša immeri* (20) *ša šarri i-kaš-ša-du-nu* (21) *su-tir-ra-ma ḫarrana* ^{II} (22) *a-na šepâ* ^{II} (23) *ša* ^{m}*Lu-ud-du-a-na-ṣabi* (24) *šuk na-' a-na* (25) *šim-tum ša* ^{m}*Ku-na a* (26) *a-na muḫ-ḫi alpi* ^{pl} (27) *lil-lik* (Left hand edge) (28) *I ma-na kaspi ina lib-bi a-na* (29) ^{m}*Lu-ud du-ana-ṣabi in-na-' ma rig-gam-* . . .

[No. 63,142]

NO. **132**.—OBV: (1) *Duppi* ^{m}*Mu-še-zib-* ^{ilu}*Bêl a-na* (2) ^{am}ŠA-TAM *abi-ia* ^{ilu}*Bêl u* ^{ilu}[*Nabû*] (3) *šu-lum abi-ia lik-ru-u* (4) *a-na eli iṣ* (?)*-la-* (?)*-li-* . (5) *ša bêl aḳ-bu-u* ^{m}*Šuma-uṣur* (6) . . *iš-mu-u* (7) . *-gi-li-bu* (8) . . *-ru-tu* (Top of rev. broken) REV. (9) . . *nu* (10) *ša* . . . (11) . . . (12) *ša* ${}^{m\,ilu}$*Bêl-iddin* . . . (13) *ina ḳatâ* ^{II} ^{m}*Mu-še-zib-* . . .

[No. 53,133]

NO. **133**—OBV.: (1) *Duppi* ^{m}*Mu-še-zib-* ^{ilu}*Marduk* (2) *a-na* ^{am}*šangi* ^{pl} (3) *aḫi* ^{pl}*-e-a* ^{ilu}*Bêl u* ^{ilu}*Nabû* (4) *šu-lum ša aḫi* ^{pl}*-e-a* (5) *lik-bu-u mi-nam-ma* (6) *ina muḫ-ḫi dul-lu* ^{am}*ušpari* (7) *ša* ^{alu}*Airi sil-la-*[*ti*] (8) *ta-bar-ri-* . . (9) *a-na* ^{m}*Su-* . . . (10) *ša* (?) . . (Remainder of obv. and top of rev. broken off) REV.: (11) . . (12) *šu* . . . (13) *kaspi a-na* ^{am}*agiri* ${}^{pl(?)}$ (14) *lid-din* ^{am}*agiri* ^{pl} (15) *la-mu-u-in-ni* (16) *u dul-la-a* (17) *ina la* ^{am}*agiri* ^{pl} (18) *baṭ-ṭil* (19) *ina muḫ-ḫi dul-la ša* ^{alu}*Airi* (20) *la ta-sil-la-'* (21) *te-ik-tum* ^{m}*Ba-ku-u* (22) *ina lib-bu-šu-nu* (23) *la i-šak-kan* (Left-hand edge) (24) . . *-ta-a-' a-mur-' ki-i* (25) . . . *-tum a-na ni* . . (26) . . *u* . . . *ku-tal a-na ni-ip-* . . .

[No 63,142.]

Be not slack in watching over the interests of the Temple; secure the money belonging to the King's son, the money belonging to Šamaš-iddin, and all the money which is in the chest . . .

. . let him ask. Send Bêl-mušallim and Bêl- . . . that they may receive a sheep on account of the bridge. Before the King's sheep arrive, do thou write and arrange a caravan for Luddu-ana-ṣabi; for the decision of Kunâ, let him go about the oxen. Send one mana of silver for it unto Luddu-ana-ṣabi . . .

No. **132.**—Letter from Mušezib-Bêl unto the *šatam*, my father. May Bêl and Nabû grant peace unto my father.

I have spoken concerning the . . . Šuma-usur . . .

No. **133.**—Letter from Mušezib-Marduk unto the priests, my brothers. May Bêl and Nabû grant peace unto my brothers.

Why have ye caused neglect in the matter of the work of the weaver for Iyyar? . . .

. . . Let him pay the money unto the hired men; the hired men are all round me, yet my work cometh to an end without hired men.

Be not slack over the work for Iyyar, Bakû shall not cause any discontinuation among you.

. . . .

No **134**—Obv.: (1) *Duppi* ^{m}*Mu-še-zib-*^{ilu}*Marduk* (?) (2) *a-na* ^{am}[*šangi*]^{pl} (3) *aḫi*^{pl}*-e-a* (4) ^{ilu}*Bêl u* ^{ilu}*Nabû šu-lum* (5) *ša aḫi*^{pl}*-e-a* (6) *lik-bu-u kap-du* (7) *III ma-na kaspi* (8) $^{m\ ilu}$*Bêl-apli-iddin* (9) *u* $^{m\ ilu}$*Samšu-aḫi-iddin* (10) ^{am}*rab-banûti*^{pl} *liš-ša-'* (11) *u lil-lik-ki* (12) . $^{m\ ilu}$*Bêl-apli-* . . . (13) . . . (Remainder of obv and top of rev broken off.) Rev.: (14) . . *-ia* . . . (15) *ša um* . . . (16) . . *du* . . (17) . . . (18) *V* . . . *du* . . (19) *III ma-*[*na*] . . (20) *it-* . (21) *ša* . . . (22) *ul* . (23) *ḫarrana*^{II} *a* (24) *a-ta* (?) . . (Left-hand edge) (25) (26) . *bîtâti*^{pl} $^{m\ ilu}$*Šamšu-aḫi-iddin apil-šu* (?) *ša* $^{m\ ilu}$*Šamšu-id* . .

[No 84,976]

No. **135**—Obv: (1) *Duppi* ^{m}*Mu-še-zib-*^{ilu}*Marduk* (2) *a-na* ^{m}*Mu-še-zib-*^{ilu}*Marduk* (3) *aḫi-ia* ^{ilu}*Nabû u* ^{ilu}*Marduk* (4) *a-na aḫi-ia lik-ru-bu* (5) [*ina eli*] ^{m}*Šuma-iddina*(*na*) (6) [*ša aš-pur*]*-rak-ka* (7) . . . *i-ši-iz-ma* (8) [*šu* ?]*-bi-lu* (9) . . *bi-la* (10) . . . *ut* (?) (Remainder of obv. broken off: what remains of rev is blank) [No 84,992]

No **136**—Obv.: (1) *Duppi* ^{m}*Mu-še-zib-*^{ilu}[*Marduk* (?)] (2) *a-na* ^{am}*šangi* UD-KIB-NUN-KI (3) *bêli-ia* ^{ilu}*Bêl u* ^{ilu}*Nabû šu-lum* (4) *ša bêli-ia lik-bu-u* (5) *ûmu*(*mu*)*-us-su* ^{ilu}*Šamši u* ^{ilu}*A-a* (6) *a-na balaṭ napšâti*^{pl} *ṭu-ub šeri* (7) *a-ra-ku ûmu*(*mu*) [*ša bêli-ia*] (8) [*u-sal-la*] . (Remainder of obv. broken off: what remains of rev. is blank) [No. 71,783]

No. **137**—Obv.: (1) *Duppi* $^{m\ ilu}$*Nabû-aḫi*^{pl}*-iddin* (2) *a-na* ^{m}*Ri-mut bêli-šu* (3) ^{ilu}*Nabû u* ^{ilu}*Marduk šu-lum* (4) *u ba-la-ṭu ša bêli-ia* (5) *lik-bu-u a-na eli* (6) *a gur-ru ša ina pani* $^{m\ ilu}$*Nabû-apli-iddin* (7) *ša be-lum iš-pur-ru* (8) *at-ta be lum* (9) *iḳ-ta-ba-a um-ma* (10) *la ta-da-al-laḫ šu* (11) *šu-u iḳ-ta-ba-a* (12) *um-mu ina ḳatâ*^{II} (13) $^{m\ ilu}$*Nergal-uṣur* (14) *al* (?)*-ṭir-ka*

No **134**.—Letter from Mušezib-Marduk (?) unto the [priests], my brothers May Bêl and Nabû grant peace unto my brothers.

Speedily let Bêl-apli-iddin and Šamaš-aḫi-iddin, the architects, receive three mana of silver, and let them come . . .

No **135** — Letter from Mušezib - Marduk unto Mušezib - Marduk, my brother. May Nabû and Marduk be gracious unto my brother. (*Remainder mutilated*)

No. **136**—Letter from Mušezib-Marduk (?) unto the Priest of Sippar, my lord. May Bêl and Nabû grant peace unto my lord. Daily [I pray] unto Šamaš and Aa for the life, health, long days . . . [of my lord] . . .

No. **137**.—Letter from Nabû-aḫi-iddin unto Rimut, his lord. May Nabû and Marduk grant peace and life unto my lord.

In the matter of those burnt bricks which are in the hands of Nabû-apli-iddin, of which my lord hath sent, thou, my lord, didst say "trouble him not"; but he hath spoken thus, "By the hands of Nergal-usur I am

REV: (15) ^{m}Ikiša(ša)-apli apil-šu ša (16) ^{m}Itti-^{ilu}Šamši-balaṭa šu u (17) u-di ša tim- . (18) ina eli ra-ba-a-ka (19) u da-la-ḫa ša ameli (20) ina katâ^{ll} šak-na ûmu III^{kam} (21) a-na pani be-ili-ia (22) it (?)-[tal]-ka ki-i (23) -di (24) . . a (?) na (?) . (25) . ka (?) a . (26) a-ma-ḫa-ar-ka (?) (27) a-na ^{m}Ri-mut (28) a-nam-din (29) $^{m\,ilu}$Marduk zii a-ibni (30) i-na-an-na (Left-hand edge) (31) um-ma mimma i-bi (?)- . . . [No 46,705.]

No. 138 —OBV.: (1) Duppi $^{m\,ilu}$Nabû-aḫi- . . (2) a-na ^{m} . . -apli (3) aḫi-ia ^{ilu}Nabû u ^{ilu}Marduk (4) a-na aḫi-ia lik-ru-bu (5) dib-bi [a]-ga-['] (6) ša bêl iš-pur-ru (7) a-na . ša ḫi-ib-bi (8) in- . (9) . . -ki (10) ul-tir (?)-bu REV.: (11) it-ti-šu (12) ul a-kab (?)-bu (13) a-na ûmu XVI^{kam} (14) it-ti-šu (15) u-ka-at (16) ^{am}gal-la ša bêli-ia (17) lu-mur ma mi-nu (18) ki-i u-ka-at (19) a-na bêli-ia (20) lu-šu-pur ru (21) . . . [No. 31,288]

No 139.—OBV : (1) Duppi $^{m\,ilu}$Nabû-aḫi- . . . (2) a-na ^{m}Šad-din-nu aḫi-[ia] (3) ^{ilu}Bêl ^{ilu}Nabû šu-lum balaṭi ša aḫi-ia [lik-bu-u] (4) a-mur ši-pir-tum a-na ^{m}Eriba-apli (5) al-tap-par um-ma at-ta (6) u ^{m}Šad-din-nu ŠE-BAR at-tu-u a (7) ša-kin (?) ut tim a-na ešten(en) man-am-ma (8) ša ina pani-ku-nu ba-nu u ki-i (9) esten(en) mârâni^{pl} ša $^{sal\,ilu}$Na-na-a-itti-ia (10) i-lik (?)-ku tu . . -ti (11) ^{m}Ki-i ^{ilu}Šamši ^{am}gal-la (12) in-da-ḫar ki-i man-am-ma (13) ia-a-nu a-na ^{m}Lib-luṭ (14) ^{m}Su-ḫa-a-a (15) . . . ut. (A few lines broken away) REV (16) . . (17) . . . -li-' . (18) [at]-ta te-i di (19) ša man-am-ma e-la-ti . (20) la da-ga-la-ka (21) . . . bîti u ^{am}la-mu-ta-nu (22) . . . -u-a la i-liš-ši (23) GIŠ-MA u uddi a-pi (24) u i- . ša i-na (25) . -mi-ti i ba-aš-šu-u (26) . . dul-lu (27) . . . ut (?) mi-na-[a a]-na (28) $^{m\,ilu}$Nabû-di-i-ni . (29) . ka-li-e (30) ma (?) la . . . -ka (31) bêl li- . . -mu (32) ša E-babbar-[ra] . . (33) bêl li- . . . (34) . (35) a-na . . . (36) . . . lid . . . [No 29,495]

writing to thee." Ikišа-apli, the son of Itti-Šamaš-balatu . . . As for thy greatness (?) and the troubling of the man, the matter is settled; on the third day [he shall come] into my lord's presence . . .

No. **138.**—Letter from Nabû-aḫi- . . . unto . . . -apli, my brother. May Nabû and Marduk be gracious unto my brother.

That matter on which my lord hath sent . . . . . . with him I have not spoken (?). I shall finish with him by the sixteenth day. Let me see my lord's servant that I may send unto my lord how I shall have completed (the affair).

No. **139.**—Letter from Nabû-aḫi- . . . unto Šaddinnu, my brother. May Bêl (and) Nabû grant peace and life unto my brother.

Now behold, I am sending a letter unto Eriba-apli, saying, "Do thou and Šaddinnu . . . my corn unto someone who is with you, and if one of the sons of Nanâ-ittia is coming . . ."

Kî-Šamaš, the servant, hath received . . . If there be no one, [speak] unto Liblut . . . (*Remainder mutilated.*)

No. **140** — Obv (1) [*Duppi*] ${}^{m\ ilu}$*Bêl-aḫi*^{pl}*-ikiša(ša)* (2) *a-na* ^{am}*šangi* UD-KIB-NUN-KI (3) *abi-ia* ^{ilu}*Nabû u* ^{ilu}*Marduk a-na* (4) *abi-ia lik-ru-bu* (5) *a-mur* ${}^{m\ ilu}$*Šamšu-it-ti-ia* (6) *a-na pa-ni bêli-ia al-tap-ra* (7) *I gur* ŠE-BAR *ina kurummati* (8) ^{arhu}*Nisanni bêli lid-da-aš-šu.* Rev.: (9) *dul-lu ina la-* (or *te-*) *ḫi-ri* (10) *ip-pu-uš X zab-bil-lu* (11) *bêli lu-še-bi-li tam-lu-u* (12) *nu-kal-la.*

(Seal)

[No 74,741.]

No **141**.—Obv.: (1) *Duppi* ${}^{m\ ilu}$*Nabû-apli-*[*iddin*?] (2) *a-na* ^{m}*Ardi-ia* [*aḫi-ia*] (3) ^{ilu}*Bêl u* ^{ilu}*Nabû šu-*[*lum*] (4) [*u balaṭi ša aḫi-ia*] (5) [*lik-bu-u*] . . . (6) . . . [*dul-lu*] (7) [*ana*] *ṣi-bu-*[*ti*] (8) *ša* [*bêli*] *lu-ma-a-du* (9) *šak-na-at ina ḳatâ*^{II} (10) *man-ma ka-a-a-ma-nu-u* (11) *ša kap-du i-na-aš-šu-u* (12) *i-nam-da-aš-šu u* (13) *ga-ba-ru-šu* (14) *i-na-aš-ša-'* (15) *bêl lu-še-bi-il* (16) *bêl la i-sil-li* (17) *a-na ṣi-bu-ti-šu* Rev: (18) *lu-ma-a-du šak-na-at* (19) *ša* ^{am}*u-ra-šu ša* (20) *mâr* ^{sal}*Na-ki-ia-a-tum* (21) *man-ma a-gan-na ia-a-nu* (22) ^{m}. . . *i-kab-ba-'* (23) *um-ma ana* ^{m}*Ardi-ia ip-te-iḳ-du* (24) . . . *-tal*(?)*-lak* (25) . . . (26) . . . (27) *bêl* . . . (28) *ṭe-en* . . . (29) *ma-* . . (30) *ša* ^{am}*u-ra-*[*šu*] . . . (31) *ma-ṭu-u.*

[No. 54,165]

No. **142** — Obv: (1) *Duppi* ${}^{m\ ilu}$*Nabû-apli-iddin a-na* (2) ^{m}*Mu-ra-nu aḫi-ia* (3) ^{ilu}*Nabû u* ^{ilu}*Marduk a-na* (4) *aḫi-ia lik-ru-bu* (5) *mi-na-a šu-gar-ru-u* (6) *ša* ^{arhu}*Nisanni* (7) *ul*

No. **140**.—[Letter] from Bêl-aḫi-ikiša unto the Priest of Sippar, my father. May Nabû and Marduk bless my father.

Now behold, I am sending Samaš-ittia unto my lord's presence; let my lord give him one *gur* of corn as his provisions for the month of Nisan. He is doing the work on the . . . ; let my lord send ten baskets (and) we will finish the terrace.

No. **141**.—Letter from Nabû-apli-iddin(?) unto Ardia, [my brother]. May Bêl and Nabû grant peace [and life unto my brother] . . .

[According to the] wish [of my lord, the matter] hath been carefully arranged. He shall deliver it into the hands of some trustworthy person who will bring it speedily, and take the answer thereof. Let my lord send; let not my lord be slack, it hath been carefully arranged according to his wish. Concerning a *urašu*-man for the son of Nakiatum, there is no one here . . . hath said that Ardia hath ordered . . .

No. **142**.—Letter from Nabû-apli-iddin unto Muranu my brother. May Nabû and Marduk bless my brother.

Why hast thou not sent the *šugarrû* of the dates for Nisan? Now behold, I am come to Babylon to the

tu (?)-*še-bi-lu* (8) *en*-(*na*) *a-mur* (9) *a-na* TIN-TIR-KI. REV.: (10) *a-na pani* (11) ^{am}*bêl-piḫati* (12) *a-tal-lak-ku* (13) *IV ka-lu-mu* (14) *kur-ba-nu-u* (15) *aš-ši-zib it-ti* (16) ^{m}*Ku-ban-na* ^{ilu}*Marduk* (17) *i-ša-' a-na* (18) TIN-TIR-KI *ir-bi* (19) *ki-i na-kut-tum* (20) *al-tap-par-ka.*

(Envelope of the above)

Dup-pi $^{m\ ilu}$*Nabû-apli-iddin a*-[*na*].

(Seal)

[^{m}]*Mu-ra-nu.*

[Nos. 78,100 and 78,100 A]

NO. **143**—OBV.: (1) [*Duppi* $^{m\ ilu}$*Bêl*]-*apli-iddin* ^{m}*Na-ṣir* (2) [*u*] ^{m}*Ki-i*-^{ilu}*Nabû a-na* (3) ^{m}*Šu-la-a aḫi-i-ni* (4) *I ka šam-ni a-na* (5) $^{m\ ilu}$*Šamšu-šarri-usur* (6) *a-na bît kâre*^{pl} REV.: (7) *i-din* ^{arḫu}*Ululu ûmu IV*^{kam} (8) *šattu XVI*^{kam} ^{ilu}*Nabû-na'id* (9) [*šar*] TIN-TIR-KI.

[No. 60,502.]

NO. **144**—OBV.: (1) *Duppi* $^{m\ ilu}$*Nabû-etir-napšâti*^{pl} (2) *a-na* $^{m\ ilu}$*Bêl-ibni aḫi-ia* (3) ^{ilu}*Bêl u* ^{ilu}*Nabû šu-lum u balati* (4) *ša aḫi-ia lik-bu-u* (5) *nar-bu-u ameli ša it-ti* (6) *bêl da-ba-bi-šu ḫarrana*^{II} (7) *il-la-ku nar-bu-u-šu* (8) *ḫarrana*^{II} *it-ti-ia* (9) *ta-at-ta-lak* (10) *ṣi-bu-ta-a ul te-pu-uš* (11) *a-di muḫ-ḫi ša* (12) *ta* (?)-*gi-ri pa-ni-ma* (13) . . . *tu* . . . (?) *la-nu* (14) . . . *il-ku* . . . REV.: (15) *en-na a-mur* (16) [*a*]-*na aḫi-ia al-tap-ra* (17) *II ma-na kaspi piṣû*(*u*) (18) ^{m}*Ṣal-lum* ^{am}*rik-ki* (19) *mâr ša* ^{m}*Ki-na-a i-din* (20) *lu-ma-a du a-na* (21) *ṣi-bu-ti-ia* (22) *ša-ki-in ia-a-nu-u* (23) *il-la-nu-uš-šu* (24) *mi-di-ta-a* (25) *ta ša-ak-ka-an.*

[No. 65,236]

presence of the Governor. Send four lambs as a present for the milk[1] with Kubanni-Marduk; come into Babylon, although I am sending what is a trouble (unto thee).

Envelope. — "Letter from Nabû - apli - iddin to Muranu."

No. **143.**—[Letter from Bêl]-apli-iddin, Nasir, [and] Kî-Nabû unto Šulâ, our brother.

Give one ka of oil to Šamaš-šarri-uṣur for the granary.[2]

(Dated) Elul, fourth day, sixteenth year of Nabû-na'id, [King] of Babylon.

No. **144.**—Letter from Nabû-eṭir-napšâti unto Bêl-ibni, my brother. May Bêl and Nabû grant peace and life unto my brother.

"The strength of a man who goeth on a journey with his enemy is his strength," but thou hast gone on a journey with me and yet dost not do my behest. Before thou displeasest me (?) . . . Now, behold! I send unto my brother two manas of white silver; give them to Ṣallum, the herb-seller (?), the son of Kinâ. This is my particular wish; (though thou doest) nothing else besides, thou shalt settle my accounts.

---

[1] *Aš-ši-zib = ana ši-zib ?*

[2] The character here is probably No. 10,809 in Brunnow's *List.*

NO **145**—OBV: (1) *Duppi* [m]. . . (2) *a-na* [m]*La-ba-ši* (3) *abi-ia* [ilu]*Bêl u* [ilu]*Nabû* (4) *šu-lum u balati ša abi-ia* (5) *lik-bu-u* (6) [*dul*?]-*la* [m ilu]*Nabû-šuma-iddin* (7) [*mâru*]-*u-a ḫu-si-ka* (8) *a-ka-lu* (9) *in-na-* . . . (10) [m ilu]*Nabû-šuma-iddin* (11) *mâru-u-a ana libbi* . . . (12) *ša a-na-ku* (Reverse mutilated) [No. 77,448]

NO. **146**—OBV.: (1) *Duppi* [m ilu]*Nabû-bani-aḫi* (2) *a-na* [m]. . . *-etir* (3) *abi-ia* [ilu]*Nabû u* [ilu]*Marduk* (4) *a-na abi-ia lik-ru-bu* (5) *ki-i aš-mu-u.* (Remainder of obv. and top of rev. broken off) REV: (6) . . . (7) *man-ma tap-pu-da-ni-ni* (8) *la ub-ba-lu*(?) (9) *šu-u tâbti* (10) *ša bêli-ia ina muḫ-ḫi-ia* (11) *ra-ba-a-ta* [No. 84,920.]

NO **147**—OBV.: (1) *Duppi* [m ilu]*Nabû-da-a-nu* (2) *a-na* [sal]*Tu-na-a* (3) *aḫati-ia* [ilu]*Bêl u* [ilu]*Nabû* (4) *šu-lum u balaṭi ša aḫati-ia lik-bu-u* (5) *šu-pur-'-ma* [m]*Kas-bi-ba-nu* (6) *ab-ku u mi-nu-u* (7) *ki-i* . . . *-ti-'* (8) *ḫar-ra-* . . . (9) *ad-* . . (Remainder of obv. and top of rev. broken off) REV: (13) *ina eli* . . . (14) *ša bîti-* . . . (15) *ina ḫa-tu-* . . . (16) *a-na* [[m]*Kas*]-*bi-ba-nu* (17) *ul aš-pur* (18) *mimma*(*ma*) *na-kut-ta-a* (19) *la tu-* . . . *ša-'.* [No. 46,441.]

NO. **148**—OBV.: (1) *Duppi* [m ilu]*Nabû-di-i-ni-šarri* (2) *a-na* [m]*Iddina-*[ilu]*Marduk* (3) *abi-ia* [ilu]*Bêl u* [ilu]*Nabû* (4) *šu-lum balaṭi ša abi-ia* (5) *lik-bu-u bêl a-mur* (6) [m ilu]*Nergal-uṣur al-tap-par-ka* (7) *u* [m ilu]*Bêl-ri-man-ni* (8) *bêl-pi-kit-ti-ia* (9) *it-ti-šu a-di muḫ-ḫi* (10) $\frac{1}{3}$ *ma-na kaspi bêli* (11) *lid-da-šu kaspi a-na* (12) *ša-a-šu u* [m ilu]*Bêl-ri-man-ni* (13) *id-din-nu* (14) *a-na kur-ba-nu-u* REV.: (15) *lid-din-nu-'* (16) *kap-da in-na-šu-'* (17) *a-di la-' kur-ba-nu-u* (18) *ik-ki-ir bu-da* (19) *ša ta-ad-din-nu* (20) *a-na* [m ilu]*Daîan-bêli-uṣur* (21) *at-ta-din-nu* [No 30,942.]

No. **145**.—Letter from . . . unto Labaši, my father. May Bêl and Nabû grant peace and life unto my father. (*Remainder mutilated.*)

No. **146**.—Letter from Nabû-bani-aḫi unto . . . -eṭir, my father. May Nabû and Marduk bless my father.

When I heard . . .

[And] none hath brought us help (?). [But] the kindness of my lord towards me is great.

No. **147**.—Letter from Nabû-dânu unto Ṭunâ, my sister. May Bêl and Nabû grant peace and life unto my sister.

Send and fetch Kasbibanu, and whatever . . . . . . Unto Kasbibanu I sent not. Do not [put thyself] to any trouble [over it].

No. **148**.—Letter from Nabû-dîni-šarri unto Iddina-Marduk, my father. May Bêl and Nabû grant peace and life unto my father.

Behold, now, my lord, I am sending Nergal-usur unto thee, and Bêl-rimanni, my overseer, with him. Let my lord give him as much as one-third of a mana of silver, but let him give the money (which he giveth to him and Bêl-rimanni) as a present; send him quickly before he hath changed the present. The receipt which thou hast given, I will give unto Daîan-bêli-usur.

No. **149**. — Obv.: (1) *Duppi* $^{m\,ilu}$*Nabû-aḫi*(?)- . . . (2) *a-na* ^{sal}*Be-lit* . . . [*aḫati-ia*] (3) ^{ilu}*Bêl u* ^{ilu}*Nabû* [*šu-lum u balaṭi ša aḫati-ia*] (4) *lik-bu-u CXX ma-ši-ḫu* (5) *ša saluppi ip-* . . . (6) *X ma-ši-ḫu a-na* . . . (7) *XX ma-ši-ḫu a-na* . . . (8) *X ma-ši-ḫu a-na* ^{ilu}*Bêl* (9) *LXXX ma-ši-ḫu a-na* $^{m\,ilu}$*Bêl-ibni* (10) . . . *-ta* . . . (11) *lid-din-nu-' XLIII gur* (12) *ša* ŠE-BAR *XXII ma ši-ḫu* (13) *a-na pani-ka a-* . . . (14) . . . Rev: (15) . . . (16) *a-na ru-uḫ-*[*ti*] (17) *lid-ku-u* ŠE-BAR (18) . . *-ra-'* (19) *a-na man-ma* (20) *la ta-nam-*[*din*] (21) ŠE-BAR *a-na pa*(?)*-nu-šu* (?) (22) *ul dag-gal* (23) *a-na eli* ŠE-BAR *ša* ^{m}. . . . (24) *al-li-ki man-ma* (25) *ul i-din-nu* (26) *ḳimi a-gan-na-ka* (27) *li-ḫi-ru ḳimi* (28) *a-gan-na ul* [*ṭâbi*?] (29) *mimmu*(*mu*) . . . (30) . . (31) *a-na* . . . (Left-hand edge) (32) [*šup*?]*-ra-' a-na* $^{m\,ilu}$*Bêl-uballiṭ ḳi-bi-i* (33) *ina eli* ^{iṣu}*elippi liš-is-bat nu-bat-tum la* (34) . . . *i-ba-tum.* [No. 74,045]

No. **150**—Obv.: (1) *Duppi* $^{m\,ilu}$*Nabû-zira-ukin* ^{am}E-GAL (2) *a-na* ^{am}E-BAR UD-KIB-NUN-KI (3) *aḫi-ia* ^{ilu}*Nabû u* ^{ilu}*Marduk* (4) *a-na aḫi-ia lik-ru-bu* (5) $^{m\,ilu}$*Nergal-suma-epuš dup šar* (6) *ša ina pa-ni-ka mi-na-a* (7) *kurummat-su ta-kil-*[*lu*] (8) *ki-i dul-la-šu i-*[*pu-uš*] (9) *kurummat-su ša* (?) . . . (10) *lib-bu* . . . (11) *la tu-*[*še-ti-iḳ*] (12) *u dul-la* . . . Rev.: (13) [*ki*]*-i dul-*[*la*] . . . (14) *ina Ekurri ia-a* [*nu*] (15) *šu-pur-ši-ma dul-la* . . . (16) *a-šar i-ba-aš-šu-u li-*[*pu-uš*] (17) *mi-na-a i-nam-ziḳ* (?) . . . (18) *um-ma dul-la-a i-ba-aš-ši* (19) *u kurummati-a ik-kal-*[*lu*] (20) *a-na mâr šarri ana muḫ-ḫi-šu* (21) *a-kab-bi šarru kurummati il-ta-kan* (22) *dul-lu uk-tal-lim-šu* (23) *a-na ša ina pa-ni-ka* (24) [*ba*]*-nu-u e-pu-uš.* [No. 60,644]

No. **149.**—Letter from Nabû-aḫi (?) . . . unto the lady Bêlit . . . [my sister]. May Bêl and Nabû grant [peace and life unto my sister].

One hundred and twenty measures of dates . . . ; let them give ten measures to . . . , twenty measures to . . . , ten measures to Bêl, eighty measures to Bêl-ibni. Of the forty-three *gur* of corn, twenty-two measures unto thee . . . for the residue (?) let them collect ; the corn . . . do not give to anyone, entrust not the corn to . . . As regards the corn for [So-and-so], do not give it to some traveller ; let them inspect the flour there with you, (for) the flour here is not [good ?] . . . Speak unto Bêl-uballiṭ (?) about a boat that it may take (it) ; let him not hold holiday.

No. **150.**—Letter from Nabû-zira-ukin, the Chamberlain, unto the Priest of Sippar, my brother. May Nabû and Marduk bless my brother.

Nergal-šuma-epuš, the scribe, who is with thee—why hast thou withheld his rations ? If [he doeth] his work [give him] his rations. Be not neglectful in this matter, or [his] work [will cease ?]. [If] there is no work in the Temple, send him, and wherever there is work to be done, let him do it. For why should he complain (?) thus, " I have work to do, yet he withholdeth my rations " ? I will speak to the King's son on his behalf ; the King will order his rations (to be given), (and) will shew him work, (and) he shall do that which is pleasing to thee.

No. **151**—Obv.: (1) *Duppi* $^{m\,ilu}$*Nabû-zira-ibašši(ši)* (2) *a-na* ^{sal}*Sik-ku-u* (3) *aḫati-ia* ^{ilu}*Bêl u* ^{ilu}*Nabû šu-lum* (4) *u balatu(tu) ša aḫati lik-bu-u* (5) *ina silli ša ilâni*^{pl} *šu-lum* (6) *a-na-ku u šu-lum a-na* (7) $^{m\,ilu}$*Bêl-iddin a-mur ši-pir-tum* (8) *a-na* ^{m}*Iddina-*^{ilu}*Marduk apil-šu ša* ^{m}*Iḳiša(ša)-apli* (9) *al-tap-par X gur* ŠE-BAR (10) *i-nam-dak-ka* (11) *ina muḫ-ḫi bîti* (12) *la ta-sil-li* Rev.: (13) *at-ta pal-sa-'* (14) *ilâni*^{pl} *a-na muḫ-ḫi-ia* (15) *su-ul-li-'* (16) *kap-du ṭe-en-ka* (17) *ina ḳatâ*^{II} *man-ma* (18) *al-la-ku lu-uš-me.*

[No. 31,290.]

No **152**—Obv.: (1) *Duppi* $^{m\,ilu}$*Nabû-zira-ibni* (2) *a-na* ^{m}*Ri-mut* (3) *aḫi-šu* ^{ilu}*Bêl u* ^{ilu}*Nabû* (4) *šu-lum aḫi-ia* (5) *liḳ-bu-u kaspi* (6) *ša* ^{ilu}*Samši ša a-na* (7) ^{kanû}*bu-ra-ni-e nadnu(nu)* (8) *ṣabi*^{pl} *ša iš-šu-ma* (9) *am-li-lik* Rev.: (10) *al-kam-ma* (11) *lu-kal-lim-ka* (12) *a-mur ḫar-ra* (13) *ša* ^{kanû}*bu-ra-ni-e* (14) *ešten(en) amelu ina ku-tal-li-ka* (15) *is-si-ir* (16) *al-kam-ma sabi*^{pl} (17) *a-na bêli-ia* (18) *lu-kal-lim* (19) *VIII C* ^{kanû}*bu-ra-ni-e ina pani bêli-nu.*

[No 49,180.]

No. **153**—Obv.: (1) *Duppi* $^{m\,ilu}$*Nabû-šuma-ibni* (2) *a-na* ^{am}*šangi* UD-KIB-NUN-KI (3) *abi-ia* ^{ilu}*Bêl u* ^{ilu}*Nabû* (4) *šu-lum u balati ša aḫi-ia* (5) *liḳ-bu-u I alpu* (6) *II immeru šuk-lu-lu* (7) *a-na eš-ru-u* (8) *a-na* . . . (Remainder of obv. broken off: traces of one line on rev.)

[No 64,830]

No. **151**.—Letter from Nabû-zira-ibašši unto the lady Sikkû, my sister. May Bêl and Nabû grant peace and life unto my sister.

I am well, by the protection of the gods—as also is Bêl-iddin. See, I am sending a letter unto Iddina-Marduk, the son of Iḳiša-apli, that he may give thee ten *gur* of wheat, be not remiss in the housework. Be observant; pray the gods on my behalf, and let me speedily have news of thee by the hand of some traveller.

No. **152**.—Letter from Nabû-zira-ibni unto Rimut, his brother. May Bêl and Nabû grant peace unto my brother.

As regards the money of Šamaš which was paid for the canes (?),[1] I took counsel with the labourers who brought them. Come and let me shew (them) to thee; behold, someone hath shut up the canal of the canes (?) behind thy back; come and I will shew the labourers unto my lord. There are eight hundred canes for our lord.

No. **153**.—Letter from Nabû-šuma-ibni unto the Priest of Sippar, my father. May Bêl and Nabû grant peace and life unto my father.

One ox and two complete sheep as the tithe for . . .

---

[1] *kanû burani* occurs without the determinative for "reed" in Strassmaier, *Nabonidus*, Nos. 746, 11: 748, 16.

No. **154**.—Obv.: (1) *Duppi* $^{m\,ilu}$*Nabû-šuma-ibni* (2) *a-na* ^{m}E-BAR UD-KIB-[NUN-KI] (3) *abi-ia* ^{ilu}*Bêl u* ^{ilu}*Nabû šu-lum* (4) *u balaṭi ša abi-ia lik-bu-u* (5) *II-ta šanâti*^{pl}*-'* (6) *V C gur L gur* ŠE-BAR *si-bu-ut* (7) *ša bêli-ia ki-i aš-šu-u* (8) *a-na-ku ḫar-ra-bi* (?)*-tu* (9) *bîti u-šal-lam* (10) *at-ta* ŠE-BAR *bêli* . . (11) *en-na a-mur* $^{m\,ilu}$. . . (Remainder of obv and top of rev. broken off) Rev.: (12) . . . *ši* (?) *du* (?) . . .

[No. 65,393.]

No. **155**.—Obv.: (1) *Duppi* $^{m\,ilu}$*Nabû-zira-ibni* (2) *a-na* ^{m}*A-ḳar-apli* (3) ^{m}*Balatu* $^{m\,ilu}$*Nabû-bêl-zikri*^{pl} (4) *u* $^{m\,ilu}$*Šamšu-udammiḳ*(*iḳ*) *aḫi*^{pl}*-šu* (5) *a-du-u* ^{ilu}*Nabû u* ^{ilu}*Na-na-a* (6) *a-na balat napšâti*^{pl} *ša aḫi*^{pl}*-e-a* (7) *u-ṣal-la* $^{m\,ilu}$*Bêl-epuš*(*uš*) (8) *ša a-gan-na-ku-nu* (9) *aḫu-u-a šu-u* (10) *man-ma dib-bi-šu* (11) *bi-'-šu-tu* Rev.: (12) *i-dib-bu-bu* (13) *ki-i ša aḫi*^{pl}*-e-a* (14) *i-li-'-u* (15) *lu-šak-ki-tu* (16) *šu-u ul-tu ri eš* (17) *a-di ki-it aḫi*^{pl} (18) *a-ha-miš ni-ni* (19) *ki-i na-kut-ti a-na aḫi*^{pl}*-a* (20) *al-tap-ra a-ga-a* (21) *lu-u tâbti ša aḫi*^{pl}*-e-a* (22) *ip-pu-šu-nu* (Left-hand edge) (23) *gab-ri ši-pir-ti ša aḫi*^{pl}*-e-a lu-mur.*

[No. 49,934.]

No. **156**.—Obv.: (1) *Duppi* $^{m\,ilu}$*Nabû-ḫi-li-ilâni*^{pl} (2) *a-na* ^{m}*Ki-na-a bêli-šu* (3) ^{ilu}*Bêl u* ^{ilu}*Nabû šu-lum ša bêli-ia* (4) *lik-bu-u ul-tu eli* (5) *ša* ^{isu}*elippi bêl iš-pu-ra* (6) *šarru ki-i il-li-ku* (7) *kap-da ši-pir-ti ana bêli-ia* (8) *ul aš-pu-ra* . . . (9) . . . (Remainder of obv and top of rev. broken off) Rev.: (10) *il-li-*[*ka*] . . (11) *u ki-i* ^{m}. (12) *bêl liš-pur-am-*[*ma*] (13) *lil-lik.*

[No 72,691]

No. **154**.—Letter from Nabû-šuma-ibni unto the Priest of Sippar, my father. May Bêl and Nabû grant peace and life unto my father.

For two years, when I received the five hundred and fifty *gur* of wheat according to my lord's wish, I restored the house which was in ruins . . .

No. **155**.—Letter from Nabû-zira-ibni unto Aḳar-apli, Balaṭu, Nabû-bêl-zikri, and Šamaš-udammiḳ, my brothers. Now for the life of my brothers to Nabû and Nanâ I pray.

Bêl-epuš, who is with you, is my brother, (and) someone hath maliciously slandered him. If it be the will of my brothers, let that person hold his peace—for we have been as brothers together from the beginning to the end. If I be sending what is a trouble unto my brothers, then let this be a favour which my brothers shall grant. Let me see an answer to my letter from my brothers.

No. **156**.—Letter from Nabû-ḫili-ilâni unto Kinâ, his lord. May Bêl and Nabû grant peace unto my lord.

After my lord had sent the boat, when the King came, I did not immediately send a letter unto my lord . . .

. . let my lord send and come.

No **157**.—Obv : (1) *$^{m\ ilu}$ Nabû-ku-ṣur-an-ni* (2) *šu-lum ša ^{m}Iddına-^{ilu}Marduk* (3) *bêli-šu ı-ša-a-lu* (4) *IV V šıḳlı kaspı* ŠE-BAR (5) *a-na I gur* 12 *ka$^{a\ an}$* (6) *a-gan-na a-ta-mar* (7) *V šıḳli kaspı pi-su-u* (8) *bêl lı-ık-nu-uk* (9) *u zir-mu-u parzıllı* (10) *u ša-gal-la* (11) *ına ḳatâ^{II} $^{m\ ilu}$Bêl-iddın* (12) *bêl lu-še-bı-la* Rev : (13) *kap-du ḫarrana^{II}* (14) *a-na šepâ^{II}-šu bêl* (15) *lıš-kun-nu amelu a-na* (16) *ma-dak-tum ıl-lak* (17) *ša I šıklu kaspi šıpâti* (18) *bêl lu-še-bı-la* (19) ŠE-BAR *at-ta-ša-a.*

[No. 31,199.]

No. **158**—Obv : (1) [*Duppı*] *$^{m\ ilu}$Nabû-lu-ud-da* (2) *a-na ^{am}šangı* UD-KIB-NUN-KI (3) *abı-ia ^{ilu}Nabû u ^{ilu}Marduk* (4) *a-na abı-ıa lık-ru-bu* (5) *a-mur ^{m}Du-muk* (6) *a-na pa-ni bêlı-ıa* (7) *al-tap-ra* (8) *^{isu}duppı* MA-GAN-NA (9) *a-na dul-lu$^{a\ an}$* (10) *ma-la* Rev. : (11) *u-kal-la-mu-ka* (12) *ı-na eštenit(ıt)* (13) *^{isu}elıppı bêl* (14) *lu-še-la-'* (15) *lu-še-bı-lu* (16) *kap-du ḫarrana^{II} a-na* (17) *šepâ^{II}-šu bêl lıš-kun* (18) *dul-la-šu a-gan-na* (19) *ı a-bı.*

[No. 61,718]

No **159**—Obv : (1) *Duppi $^{m\ ilu}$Nabû-nu-u-ru* (2) *a-na ^{m}Mu-še-zıb-^{ilu}Marduk* (3) *abı-ıa ^{ilu}Nabû u ^{ilu}Marduk* (4) *a-na abı-ia lık-ru-bu* (5) *a-na elı* ŠE-BAR *u saluppı* (6) *ša bêl ıš-pur-ru* ŠE-BAR (7) *ša bêlı-ıa ına panı-ıa ıa-a nu* (8) *al la-' XX gur* . . (9) *mı-na-a a-na* . . . (10) *bêl u-sil-[la]* . . . (11) . . (12) . Rev (13) . . *-ga-* . . . (14) *a-na ^{m}*. . . (15) *a-nam-dın ıa-a-nu um-* . . . (16) *ul-tu ım-ma-ka a-* . . (17) *a-na bêlı-ia at-ta-ḫar* (18) *a-na eli ^{am}gal-la ša bêl* (19) *ıš-pur-ru a-ga-an-nu-tu* (20) *ṣabı^{pl} ša ^{am}šanû(u)* (21) *ša Dur-ilı^{ki} a-na muḫ-ḫi-šu-nu* (22) *a-na bêlı-ıa ıḳ-bu-u* (23) *a-na mar-ra al-la* . . . (24) *a-na elı ıt-tı(?)* . . . (25) *a-dıb-bu-ub mı-[na-a]* (26) *ı-'-* . . . (27) *ına puḫrı i-šak-kan.* [No. 38,170]

No. **157**.—Nabû-kuṣur-anni greets his lord Iddina-Marduk.

I see wheat here is four or five shekels of silver for one *gur*, twelve *ḳa*. Let my lord seal five shekels of white silver, and send them by the hand of Bêl-iddin; also an iron hoe and a *šagalla*. Let my lord speedily set him on his way.

A man is going to the fortress. Let my lord send a shekel of silver for wool (and) I will get the corn.

No. **158**.—[Letter from] Nabû-ludda unto the Priest of Sippar, my father. May Nabû and Marduk bless my father.

See, I am sending Dumuk unto the presence of my lord; let my lord bring up and send all the logs of *magan*-wood for the work, that I did shew thee, in a boat. Let my lord speedily despatch him on his way, for he hath much work (to do) here.

No. **159**.—Letter from Nabû-nûru unto Mušezib-Marduk, my father. May Nabû and Marduk bless my father.

As regards the wheat and dates about which my lord sent, I have no wheat here for my lord, except twenty *gur*. Why . . .

. . . unto . . . I will give. There is none, but henceforth (?) for my lord I will buy (some).

In the matter of the slave about whom my lord sent, these are the labourers of the prefect in Durili, (who) had spoken unto my lord concerning them . . .

No. **160**. — Obv.: (1) *Duppi* ${}^{m\ ilu}$*Nabû-si-lim* (2) *a-na* ^{am}ŠA-TAM *ahi-ia* (3) *lu-u šu-lum a-na ahi-ia* (4) ^{ilu}*Nabû u* ^{ilu}*Marduk a-na* (5) *ahi-ia lik-ru-bu* (6) ${}^{m\ ilu}$*Nabû-šarri-uṣur apil-šu ša* ^{m}*Suma-usur* (7) *šarru a-na eli* ^{am}*ṣabi*^{pl}*-šu ul-te-ziz* (8) *um-ma* ^{am}*ṣabi*^{pl} *ul i-man-gur-ma* (9) *dul-lu ša šarri ul ip-pu-uš* (10) *šarru iḳ-ta-ba-' um-ma* (11) *a-na* ^{am}ŠA-TAM *šu-pur-ma* (12) *liš-pur-ra-ak-aš-šu-nu-tu* (13) *en-na a-na bêli-ia* (14) *al-tap-ra ḫa-an-tiš* (15) ${}^{m\ ilu}$*Ba-u-na'id* (16) *apil-šu ša* ${}^{m\ ilu}$*Šamšu-iddin* Rev.: (17) ^{m} . . . *-etir apil-šu ša* ^{m}*Ri-mut* (18) ^{m}*Ri-mut apil-šu ša* ^{m}*Ša-pî-*^{ilu}*Bêl* (19) ${}^{m\ ilu}$*Nabû-na'id apil-šu ša* ${}^{m\ ilu}$*Nabû-iddin* (20) *ina is-ḳa-tum be-ili* (21) *liš-pur-ra-aš-šu-nu-tu* (22) *a-na da-[a]-ni-ka šarru* (23) *ki-i u-dan-ni-in* (24) *a-na muḫ-ḫi ip-te-kid* (25) ^{am}*[ḫar]-ra-ku gab-bi* (26) *gaš-ru-u i-ka-bu-u* (27) *um-ma dal-ḫa-an-ni* (28) *ša* ^{arḫu} *Simani u* ^{arḫu} *Du'uzi* (29) *man-ma ul id-di-ni-an-na-šu* (30) *bêl lik-bi-i-ma* (31) *lid din-nu-ni-iš-šu-nu-tu* (32) *lu-u-ma-a-du* (33) *pa-ni-šu-nu* (Left-hand edge) (34) *bi-šu-'*.

[No 38,236]

No **161**—Obv.: (1) *Duppi* ${}^{m\ ilu}$*Nabû-ni-ip-šu-uṣur* (2) *u* ^{m}*Mu-še-zib-*^{ilu}*Marduk* (3) *a-na* ^{m}*Na'id-*^{ilu}*Marduk* (4) ^{m}*Arad-*^{ilu}*Bêl* (5) *u* ${}^{m\ ilu}$*Nabû-aḫi*^{pl}*-ukin* (6) *aḫi*^{pl} ^{ilu}*Nabû u* ^{ilu}*Marduk* (7) *a-na aḫi*^{pl} *lik-ru-bu* (8) *ina muḫ-ḫi iṣṣuri* (9) *ša a-ḳa-ba-ka-nu-šu* (10) [*la*] *ta-sil-la-'* (11) . . [*iṣṣuri*] *ša li-i-šu* (12) . . . *tu* (13) . . . *tu* (14) *u* (15) . . Rev: (16) . . . (17) . [*E*]*-zi-da* (18) . . *-ni ina muḫ-ḫi* (19) *iṣṣuri la ta sil-la-'* (20) *iṣṣuri ab-ka ni* (21) *kap-du te-en-ku-nu* (22) *lu-uš-mu*.

[No 75,585]

No. **160**.—Letter from Nabû-Silim unto the *šatam*, my lord. Peace be upon my brother; may Nabû and Marduk bless my brother.

The King appointed Nabû-šarri-uṣur, the son of Šuma-uṣur, over his workmen, but the men are not pleased, and consequently will not do the King's work. The King hath therefore spoken (to me) thus, "Send unto the *šatam*, that he may send them unto you." Wherefore unto my lord I now send, that my lord may speedily send Ba'u-na'id, the son of Šamaš-iddin, . . . -eṭir, the son of Rimut, Rimut, the son of Ša-pî-Bêl, and Nabû-na'id, the son of Nabû-iddin, under guard for thy judgment. The King, after he hath confirmed (this), will arrange the matter.

All the stonemasons have spoken discontentedly,[1] saying, "He oppresseth us, for none hath paid us for the months of Siwan and Tammuz." Let my lord give orders and pay them, for they are very threatening.

No. **161**. — Letter from Nabû - nipšu - uṣur and Mušezib-Marduk unto Na'id-Marduk, Arad-Bêl, and Nabû-aḫi-ukin, my brothers. May Nabû and Marduk bless my brothers.

In the matter of the birds about which I spoke to you, be not neglectful, . . .

. . . be not neglectful about the birds; send me the birds. Speedily let me hear news of you.

---

[1] *Gašrû*, literally "treason"

NO. **162**.—OBV.: (1) *Duppi* [m ilu] *Nabû-šuma-usur* (2) *a-na* [m] *Ši-rik aḫi-ia* (3) [ilu] *Marduk u* [ilu] *Ṣar-pa-ni-tum* (4) *a-na aḫi-ia lik-ru-bu* (5) ŠE-BAR-*a XV gur ša pani-ka* (6) *a-na* [m ilu] *Bêl-id-dan-nu* REV.: (7) *u* [m ilu] *Šamšu-etir* (8) *i-din*.

(Seal.)

[No. 30,855.]

NO **163**.—OBV.: (1) *Duppi* [m ilu] *Nabû-šuma-ešir* (2) [m ilu] *Bêl-apli-iddin u* [m] *Ki-i-*[ilu]*Bêl* (3) *a-na* [am] *šangi Sip-par* [ki] (4) *bêli-ni* [ilu] *Bêl u* [ilu] *Nabû* (5) *šu-lum ṭu-ub lib-bi* (6) *u a-ra-ku ûmu*(*mu*) (7) *ša bêli-ni lik-bu-u*. (Remainder broken off: what remains of rev. is blank)

[No. 84,991.]

NO. **164**.—OBV.: (1) *Duppi* [m ilu] *Nabû-šuma-ešir* (2) [m ilu] *Bêl-uballit*(*iṭ*) *u* [m] *Ki-i-*[ilu]*Bêl* (3) *a-na* [am] *šangi Sip-par* [ki] *bêli-ni* (4) [ilu] *Bêl u* [ilu] *Nabû šu-lum ša bêli-ia* (5) *liḳ-bu-u a-na muḫ-ḫi* (6) [am] . . . [pl] *ša bêl iš-pur-an-na-šu* (7) *u* [am] . . . *ina ḳatâ* [II] (8) [m] . . . (9) *ûmu*(*mu*) . . . (10) *bêli-ia ir-* . . . (11) *VI gur* . . . (12) *ša XVI* [am] *ṣabi* [[pl]] (13) . . . [arḫu] . . (14) *apil* [m] *Zir-tu* . . . (15) *ekurri-ia* [am] . . . [m ilu] *Bêl-imḳut*(*ut*) (16) BAR *a-na ûmu XV* [kam] . . . (17) BAR *XV* [am] *sabi* [pl] . . . (18) *a-na* [m] *A-na-a-mat-* . . (19) *ni-id* . . . REV.: (ll. 20, 21 obliterated) (22) *ina ḳatâ* [II] [m ilu] *Šamšu-eriba* [am] *šakû* . (23) *u* [m] *Ri-mut* [am] . . . (24) *aḫi-ia nu-ul-te-*[*bi-lu*] (25) . . . *u* [am] *šakû* . . . (26) . . . [*a*]*-šap-pa-ra* (27) *a-di muḫ-ḫi ṭe-*[*e*]*-ma* (28) *ša* ŠE-BAR *te-me ša bêlu*(*lu*) (29) *ni-iš-me ka-lak-ku* (30) *ša bêl u-kal-lim-an-na-šu* (31) *ul i-man-gur-ma* (32) . . . *ul i-na-aš-ši* (33) . . . [*ka*]*-lak-ku a-a-* . . (34) . . . *-aš-šu* (35) . *bêli-ia* (36) *ni-*[*iš*]*-mu* . . .

[No. 56,007.]

NO **165**.—OBV: (1) *Duppi* [m ilu] *Nabû-šuma-ešir* (2) *a-na* [m ilu] *Bêl-uballit*(*iṭ*) *u* [m] *Ki-i-*[[ilu]*Bêl*] (3) *aḫi* [pl]*-e-a* [ilu] *Bêl u* [ilu] *Nabû*

No. **162**.—Letter from Nabû-šuma-usur unto Širik, my brother. May Marduk and Ṣarpanitum bless my brother.

Give my wheat—the fifteen *gur* which thou hast—unto Bêl-iddannu and Šamaš-eṭir.

No. **163**.—Letter from Nabû-šuma-ešir, Bêl-apli-iddin, and Kî-Bêl unto the Priest of Sippar, our lord. May Bêl and Nabû grant peace, happiness, and long life unto our lord . . .

No. **164**.—Letter from Nabû-šuma-ešir, Bêl-uballiṭ, and Kî-Bêl unto the Priest of Sippar, our lord. May Bêl and Nabû grant peace unto my lord.

Concerning the . . . (men) of whom our lord sent us and the men . . .

. . . concerning the instructions for the wheat; we have heard the instructions of our lord, but the cellar which our lord shewed us is not fitting . . .

No. **165**.—Letter from Nabû-šuma-ešir unto Bêl-uballiṭ and Kî-[Bêl], my brothers. May Bêl and Nabû grant peace unto my brothers.

(4) *šu-lum ša aḫi*^{pl}*-e-a* (5) *lik-bu-u II gur* (6) *saluppi a-na* REV : (7) $^{m\ ilu}$*Bêl-usur II gur a-na* (8) $^{m\ ilu}$*Šamšu-pir-'-uṣur* (9) *ša ḳu-up-pu i-na-ṣa-ri* (10) *bêli*^{pl} *lid-din* ^{arḫu}. . . (11) *ûmu IX*^{kam} *šattu XI* (?) (12) $^{m\ ilu}$*Nabû - na'id šar* TIN-[TIR-KI].

[No. 74,350.]

NO **166**.—OBV.: (1) *Duppi* $^{m\ ilu}$*Nabû-šuma-ešir* (2) ^{m}*Ki-i-*^{ilu}*Nabû a-na* (3) $^{m\ ilu}$*Šamšu-epuš(uš) aḫi-ni-ia* (4) ^{ilu}*Bêl u* ^{ilu}*Nabû šu-lum-ku* (5) *lik-bu-u XX gur saluppi* (6) *a-na* $^{m\ ilu}$*Nabû-* . . . (7) ^{am}*rab-*^{isu}. . . (8) *i-din(in)* ^{arḫu}. . . REV.: (9) *ûmu XXI*^{kam} *šattu VII*^{kam} (10) ^{m}*Ku-raš šar* TIN-TIR-KI (11) *šar mâtâti*^{pl}.

[No. 60,078.]

NO **167**.—OBV: (1) *Duppi* $^{m\ ilu}$*Nabû - šuma - iškun(un)* (2) *a - na* ^{am}*šangi Sip - par*^{ki} (3) *abi - ia* ^{ilu}*Bêl u* ^{ilu}*Nabû* (4) *šu-lum ša abi-ia* (5) *lik-bu-u* (6) *ki-i ûmu(mu)* (7) *kun-nu u ki-i* (8) *tur-ru* (9) *kap-da* REV.: (10) *te-e-mu* (11) *ša bêli-ia* (12) *lu-uš-mu*.

[No. 61,719.]

NO **168**.—OBV.: (1) *Duppi* $^{m\ ilu}$*Nabû-šuma-iškun(un) a-[na]* (2) ^{am}E-BAR *Sip-par*^{ki} *abi-ia* (3) ^{ilu}*Nabû u* ^{ilu}*Marduk a-na* (4) *abi-ia lik-ru-bu* (5) ^{m}*Ta-li-mu* ^{am}*ri'u* (6) *ša* ^{ilu}*Šamši u* ^{m}*Arad-*^{ilu}*Bêli mâri-šu* (7) *XXX ṣi-e-nu pu-kud-di-tum* (8) [*ina*] *katâ*^{II}*-šu iṣ-sa-bat* (9) . . . *-ta ina lib-bi [a]-na kaspi* (10) [*it*]*-ta-din u* (11) . . . *su* (Remainder of obv. and top of rev. broken off) (12) . . *-su* (13) [*si-e*]*-nu* (14) . *-ku gab-bi* (15) *a-na kaspi i-nam-din* (16) *u sa-bit*

[No. 61,584.]

Let my lords give two *gur* of dates unto Bêl-uṣur, and two *gur* unto Šamaš-pir'-usur, who is Keeper of the Chest.

(Dated) in the month of . . . , the ninth day, the eleventh (?) year of Nabû-na'id, the King of Babylon.

No. **166**.—Letter from Nabû-šuma-ešir (and) Kî-Nabû unto Šamaš-epuš, our brother. May Bêl and Nabû grant thee peace.

Give twenty *gur* of dates unto Nabû- . . . , the chief of the . . .

(Dated) in the month of . . . , the twenty-first day, the seventh year of Cyrus, the King of Babylon, King of countries.

No. **167**.—Letter from Nabû-šuma-iškun unto the Priest of Sippar, my father. May Bêl and Nabû grant peace unto my father.

Let me speedily hear word of my lord as to whether the day is fixed or omitted.[1]

No. **168**.—Letter from Nabû-šuma-iškun unto the Priest of Sippar, my father. May Nabû and Marduk bless my father.

Talimu, the herdsman of Šamaš, with Arad-Bêl, his son, hath carried off thirty sheep entrusted to his care, and hath sold them for silver . . . He hath sold all for silver and taken it.

[1] This refers to the length of the month, as to whether it will contain twenty-nine or thirty days.

No 169 —Obv.: (1) *Duppi* $^{m\ ilu}$*Nabû-šuma-*[*iškun*?] (2) *a-na* ^{am}*šangi* UD-KIB-NUN-KI (3) *abi-ia* ^{ilu}*Bêl u* ^{ilu}*Nabû* (4) *šu-lum u balati ša abi-ia* (5) [*lik*]-*bu-u a-na* (Remainder of obv. and top of rev. broken off) Rev.: (6) . . . *zi* (?).

[No. 84,969]

No. 170. — Obv.: (1) *Duppi* $^{m\ ilu}$*Nabû-*[*šuma*]*-iškun*(*un*) (2) *a-na* ^{am}*šangi Sip-par* ^{ki} (3) *abi-ia* ^{ilu}*Nabû u* ^{ilu}*Marduk* (4) *a-na abi-ia* (5) *lik-ru-bu dul-lu* (6) *ina muḫ-ḫi V* . . . ^{isu}*dalti* (7) . . . (Remainder of obv. and top of rev. broken off) Rev.: (8) *ša bêl iš-pur* . . . (9) *um-ma kaspi i-ba-aš* (10) *ultu lib-bi na-din* (11) GIŠ-DA *bêl li-mur* (12) *u ri-iḫ-*[*ti*] (13) *ina lib-bi* . . .

[No. 84,948.]

No 171 —Obv: (1) *Duppi* $^{m\ ilu}$*Nabû-šuma-*[*iškun*?] *a-na* (2) ^{am}*šangi* ^{alu}UD-KIB-NUN-KI (3) *bêli-ia* ^{ilu}*Bêl u* ^{ilu}*Nabû* (4) *šu-lum balati ša bêli-ia* (5) *lik-bu-u a-mur* ^{m}*Bul-lu-ṭu* (6) *apli-šu ša* $^{m\ ilu}$*Nabû-zira-ukin a-na* (7) *pa-ni bêli-ia al-tap-ra* (8) *II C* ŠE-BAR *ina* ŠE-BAR-*ia* (9) *ša ina pa-ni bêli-ia bêl lid-da-aš-šu* (10) *kap-du ḫarrana* ^{II} *a-na sepâ* ^{II}*-šu* (11) *bêl liš-kun* ŠE-BAR (12) . . . *-ni-ti bêl lid-da-aš-šu.* (Remainder of obv and top of rev broken off.) Rev.: (13) . . . (14) ŠE-BAR-*ma* . . . (15) *bêli-ia i-tik-šu* . . . (16) *bêl lid-da-ni-im-ma* (17) *a-na* . . . *-šu-nu* (18) *lid-din* ŠE-BAR-*ia u* ŠE-BAR (19) $^{m\ ilu}$*Nabû-zira-ukin* [*li*]*-im-ḫur* (20) *kap-du ḫarrana* ^{II} (21) *a-na šepâ* ^{II}*-šu* (22) *bêl liš-kun.*

[No. 64,900.]

No. 172.—Obv.: (1) *Duppi* $^{m\ ilu}$*Nabû-* . . . (2) *u* $^{m\ ilu}$*Nabû-šuma-iddin* (?) . . . (3) *ana aḫi* ^{pl}*-ia lik-ru-bu* . . .

No. **169.**—Letter from Nabû-šuma-[iškun?] unto the Priest of Sippar, my father. May Bêl and Nabû grant peace and life unto my father . . .

No. **170.**—Letter from Nabû-[šuma]-iškun unto the Priest of Sippar, my father. May Nabû and Marduk bless my father.

The work on the . . .

. . . of that which my lord sent, saying, "Here is the money, paid down for it. Let my lord see (for himself) the temple gift, and the rest . . ."

No. **171.**—Letter from Nabû-šuma-[iškun?] unto the Priest of Sippar, my lord. May Bêl and Nabû grant peace unto my lord.

See, now, Bulluṭu, the son of Nabû-zira-ukin, I am sending unto the presence of my lord. Let my lord deliver unto him two hundred measures of wheat from my wheat which my lord holdeth. Let my lord speedily set him on his way, and let my lord give him the wheat . . .

. . . let my lord give and he shall pay money for them. Let him buy the wheat which belongeth both to me and to Nabû-zira-ukin. Speedily let my lord set him on his way.

No. **172.**—Letter from Nabû- . . . and Nabû-šuma- . . . May [Nabû and Marduk] bless my brothers.

(4) bît a-na-a-'-tu ma-lu-u mul- . . (5) mê^(pl) šu-ṣu-a-an
(6) ina muḫ-ḫi la ta-sıl-la-a-an (7) ^(subatu) sır-a-am-e-ti gab-bi
ša . . . (8) ^(sal)Ka-ra-na-ti u ^(sal)Ina-a-šar-ši-i- . . .
(9) ḫi-tu u šu-bı-lu ^(ḫru)pi-ni-e (10) ta- . . . -ka-ta u pi-e-nu
(11) gı-ni-e ša ûmu VI^(kam) (12) šu-bı-la-a-an . . .
(13) ^(m)Pı-ki . . . (14) šu-bi-[la] . . . (15) ^(karpatu) . .
(16) mu-ru- . . (17) ma- . . (18) ^(am) karpatı
(19) saluppi . (20) . . . -a-a ı- . . .
[No. 46,730.]

No. 173.—OBV.: (1) Duppi ^(m ilu)Nabû- . . . (2) ^(m ilu)Marduk-
. . . ^(m)Kı-i- . . (3) ^(m)A-na-a-[mat-^(ilu)Bêlı]-ad-gal . . .
(4) ^(m ilu)Nabû u [^(ilu)]Marduk a-na aḫi-ı[a lık-ru-bu] (5) XL gur
V ka saluppi a-na . . . (6) BAR ma-na V šıkli a-na
^(m)Ka- . . . (7) bêl lid (sic) kaspi ni-in-da-bu (8) ^(arḫu)Kisilımu
umu XVI^(kam) šattu XV[^(kam)] (9) ^(ilu)Nabû-na'ıd šar TIN-[TIR-KI].
[No. 65,352.]

No. 174.—OBV. (1) Duppi ^(m ilu)Nabû- . . . [ana] . . .
(2) bêlı-ıa ^(ilu)Bêl u ^(ilu)Nabû [šu-lum balati] (3) ša bêlı-ia lik-bu-u
ina elı . . . (4) ša ^(ilu)Bêli a-na elı IC ^(am) ṣabi^(pl) a-gan-na
(5) a-ma tum aš-ša-a mı-ta-ak-ka ina lıb-bı-ıa (6) ul ta-tal-
la-ka ^(ilu)Bêl u ^(ilu)Nabû ki-i (7) ina eli mi-tu-u-tum la ak-ka
(8) en-na a-na bêlı-ıa al-ta-par (9) III ma-na kaspi la-pa-ni
mârı-šu ša ^(m)Kas ba(?)-an-na (10) V ma-na kaspi la-pa-ni
^(m). . . apıl (11) ^(m ilu)Nabû-mu-še-zib bêl lı-ıš-[ša-am-ma]
lu-še-bıl-am-ma (12) a-na . . . dul-lu (13) . . . (14) a-na
dul-la la a-nam-dın u a- . . -tum (15) ma-la ıt-ti-ıa
a-na kaspı la ad-dı-nu (16) IV C saluppi ına eli bêlı la
aš-kun-nu (17) ^(am) ṣabi^(pl) banı-tı bêl liš-pu-ur-ru ^(m)Mu-gal-lu
(18) apıl ^(m)Na-ba-an-nu ul-tu elı ûmu(mu) ša bêl (19) lıl-lı-ku

The . . . -house is full of water—take it out, and be not slack in the matter, for all the jackets of the ladies Karanati and Ina-ašar-šî . . . are spoiled. Send some *pinî*-flesh . . .

No. **173**. — Letter from Nabû - . . . [unto] Marduk- . . . , Kî- . . . , Ana-a[mat-Bêli]-adgal [my brothers]. May Nabû and Marduk [bless] my brothers.

Let my lord give forty *gur* and five *ka* of dates for . . .· half a mana and five shekels of silver unto Ka- . . . The money is an offering (to the temple). (Dated) Kislew, the sixteenth day, the fifteenth year of Nabû-na'id, King of [Babylon].

No. **174**.—Letter from Nabû- . . . [unto . . .], my lord. May Bêl and Nabû grant [peace and life] unto my lord.

Concerning the . . . of Bêl, I have received instructions for one hundred workmen here ; thy dead man hath not arrived—by Bêl and Nabû I do not . . . death. So I send unto my lord. Let my lord take and send three manas of silver to the son of Kasbanna, and five manas of silver to . . . the son of Nabû-mušezib . . .

. . . I shall not pay for the work, and for the . . . (all that are with me) I have not sold. I have not deposited four hundred measures of dates on behalf of my lord. Let my lord send builders. Mugallu, the son of Nabannu, from the day that my lord departed, hath not [delivered] a single brick ; so

eštenit(it) a-gur-ru ul is- . . . -gur (20) u ^{isu}elippi ša a-gur-ru li-taš-pu-ur (21) ^{m}La-ba-ši apil ^{m}Na-ba-ṣu ina is-ḳa-tum lil-li-ku (22) ^{m}Mu-ra-nu apil ^{m}Ki-kis-ia ina is-ḳa-tum lil-li-ku (23) mârâni^{pl} . . . -din-nu^{pl} ša $^{m\ ilu}$Nabû-šuma-uṣur lil-li-ku-nu (24) araḫ ûmu(mu)^{pl} a-ga-a ^{m}Ḫa-aḫ-ḫu- . . . (25) dul-la-šu-nu ul i-pu-uš REV.: (26) $^{m\ ilu}$Bêl-aḫi-iddin apil ^{m}Ku-kur-ra BAR ma-na kaspi (27) lil-li-ku ^{m}Tab-ni-e-a apil ^{m}Ḫi-ri-tum (28) BAR ma-na kaspi lil-li-ku (29) ^{m}Ga-la-la apil ^{m}Ša-pi-i-ili-ia (30) BAR ma-na kaspi ^{m}Mu-ra-šu-u aḫu ša (31) $^{m\ ilu}$Marduk- . . . u ki-i BAR ma-na kaspi (32) BAR ma-na kaspi V ^{isu}elippi ša a-gur-ru (33) ^{m}Zir-u-tu ša I ḫu-ṣab ^{m}Gu-za-nu (34) I immer ^{ilu}Taš-me-tum ICL gur saluppi-šu (35) bêl liš-ša-am-ma ina ḳatâ^{II} ^{m}Mu-ra-šu-u (36) ša a-na bêli . . . ma bêl (37) lu-še-bil-il L gur saluppi (38) ša ^{m}Muk-ki-e-a-a I ḫu-ṣab ul-tu eḳli (39) ša E-sag-ila man-sum(?) bêl lu-še-bil-lu (40) L gur saluppi ša ^{m}Ap-la-a apli-šu ša (41) ^{m}Ri-mut bêl liš-ša-am-ma bêl lu-še-bil-lu (42) kaspi ša ^{m}Na-ar-gi-a a-na saluppi (43) at-ta-ša-a saluppi-šu ina muḫ-ḫi-ia (44) ^{m}A-ḳar-^{ilu}Nabû apil ^{m}Ki-din-^{ilu}Sin I ma-na . . . (45) u il-li-ku ^{am}ṣabi^{pl} sa-ba-tum (46) a-ki-i im- . . . ša ina a-ma-tum ša šarri (47) ša bêli-ia riš-tu . . . šat-bu-u . . . ^{ilu}Nabû ki-i (48) . . . ana pani a . . $^{m\ ilu}$Marduk- . . . (49) . . . -ia i-si-ib-bu kap-du (50) II(?) ma-na kaspi pisû(u) bêl lu-še-[bil] (51) . . te-si . . . (52) . . .

[No. 26,476]

NO. **175**—OBV: (1) Duppi ^{m}Na-di-nu (2) a-na ^{am}šangi UD-KIB-NUN-KI (3) aḫi-ia lu-u-šu-lum (4) a-na aḫi-ia ^{ilu}Bêl u ^{ilu}Nabû (5) šu-lum ša aḫi-ia lik-bu-u (6) a-mur a-na eli

do thou send a shipload of bricks. Let Labaši, the son of Nabaṣu, go to prison; let Muranu, the son of Kikisia, go to prison; let the sons . . . of Nabû-šuma-uṣur go.

All this month Ḫaḫḫu- . . . have not done their work.

Bêl-aḫi-iddin, the son of Kukurra—half a mana of silver. Let him go. Tabnîa, the son of Ḫiritum—half a mana of silver. Let him go. Galala, the son of Ša-pî-ilia—half a mana of silver; Murašû, the brother of Marduk- . . . —half a mana of silver—half a mana of silver, five shiploads of bricks. Tirutu—one palm-tree; Guzanu—one lamb for Tašmetum. One hundred and fifty *gur* of his dates let my lord receive, and let my lord despatch them by the hand of Murašu . . . Let my lord despatch fifty *gur* of dates belonging to Muḳḳîa, one palm-tree from the fields of E-Saggila . . .

Let my lord take and forward fifty *gur* of dates belonging to Aplâ, the son of Rimut.

I have received the money from Nargia for the dates; his dates (are here) before me. Aḳar-Nabû, the son of Kidin-sin—one mana . . . and the workmen who are prisoners have come, according to the . . . the command of the king . . .

No. **175.**—Letter from Nadinu unto the Priest of Sippar, my brother. May there be peace unto my brother. May Bêl and Nabû grant peace unto my brother.

. . . (7) *a-na pa-ni bêli* . . . (Remainder of obv. and top of rev. broken off) REV.: (9) . . . (10) *at-ta bêl i-di* (11) *ša a-na eli ḳanî* (12) *ša* *am* *ki-i-pi la* (13) *ra-aḫ-ṣa-ki a-šap-par-ma* (14) *kaspi ša a-na ḳanî*pl *ad-da-aš-šu* (15) *a-maḫ-ḫar-šu te-e-mu* (16) *u šu-lum ša aḫi-ia* (17) *lu-uš-me*
[No. 60,083.]

NO. **176**—OBV.: (1) *Duppi* m*Na-di-nu a-na* (2) m ilu*Nabû-šuma-iškun aḫi-ia* (3) ilu*Nabû u* ilu*Marduk a-na aḫi-ia* (4) *lik-ru-bu ana-ku u* m ilu*Nabû-eṭir* (5) *a-na pa-ni šarri ni-il-lak* (6) m*Ardi-ia a-gan-nu ina ṭe-me-šu* (7) *mâri-ka nu-bat-ti* (8) *la i-ba-a-tu ḫa-an-tiš li-ik-šu-du* (9) *a-mur kurummati bi-riš u šeri* (10) *a-gan-nu ina pa-ni-šu-nu* (11) ilu*Bêl a-na lib-bi* (12) . . . *-pa* (One or two lines wanting.) REV.: (13) . . . *at* (?) *su-'-* . . . (14) *a-na lib-bi a si ḫi* (?)-*i* (?) (15) *ina eli bêli la i-sil-li* (16) *ia-a-nu bat-la* (17) *iš šak-kan* (18) *ši-pir-ta-a lu-u mu-kin-ni-ia* (19) ilu*Nabû lu-u-i-di* (20) *ki-i gab-ri ši-pir-ti-ia* (21) *la aš-tu-ru u ina pa-ni-ia* (22) *la ad-ku-u.* [No. 62,417.]

NO **177**.—OBV. (1) *Duppi* m*Ni-din-ti-*ilu*Bêl* (2) *a-na* m ilu*Nabû-bêl-usur* (3) *aḫi-ia* ilu*Bêl u* ilu*Nabû* (4) *šu-lum u balaṭi ša aḫi-ia* (5) *lik-bu-u en-na* (6) [*lu*]-*u-ti-i-di* (7) . . . (Remainder of obv. broken off) [No. 73,472.]

NO. **178**—OBV.: (1) *Duppi* m*Ni-din-*[*ti-*ilu*Bêl*(?) *a-na*] (2) m*Eṭir-*ilu*Marduk abi* (?)-[*ia*] . . . (3) *šu-lum u balaṭi ša abi-*[*ia lik-bu-u*] (4) *I immeru I dannu* (?) *a-* . . . *-gal* . . . (5) *ša bi-ri-ni mu-ṣur-* . . . (6) *ana* GIŠ-DA *ša* ilu*Šamši* (7) *I immeru ana* GIŠ-DA *ša* ilu. . . REV.: (8) *I immeru ana* GIŠ-DA *ša* ilu. . (9) *ša* m*Arad-*ilu*A-nu* . . . (10) *I immeru ana* GIŠ-DA ilu. . . (11) *napḫariš V immeri* . (12) *šu-lu-u ri-ša-* . . (13) *šu-bi-la* . . . (14) *immeru ul* . . (15) *ûm*(*um*) *u-* . . . [No. 84,952]

See, concerning the . . . unto the presence of my lord . . .

. . . thou, O my lord, knowest that with regard to the reeds for the warden, I have not washed (them). I will send that I may receive the money which I am to pay for the reeds. Let me hear the instructions and greeting of my lord.

No. **176.**—Letter from Nadinu unto Nabû-šuma-iškun, my brother. May Nabû and Marduk be gracious unto my brother.

I and Nabû-eṭir are going unto the presence of the King, Ardia being here in charge, (and) thy son taking no holiday. May they speedily finish. Behold, their allowance of food and meat is here in plenty (?). Bêl unto . . .

. . . let my lord not be slack therein, for there is none, and there is a deficiency. May my letter be my witness; I call Nabû to witness that I have written my answer and have had it prepared (?) before my eyes.

No. **177.**—Letter from Nidinti-Bêl unto Nabû-bel-uṣur, my brother. May Bêl and Nabû grant peace unto my brother.

Now . . . thou knowest . . .

No. **178.**—Letter from Nidin[ti-Bêl ?] unto Eṭir-Marduk. May Bêl and Nabû grant peace and life unto my father.

(*Remainder mutilated, but containing a list of offerings of sheep to Šamaš.*)

NO. **179**. — OBV.: (1) *Duppi* ^{m}*Na-sir u* ^{m}*Ki-i-*^{ilu}*Nabû* (2) *a-na* $^{m\,ilu}$*Šamšu-iddin aḫi-i-ni* (3) *LX* (?) *ḳa ki-me a-na na-še-e* (4) . . . *ša ûmu XXVIII*^{kam} *ša* ^{arḫu}*Kisilimi* (5) . . . ^{am}. *zu* . .^{pl} (6) . . . UD-[KIB]-NUN-KI (7) *i-din* ^{arḫu}*Kisilimi* REV.: (8) *umu XXVIII*^{kam} *šattu III*^{kam} (9) ^{m}*Ku-ra-aš šar E*^{ki} (10) *šar mâtâti.*

[No. 75,727]

NO **180**.—OBV: (1) *Duppi* ^{m}*Ni-ḳu-du* (2) *a-na* ^{am}*šangi Sip-par*^{ki} (3) *abi-ia* ^{ilu}*Bêl u* ^{ilu}*Nabû* (4) *šu-lum u balati* (5) *ša abi-ia* [*lik-bu*]-*u* (Remainder of obv and top of rev. broken off) REV.: (6) . . . ^{ilu}*Nabû* . . . (7) *ki u-še-ṣa-'* (8) *pur-ru-su-nu* (9) *il-ta-kan-'* (10) *III* $\frac{5}{6}$ *ma-na kaspi* (11) *šu-zir* (?)-*bi-šu-nu.* [No. 84,914]

NO. **181**. — OBV.: (1) *Duppi* ^{m}*Nu-ur* ^{am}*ri'u* (2) *apil* $^{m\,ilu}$. . . -*eṭir apil* $^{m\,ilu}$. . . (3) *II gur I pi saluppi* [*ana*] ^{m}*Ši-ri-ša-*^{ilu}*Bêl* (4) *apil* $^{m\,ilu}$*Nabû-aḫi-šu apil* . . . (5) *aḫi ša* ^{am} . . (6) *ûmu XIII*^{kam} . . . (7) . . . REV.: (8) *un-*[*ḳu*] (Seal) (9) ^{m}*Nu-ur.* [No. 46,747.]

NO. **182**—OBV.: (1) *Duppi* $^{m\,ilu}$*Nergal-aḫi-iddin a-na* (2) ^{m}*Iddina-*^{ilu}*Marduk abi-ia* (3) ^{ilu}*Bêl u* ^{ilu}*Nabû šu-lum u balaṭi ša* (4) *ša abi-ia liḳ-bu-u* (5) *a-na eli kaspi ša abu-u-a* (6) *iš-pu-ru kaspu ḳa-al-la-al* (7) *ša a-na saluppi* (8) *in-na-di-in* (9) *II ma-na kaspi kap-du* (10) *abu-u-a lu-še-bi-lu* (11) *al-la a-ga-'-i* (12) *ki-i ṭâbti-ka* REV.: (13) *ina eli-ia ia-a-nu* (14) *a-mur* $^{m\,ilu}$*Nabû-ba-at-tu-u-a* (15) *a-na abi-ia al-tap-par* (16) ^{am}ŠA-TAM *a-na* TIN-TIR-KI (17) *it-tal-lak a-di la* (18) *a-na ku-tal-la i-ni-ḫi-si* (19) *ṭe-me ša abi-ia lu-uš-me* (20) *ki-i* ŠE-BAR *u ki-i* (21) *mimmu*(*mu*) *ma-la pa-ni-ka ma-ḫar* (22) *a-na abi-ia a-nam-din* (23) *a-mat-ka it-ti-ia* (24) *la ta-ša-an-na* [No. 34,556.]

No. **179**—Letter from Naṣir and Kî-Nabû unto Šamaš-iddin, our brother. Give sixty (?) *ḳa* of flour for receiving . . . twenty-eighth day of Kislew [unto] . . . (Dated) Kislew, the twenty-eighth day, the third year of Cyrus, the King of Babylon, King of countries.

No. **180**.—Letter from Niḳudu unto the Priest of Sippar, my father. May Bêl and Nabû grant peace and life unto my father . . .

. . . [I call Bêl] and Nabû [to witness] that I have not let it go forth. They have arranged their . . . , give (?) them three and five-sixths of a mana of silver.

No. **181**.—Letter from Nur, the herdsman, the son of . . . -etir, the son of . . .

[Give] two *gur*, one *pi* of dates unto . . . Širi-ša-Bêl, the son of Nabû-aḫi-šu, the son of . . .

Signet of Nur.

No. **182**. — Letter from Nergal-aḫi-iddina unto Iddina-Marduk, my father. May Bêl and Nabû grant peace and life unto my father.

In the matter of that money which my father sent, the money which hath been paid for the dates is (too) little; so let my father speedily send two manas of silver in addition to this, for otherwise there is no advantage from thee towards me.

See, I am sending Nabû-battûa unto my father. The *šatam* is coming to Babylon; before he sets out for his return, let me have word from my father; if wheat or anything be acceptable to thee, I will give it unto my father. Change not thy orders with me.

No. **183**—Obv.: (1) *Duppi* $^{m\ ilu}$*Nergal-mušallim* (2) *a-na* ^{m}*Iddina(na)-apli* (3) *abi-ia* ^{ilu}*Nabû u* ^{ilu}*Marduk* (4) *a-na abi-ia lik-ru-bu* (5) ^{am}*gal-lat-ta-a ši-i-ti* (6) *ki-i ta-ḫal-liḳ* (7) *a-gan-na-ka ina pani* (8) ^{m}*Ba-nu-nu u* ^{m}*Ḫa-ad-da-a* (9) ^{am}*ku-lu-u*^{pl} (10) *ši-pir-tum il-tap-par-ra-nu* (11) *um-ma* ^{am}*mâr-šip-ri-ka* (12) *lil-lik-kam-am-ma* (13) *li-bu-ku-šu* (14) *a-na-ku* (15) *na-aš-pir-tum* (16) *ina ali* Rev.: (17) *al-lik-ku-u* (18) *ul al-lik-ku* (19) *a-mur* $^{m\ ilu}$*Nabû-mu-li-di-im-bi* (?) (20) *a-na bêli-ia al-tap-ra* (21) *bêl li-bu-ku-ši-im-me* (22) *ina ḳatâ*^{II}*-šu bêl lid* (sic)*-pur-ru* (23) *i-na lib-bi ša abu-u-nu* (24) *at-ta a-na bêli ia* (25) *aš-pur-ru.*

[No. 85,500.]

No **184**—Obv.: (1) *Dup-pi* $^{m\ ilu}$*Nergal-iddina a-na* (2) ^{am}E-BAR UD-KIB-NUN-KI *bêli-ia* (3) ^{ilu}*Bêl* ^{ilu}*Nabû u* ^{ilu}*Nergal šu-lum u balati ša bêli-ia* (4) *liḳ-bu-u ûmu(mu)-us-su še-e-ri* (5) *u ki-is ûmu(mu)* ^{ilu}*Nergal u* ^{ilu}*La-az* (6) *a-na balaṭ napšâti*^{pl} *ša* ^{am}E-BAR ^{alu} UD-KIB-NUN-KI (7) *bêli-ia u-ṣal-la* (8) ^{šipâtu}ZAGIN-KUR-RA *ša ina ḳatâ*^{II} $^{m\ ilu}$*Šamšu-zira-ibašši(ši)* (9) *bêl u-še-bi-lu a-ta-mar* (10) *a-na muḫ-ḫi dul-lu ša bêl iš-pu-ur* (11) *ina ṣilli ša* ^{ilu}*Šamši u ina ṣilli-ka* (12) *dul-lu ḫi-i-ri* (13) *šu-lum a-na dul-lu-ia* Rev.: (14) *a-na bêli-ia al-tap-par* (15) *um-ma X ma-na šipâti* (16) *a-na* $^{m\ ilu}$*Šamšu-zira-ibašši(ši)* (17) *i-di-in bêl lu-u-id-din* (18) *bêli-ni X ma-na šipâti* (19) *in-na-aš-ši-im-ma dul-lu-a* (20) *ša i-ba-aš-šu-u a-gan-na-ka* (21) *li-pu-uš na-kut-ut-tum* (22) *ša dul-lu bêli la i-raš-ši* (23) *mi-nu-u ṣi-bu-tu* (24) *ša bêli-ia bêl liš-pu-ru*

[No. 67,365]

No. **183.**—Letter from Nergal-musallim unto Iddina-apli, my father. May Nabû and Marduk bless my father.

After that female slave of mine ran away over yonder to Banunu and Ḫaddâ, the . . . -men, they sent us a letter, saying, "Let your messenger come and fetch her." (Now) I myself have business in the city; shall I go or shall I not? See, I send unto my lord Nabû-mulidi-imbi (?); let my lord fetch her and send her in his hands. Thou art instead of our father; unto my lord I send.

No. **184.**—Letter from Nergal-iddina unto the Priest of Sippar, my lord. May Bêl, Nabû, and Nergal grant peace and life unto my lord. Daily in the morning and at the end of the day I pray unto Nergal and Laz for the life of the Priest of Sippar, my lord.

I have seen the blue wool which my lord hath sent by the hand of Šamaš-zira-ibašši. With regard to the work concerning which my lord sent, the digging works (my work) are going on well, thanks to the favour both of Šamaš and of thee.

I sent unto my lord thus, "Give ten manas of wool unto Šamaš-zira-ibašši; let my lord give (it)." Now the ten manas of wool have been received that I may complete my work which is yonder. My lord shall suffer no trouble over the work. What my lord desireth, that let him send.

No. **185**.—Obv. (1) *Duppi* $^{m\ ilu}$*Nergal-gimilli* (2) *a na* $^{m\ ilu}$*Bêl-mušallim* (3) *lu-u-šallim-mu ana be-ili-ia* (4) *aš-šu* ^{m}*Ad-na-lu* (5) *ša be-ili iš-pu-ra* (6) $^{m\ ilu}$*Nabû-na-id* (7) *il-tap-ra* (8) *um-ma ṣabi*^{pl} (9) *di-ka-a u* (10) *ûmu IX*^{kam} *at-ta* (11) ^{m}*Ad-na-lu* (12) ^{m}*Abu-ila-'* Rev.: (13) *a-na pa-ni-ia* (14) *al-ka-nu* (15) *a-na* ^{m}*Uruk*^{ki}*-a* (16) *u* ^{m}*Kan-na-nu* (17) *ki-i aḳ-bu-u* (18) *ul im-gur-ma* (19) *ṣabi*^{pl} *ul i-di-ku-nu* (20) *a-du-u ina pani-ka* (21) *šu-nu u ia-a-ša* (22) ^{m}*Ad-na-lu* (23) *u* ^{am}*bêl-ḫarrani*^{II}*-šu* (24) *ina še-ri* (25) *a-na pa-ni* (26) *be-ili-ia* (Left-hand edge) (27) *ni-il-la-ka*.

[No. 79,430.]

No **186**.—Obv.: (1) [*Duppi*] $^{m\ ilu}$*Nergal-* . . . (2) [*a*]*-na* ^{m}*E-babbara*(*ra*)*-ša-du-nu* (3) *aḫi-ia* ^{ilu}*Nabû u* ^{ilu}*Marduk* (4) *a-na aḫi-ia lik-ru-bu* (5) *u-il-tim ši-i* (6) *ša* $^{m\ ilu}$*Nabû-tuk-ki-na-an-nu* (7) *it-ti* ^{m}*Iḳiša*(*ša*)*-apli* (8) ^{alu}*Du-ur-ga-az-za-a-a* (9) *i-'-lu-u-* . . . (10) $^{m\ ilu}$*Nabû-ka-ṣir* (11) *apil* ^{am}*gallabi a-na* (12) *pak-da im-nu-u* (13) *a-na* $^{m\ ilu}$*Nabû-ka-ṣir* (14) *pi-ḳit-ma* Rev: (15) *u-*[*il*]*-tim a-na* (16) *man-ma i-nam-din* (17) $^{m\ ilu}$*Nabû-* . . *-ka* (18) *dul-la* . . . (19) *ma-a-du* . . . (20) *a-na* . . .

[No. 72,845.]

No. **187**.—Obv.: (1) *Duppi* $^{m\ ilu}$*Nergal-gimilli* (?) (2) *a-na* ^{m}*Na'id-*^{ilu}[*Marduk*?] (3) *aḫi-ia* ^{ilu}*Bêl* ^{ilu}*Nabû* (4) *šu-lum balaṭi ša aḫi-ia* (5) *at-ta ti-i-di* (6) *ki-i lu-u-ma-a-du* (7) *ma-sar-tum-ka* (8) [*a-na-aṣ-ṣa*?]*-ru* (Remainder of obv. and top of rev. broken off) Rev. (9) *u tâbti-a* (10) *ina muḫ-ḫi-ka* (11) *a-šak-kan* (12) *ad-da-ni-ka* (13) ŠE-BAR *ina muḫ-ḫi* (14) $^{m\ ilu}$*Šamšu-uballit*(*it*) (15) *la ta-sil*(?)-[*li*].

[No. 65,839.]

No. **185.** — Letter from Nergal-gimilli unto Bêl-mušallim. Peace be upon my lord.

In the matter of Adnalu, about whom my lord sent, Nabû-na'id hath sent thus : "Summon the workmen, and do thou, Adnalu and Abu-ila', come unto my presence on the ninth day." Though I spoke to Urukâ and Kannanu (about it), it did not seem good (to them), and they did not summon the workmen. Thou (however) hast their agreements, and I and Adnalu, with his muleteer, to-morrow will come to the presence of my lord.

No. **186.** — Letter from Nergal- . . . unto Ebabbara-šadunu, my brother. May Nabû and Marduk bless my brother.

There is a debt which Nabû-tukkinannu hath contracted with Ikiša-apli, the man from Dur-gazza ; but Nabû-kaṣir, the son of the barber, counteth it as a deposit. Give, therefore, directions to Nabû-kaṣir that he pay the debt to someone . . .

No. **187** —Letter from Nergal-gimilli (?) unto Na'id-Marduk (?), my brother. May Bêl and Nabû (grant) peace and life unto my brother.

Thou knowest that [I am] carefully [watching] thy interests . . . I will do thee a favour, I will give thee the corn. (But) be not slack in the matter of Šamaš-uballiṭ.

No. **188**.—Obv.: (1) *Duppi* $^{m\ ilu}$*Sin-na-din-aḫi* (2) *a-na* $^{m\ ilu}$*Nabû-eṭir-napšâti*^{pl} (3) *abi-ia* ^{ilu}*Bêl* ^{ilu}*Nabû* ^{ilu}*Sin* (4) *u* ^{ilu}*Šamšu šu-lum balaṭi ḫu-ud lib-bi* (5) *u arak ûmi*^{pl} *ša abi-ia* (6) *liḳ-bu-u ḫarrana*^{II} *a-ga-a* (7) *ša aḫu-u-tu ša abu-u-a* (8) *it-ti-ia ṣa-ab-tu* (9) *mi-nu-u ki-i ip-pu-šu-ma* (10) . . . *-ka* (11) . . . ^{ilu}*Sin u* ^{ilu}*Šamšu* (12) [. .]*-bu-u* Rev.: (13) . . . *ûmu(mu)-us-su* (14) [*a*]*-na muḫ-ḫi-ka* (15) *u-ṣal-lu-u ṣu-li-e-a* (16) *liš-mu-u ḫi-su-u-tu* (17) [$^{m\ ilu}$]*Marduk-mâri-* . . . *ri-* . . . (18) *il-ta-sa-an-ni* (19) *i-ḳab-ba-a um-ma* (20) *III ma-na* $\frac{1}{3}$ *šiḳli kaspi* (21) *ša* ^{ilu}*Bêl ina muḫ-ḫi-ka.*

[No. 26,690.]

No. **189**—Obv.: (1) *Duppi* ^{m}*Su-ḳa-a-a* (2) *a-na* ^{m}*Ši-rik-ki abi-ia* (3) ^{ilu}*Bêl u* ^{ilu}*Nabû šu-lum balaṭi ša* (4) *abi-ia liḳ-bu-u* (5) *kaspi piṣû(u) ša ina pani-ka* (6) *ina ḳatâ*^{II} $^{m\ ilu}$*Nabû-aḫi-id-dan-nu* (7) *bêl lu-še-bi-lu* (8) *ana muḫ-ḫi kaspi*$^{a\ an}$ (9) *ša tak-ḳa-ba-'* (10) GIŠ-DA *ki-i a-mu-ru* (11) BAR *ma-na III šiḳli* (12) *kaspi* Rev.: (13) *ša ana pani* ^{ilu}*Nabî a-dan-nu* (14) *ina* GIŠ-DA *ana muḫ-ḫi-ka* (15) *ša-ṭi-ir.*

[No. 30,643.]

No. **190**—Obv.: (1) *Duppi* ^{m}*Suḳa-a-a* (2) *a-na* $^{m\ ilu}$*Nabû-zira-ibni* (3) *abi-ia* ^{ilu}*Bêl u* ^{ilu}*Nabû* (4) *šu-lum u balaṭi ša abi-ia* (5) *liḳ-bu-u en-na* (6) *ša la imeri at-ta-lak* (7) *imeri a-na* (8) $^{m\ ilu}$*Šamšu-eṭir* (9) *i-din-ma* (10) *liš-šu-'* Rev.: (11) *pu-gu-da-ti* (12) *in-na-aš-šu.*

[No. 49,616]

No. **188.**—Letter from Sin-nadin-aḫi unto Nabû-eṭir-napšâti, my father. May Bêl, Nabû, Sin, and Šamaš grant peace, life, happiness, and long days unto my father.

This method of brotherhood which my father hath taken with me, how, when he hath done it . . . ? I pray unto . . . Sin and Šamaš daily on thy behalf—may they hear my prayers . . . Marduk-mâri . . . hath spoken to me and hath said, "Three manas and one-third of a shekel of silver for Bêl (I give) unto thee."

No. **189.**—Letter from Sukâ unto Širikki, my father. May Bêl and Nabû grant peace and life unto my father.

The white silver which thou hast, let my lord send by the hand of Nabû-aḫi-iddannu. Concerning the silver of which thou didst speak, when I saw the Temple-gift, (I found that) half a mana and three shekels of silver which I will pay into (the treasury of) Nabû, hath been written against thy name for the Temple-gift.

No. **190.**—Letter from Sukâ to Nabû-zira-ibni, my father. May Bêl and Nabû grant peace and life unto my father.

Now I am coming without an ass; (but) give an ass to Šamaš-eṭir that it may carry him, and the deposits shall be brought.

No. **191**.—Obv.: (1) *Duppı* ᵐ *Su-ḳa-a-a* [*a-na*] . . . *-a-a* (2) *bêlı-ia* ⁱˡᵘ *Bêl u* ⁱˡᵘ *Nabû šu-lum u balati* (3) *ša bêlı-ia liḳ-bu-u a-na muḫ-ḫi* (4) *ḳi-me ša taḳ-ba-' ḳi-me kı-i aš-ša-'* (5) *ša-ki-ın u a-na-ku mar-sa-ak* (6) *ma-la šu-bu-lu ul an-ṣi* (7) *ul-tu* ÙD-AB-AB *mar-ṣa-ak* (8) *ına lıb-bi kı-i ḳı-me a-na bêli-ia* (9) *la u-še-bi-lu u te-e-me-a* (10) *la taš-mu-u ina ṣıllı ša ilânı*ᵖˡ (11) *um-ma um-taš-šır-an-ni* (12) *a-mur ûmu*(*mu*)*-su* ⁱˡᵘ *Bêl u* ⁱˡᵘ *Ninıb* (13) *a-na muḫ-ḫi bêlı-ia u-sal-lu* (14) *a-na muḫ-ḫi* ᵐ *Bêli-šu-nu ša bêl* (15) *ıš-pur a-na* ᵐ *Bêlı-šu-nu kı-ı* (16) *aḳ-bu-u um-ma* . . . (17) *a-lık-ma* . . . (18) . . . (19) UD-AB-AB- . . . (20) *u a-na ku-tal-la* Rev.: (21) [*aš*]*-pur-ak-ka u a-* . . . (22) *ıl-lu* (sic) *ma-am-ma* . . . (23) *ul ad-di-šı-ı ul* . . . *-aḳ-bı* (24) *ṭe-en-ka lu-uš-mu-ma* (25) *it-ti ma-am-ma al-la-ku* (26) *ḳu-tu-lu-ka-nu il-la-ku* (27) . . . *-du-šı-i lu-uš-pur-ak-kaš* (28) . . . *-tu a-mur ık-ḳa-bu-u* (29) *um-ma ma-la al-la a-ḫa-miš* (30) *kaspı i-ša-an-nım-ma gi-mir* (31) *a-na* ᵃᵐ *šangı ıḳlı*ᵖˡ *a-ga-'* (32) *nı-id-din u iḳlı*ᵖˡ *ıt-tı* (33) *bêl pıt-ki ni-iz-kur te-en-ka* (34) *a-na muḫ-ḫi lu-uš-me mı-na-a* (35) *ṭe-en-ka ıl-lı-ık* (36) *kap-du te-en-ka* (37) *lu-uš-me.*

[No 47,413]

No **192**—Obv.: (1) *Duppı* ᵐ *Pir-' u* (2) ᵐ *Iddına* ⁱˡᵘ *Nabû a-na* ᵐ *Ki-ı-*ⁱˡᵘ*Nabû* (3) ᵐ*Na-ṣır u* ᵐ ⁱˡᵘ *Bêl-ıddına*(?) (4) *aḫı*ᵖˡ*-e-nı* ⁱˡᵘ *Nabû* (5) *u* ⁱˡᵘ *Marduk a-na aḫı*ᵖˡ*-e-ni* (6) *lik-ru-bu XLVIII I* PA *saluppi* (7) [*ina*] GIŠ-BAR *gal-la-tum VI* . . . *I* PI (8) *saluppi ša VI* AŠ-A-AN (9) *ina* GIŠ-BAR *gal-la-tum* (10) *VI gur* 78 *ḳa* [*saluppi*] (11) *ša* . . . (Remainder of obv and top of rev. broken off) Rev.: (12) . . . (13) *bi-'-*[*šu*] . . . *a-na* (14) *ısittı* ⁱˢᵘ *daltı ta-nam-dın-nu* (15) *elı ma-ak-ka-su* (16) *lıb-bu-u-a* (17) ⁱˡᵘ ŠAR-ḪU UD-KIB-NUN-KI (18) *u* ⁱˡᵘ *Bu-ne-ne* (19) *a-na isıtti* ⁱˢᵘ *daltı* (20) *ın-na-'*

[No. 61,858.]

No. **191**—Letter from Sukâ to . . . -â, my lord. May Bêl and Nabû grant peace and life unto my lord.

Concerning the flour of which thou didst speak, after I had received the flour it was put aside, I being sick (at the time). I cannot find all that was sent; I have been sick since the festival-day, (and) it is for this reason I have not sent the flour unto my lord, and thou hast not heard news of me. (But) by the grace of the gods (the sickness) hath now left me. Lo, I pray daily unto Bêl and Ninib on behalf of my lord.

Concerning Bêli-šunu, whom my lord sent: after I had spoken to Bêli-šunu thus, "Come and . . . the festival . . .," and I sent back to thee, and he hath come unto . . . Let me hear news of thee and the . . . shall come by some traveller . . . let me send it unto thee . . . Behold, (people) are saying thus, "Except with regard to each other (?) the money varieth," so we have given all unto the priest of these fields, and we have mentioned the fields to the overseer. Let me hear thine instructions in this matter. Why have thy instructions (not) come? Speedily let me hear thy instructions.

No **192**.—Letter from Pir' and Iddina-Nabû unto Kî-Nabû, Naṣir, and Bêl-iddina(?), our brothers. May Nabû and Marduk bless our brothers.

Forty-eight (*gur*), twelve *ḳa* of dates as the payment for the female slave, six . . . , one *pi* of his dates, six of corn, as payment for the female slave, six *gur*, seventy-eight *ka* [of dates] . . . for the door-sill thou shalt give. For the dues with me of Šamaš of Sippar and Bunene, for the door-sill send (it).

No. **193**.—Obv.: (1) *Duppi* ^{m}*Rı-mut a-na* (2) ^{m}*Ar-ra-bi aḫi-ıa* (3) ^{ilu}*Nabû u* ^{ilu}*Marduk a-na* (4) *aḫi-ia lik-ru-bu* (5) *šu-lum a-na-ku* (6) *a-di eli bêl ul ḳa-ba-'* (7) *ina eli dul-lu alpi* (8) . . . *la ta-sil-la* (9) *gab-bi ina îna*^{II}*-ia a-mur* (10) *bi-iḳ-ḳud ša ḫa-ab-bu-ru* (11) *ša ni-ḫu-u u iš-še-e-nu* (12) *ina lıb-bi la am-mar* (13) *mimma dul-lu li-pu-uš*^{pl} (14) *bit-li-e* (15) *ša* . . . *ki-rib* (16) *XXX* ^{am}*ṣabi*^{pl} Rev.: (17) *ıt-ti-ka* (18) *a-bu-ku-ma* (19) *ina lib-bi esten(en) ni-ši* (20) *iš-ša-'-šu* (21) *ına bîti ina elı nâri* (22) *i-di-ni-ıš-šu* (23) ^{ilu}*Bêl a-na eli ša* . . . *nârı* (24) *u-ṣal-lam* (25) *a-na eli saluppi* (26) *ša aḳ-ḳab-ba-'* (27) *mi-nam-ma ṭe-mu* (28) *ul maš-šir.*

[No. 31,197.]

No. **194**.—Obv.: (1) *Duppi* ^{m}*Rı-mu-tu a-na* (2) ^{m}*Iddina(na)-apli aḫi-ia* (3) ^{ilu}*Nabû u* ^{ilu}*Marduk a-na* (4) *aḫi-ia lık-ru-bu* (5) *ına ṣılli ša ılânı*^{pl} (6) *šu-lum a-na-ku* (7) *ilânı*^{pl} *ki-i u-ṣal-lu-u* (8) *si-bu-ta-a* (9) *ak-ta-šad a-na eli* (10) *ṣi-bu-ti-ka* (11) *ša taš-pu-ru* (12) ^{ilu}*Bêl u* ^{ilu}*Nabû kı-[i]* (13) *a-na elı-ša* (14) *la aḳ-bu-[u]* Rev.: (15) *u a-di-i a-na [eli-šu]* (16) *aḳ-bu-u* (17) *ina lib-bi u-ḫa-am-mu-ka* (18) $\frac{1}{3}$ *ma-na kaspi la-pa-ni* (19) ^{m}*Li-bu-ru ta-at-ta-ši* (20) *ri-ḫı-it kaspi a-na* (21) $^{m\,ilu}$*Nabû-apli-iddin la ta-maḫ-ḫar* (22) *a-dı muḫ-ḫi ša* (23) *ır-ru-bu-am-ma* (24) *e-dir-ru-ka* (25) *liš-mi-ma ešten(en) ši-pır-tum* (26) *ša šu-lum ša bîti* (27) *ša* ^{sal}*Ḫa-ma-ra-na-tu* (28) ^{sal}*amti-ıa* (Left-hand edge) (29) *u mâri-šu šu-pur.*

[No 31,294]

No. **193.** — Letter from Rimut unto Arrabi, my brother. May Nabû and Marduk bless my brother. I am well.

Before ever my lord speaketh about the commission of the ox, saying, "Be not neglectful," (I will send and say that) I am seeing to everything with my own eyes; I cannot (however) see to the arranging of the fodder, both soft and hard (?).[1] They shall do all the work. I have sent *bitlî* . . . for thirty men with thee, but one only hath taken it. Put it in a house near the river. I pray unto Bêl on behalf of . . . the river. Concerning the dates of which I spake, why hast thou left no instructions?

No. **194.**—Letter from Rimutu unto Iddina-apli, my brother. May Nabû and Marduk bless my brother. I am well by the grace of the gods; if I pray unto the gods I shall attain my desire.

Concerning thy desire which thou didst send, (I call) Bêl and Nabû (to witness whether) I have not spoken concerning it, and entered into agreements thereto. In this matter do I hasten thee. One-third of a mana of silver thou shalt receive before Liburu; the rest of the money do not give to Nabû-apli-iddin before he comes in, and then let him hear thy arrangement; and send a letter of greeting from the house of the lady Ḫamaranatu, my servant and her son.

---

[1] *Ḫabburu ša niḫû u iššênu.* "Husks which are soft and hard" I refer the word *niḫû* to the root *nîḫu*, "to be quiet," and *iššênu* to the Chaldee אשינא, "hard," but the whole passage is doubtful.

No. **195**—Obv.: (1) *Duppı* ^{m}*Rı-mut a-na* (2) ^{m}*Iddına-*^{ilu}*Marduk abı-ıa* (3) *ûmu(mu)-su* ^{ilu}*Bêl u* ^{ilu}*Nabû* (4) *a-na balat napšâtı*^{pl} (5) *ša abi-ıa u-sal-lam* (6) ^{m}*Ḫa-am-ba-ku* (7) *ul u-ka-* . . . (8) *u kı-i al-li-ku* (9) *aḳ-ta-bi* (10) *ta-at-tal-lak* (11) *u* ^{m}*Iddına(na)-aplı* (12) *a-na kaspi* (13) *ık-ta-ba-'* Rev.: (14) *ša la bêlı-ıa* (15) *ul ıd* [*da*]*-aš-šu* (16) *a-na-ku I ma-na* (17) *ına lıb-bı at-ba-ku* (18) *ša la bêlı-ıa* (19) *ul* [*a-na*]*-aš-šı* (20) *te-mu ša bêlı-ıa* (21) *a-na elı lu-uš-me* (22) ^{am}*mâr-šipri ša bêlı-ıa* (23) *a-na pa-nı* ^{m}*Ar-ra-bi* (24) *lıl-lak-ma* (25) *ga-dı-da-'* (26) *lı-bu-ba-kam-ma* (27) . . . (Left-hand edge) (28) *te-mu ša bêlı-ıa lu-uš-me* (29) *šı-pır-ta-ka a-na pa-ni* . . .

[No. 34,553]

No **196**—Obv: (1) *Duppi* ^{m}*Rı-mut a-na* (2) ^{am}*šangı* UD-KIB-NUN-KI (3) *bêlı-ıa ûmu(mu)-us-su* (4) ^{ilu}*Bêl u* ^{ilu}*Nabû a-na balat napšâtı*^{pl} (5) *tu-ub* (sic) *tu-ub šeri* (6) *u a-ra-ku ûmu(mu) ša bêlı-*[*ıa*] (7) *u-ṣal-la a-na muḫ-ḫi ımmerı* (8) *ša* ^{ilu}*Šamšı ša bêl ıš-pu-ru* (9) *eš-ten(en)* [*šu*] *II šu šı-pır-tum* (10) *a-na* [*bêli*]*-ıa al-tap-*[*par*] (11) . . . ŠE-KUL *a-na* . . . (12) [*ṣı* (?)]*-e-nu al-la* ŠE-KUL (13) . . . *karanu ı-ba-aš-šı* (14) . . . *bêl ıš-pu-ru* (15) ' . . . *-šı-šu* Rev: (16) . . . ŠE-KUL (17) . . . *-uš* (18) . . . *gur* ŠE-KUL (19) *bît* ^{isu}*karani* . . . [$^{m\ ilu}$*Šamšu*]*-upaḫḫır(ır)* (20) *kı-i* ^{isu}*ḳup-pu ına* . . . (21) *il-te-šı u* ŠE-KUL *ma-a-du* (?) (22) *ına lıb-bı-ša* ^{ilu}*Bêl u* ^{ilu}*Nabû za-kıp* (23) *u šattı a-ga-a III gur* ŠE-[KUL] (24) *u-šal-lam-ma ı-zak-kap* (25) *u* ^{am}*ṣabı*^{pl} *ına panı-šu ıa-a-nu* (26) *ša ı-ga-rı ıp-pu-uš-šu* (27) ^{am}*ṣabı*^{pl}

No. **195.**—Letter from Rimut unto Iddina-Marduk, my father. Daily I pray unto Bêl and Nabû for the life of my father.

Ḫambaku has not . . . and when I came, I said, "Thou shalt go"; and Iddina-apli hath said that, as regards the money, without my lord's authority he will not give it, and I for my part, therefore, cannot obtain a single mana (of silver) to deliver in the matter, without my lord's authority. Let me hear my lord's directions in the matter; let my lord's messenger go to Arrabi that he may send . . . , and . . . Let me hear news from my lord; thy letter unto . . .

No. **196.**—Letter from Rimut unto the Priest of Sippar, my lord. Daily I pray unto Bêl and Nabû for the life, happiness, health, and long days for my lord.

Concerning the sheep of Šamaš about which my lord sent, I have (already) sent one or two letters unto my lord. With regard to the seed corn . . . My lord hath sent . . .

. . . *gur* of seed corn . . . the wine-cellar. If [Šamšu]-upaḫḫir . . . the box, much (?) corn is therein; by Bêl and Nabû it is sown, and this year he will make up the total of the three *gur* of seed corn and sow it, but he hath no workmen to

bêl li-iš-pu-ra-am-ma (28) *i-ga-ri li-ip-pu-uš* (29) *u ia-a-nu-u bêl liš-pur-ra* (30) *ebur eḳli ša šatti a-*[*ga-a*] (31) [am] KU-MAL-MAL[pl] *lu-it-bu-*[*ku*] (32) *i-ga-ri li-*[*ip-pu-šu*] (33) . . . *tu* (?) *šatti* (Left-hand edge) (34) *a-na* [ilu] *Šamši li-id-din kap-du ṭe-e-*[*mu bêli-ia lu-uš-mu*].

[No. 56,033.]

No 197.—Obv.: (1) *Duppi* [m] *Ri-mut a-na* (2) [am] *šangi* UD-NUN-KIB-KI *bêli-*[*ia*] (3) *ûmu*(*mu*)*-us-su* [ilu] *Bêl u* [[ilu] *Nabû*] (4) *a-na balaṭ napšâtim*(*tim*)[pl] [*ṭu-ub libbi*] (5) *ṭu-ub šeri a-ra-ku ûmu*[(*mu*)] (6) *ša bêli-ia u-ṣal-*[*la*] (7) [*bêl lu*]*-u-i-di* [m ilu] . . . (8) . . . *-šu-nu a-na* . . . (9) . . . *-ra* (?) . . . (Remainder of obv. and top of rev. broken off.) Rev.: (10) . . . (11) *i-tab-ku* . . . (12) *ka-al-da-* . . . (13) *bêl li-iḳ-bi* . . . (14) *a-na mu-ir-ba* . . . (15) *ši-pir-tum a-na eli* . . . (16) *buši ša* [ilu] *Šamši* . . . (17) [m] *Mu-ra-šu-u* . . . (18) *a-na a-gan-na* . . . (19) *I CXX* ŠE-BAR *ina ḳatâ*[II] . . . (20) [m ilu] *Šamšu-aḫi*[pl]*-eriba* . . . (21) *ma-ḫir.*

[No. 84,956.]

No. 198—Obv.: (1) *Duppi* [[m] *Ri*]*-mut* (2) *a-na* [am] *šangi*[pl] [alu] UD-KIB-NUN-[KI] (3) *bêli-ia ûmu*(*mu*)*-us-su* (4) [ilu] *Bêl u* [ilu] *Nabû* [ilu] *Šamšu u* [ilu] *Nergal* (5) *a-na bu-lu-ṭu napšâti*[pl] (6) *a-ra-ku ûmu*(*mu*) (7) *tu-bu-ub libbi ṭu-bu-ub šeri* (8) *u bu-u-nu pa-ni* (9) [*ša šarri ḫa-du-tu it*]*-ti bêli-ia* (10) [*u-ṣal*]*-la* (11) [*bêl lu-u*]*-i-di* ŠE-KUL (12) . . . [*a*]*-na pa-ni* (Remainder of obv. and top of rev. broken off.) Rev.: (13) . . . *tâbu* (14) . . . *tâbu* (15) . . . *i-na lib-bi* (16) [[m]] [ilu] *Šamšu-upaḫḫir*(*ir*) *a-na* [isu] *karani* (17) [*li*]*-i-ip-pu-uš* (18) *lu-u-ma-a-du ba* (?)*-nu* (19) *en-na ki-i pa-ni bêli ša* (20) *maḫ-ra* . . . *V* [am] *ṣabi*[pl] (21) *bêl li-iš-pur* [*a*]*-mur* (22) *V gur* ŠE-[KUL]. (Remainder broken off)

[No. 84,916]

build a wall. Let my lord send workmen to build the wall, or if there are none, let my lord send word of it. Let the . . . -men send the crops of the fields for this year, let them build a wall ; the . . . of the year let them give to Šamaš. Speedily [let me hear] news [of my lord].

No. **197**.—Letter from Rimut unto the Priest of Sippar, my lord. Daily I pray unto Bêl and Nabû for the life, [happiness], health, and long days for my lord . . .

No. **198**.—Letter from [Ri]mut unto the Priest of Sippar, my lord. Daily I pray unto Bêl, Nabû, Šamaš, and Nergal for life, long days, happiness, health, and that the light of the [King's] countenance may be favourable unto my lord.

. . . Therein let (?) Šamaš-upaḫḫir arrange for the wine, for it is very plentiful. Now, if it is pleasing unto my lord, let my lord send five workmen. Behold, five *gur* . . .

NO. 199.—OBV.: (1) *Duppi* ^m*Ri-[mut a-na]* (2) ^{am} *šangi* ^{alu}[UD-KIB-NUN-KI] (3) *bêli-ia ûmu(mu)-[us-su]* (4) ^{ilu}*Bêl u* ^{ilu}*Nabû a-[na balat] napšâti* [^{pl}] (5) *tu-ub lib-bi* [*tu*]*-ub šeri* (6) *u a-ra-ku ûmu(mu)* (7) *ša bêli-ia u-ṣal-la* (8) *bêl lu-u-i-di* (9) . . . (Remainder of obv and top of rev. broken off) REV.: (10) . . . (11) . . . *muḫ-ḫi ekli* ^{pl} . . . (12) . . . *li-iḫ-ḫar-ṣa-an-ni-ma* (13) *bêl li-iš-pu-ra-an-šu* (14) [*ki*?]*-i ekli* ^{pl} *ku-um ekli* ^{pl} *i-nam-din-nu* (15) *ma-ṣar-tu ni-iṣ-ṣur u ia-a-nu-u* (16) *alpi* ^{pl} *a-na bît bêli-ia-a-ni* (17) *ni-iš-bu-uš u* (18) *ma-al* ŠE-KUL *ni-iz-*[*za-ḳap* (?)] (19) *ni-ik-kil-* . . .

[No. 84,965.]

No 200.—OBV : (1) *Duppi* ^m*Ri-*[*mut* . . .] (2) *a-na* ^{sal} . . . (3) *be-lit-ia* [^{ilu}*Bêl u* ^{ilu}*Nabû*] (4) *šu-lum balati* [*ša bêlti-ia*] (5) *liḳ-bu-u* [^m] . . . (6) *abi-šu ša* . . . (7) *mâr šarri* . . . *-na-nu* (8) *a-na ûmi VI* ^{kam} *a-* [*mat*] (9) *il-ta-kan a-mur it-ti-šu* (10) *a-na* E-KI *e-ru-bu* (11) *a-na* ^m*Kal-ba-a* (12) *bêl li-iš-pu-ru* REV : (13) *a-na ûmi VI* ^{kam} (14) *ša e-ru-bu* (*ši*)*-pir-ta-a* (15) *liš-ši* ^m*Bu-ur-šu-u* (16) *bêl li-iš-pu-ru-am-ma* (17) *a-gan-nu it-ti-šu* (18) *li-id-bu-ub* (19) *man-ma ša ku-tu-la-a* (20) *a-ḳab-bu im-ma-ru* (21) *i-a-ru ki-i* ŠE-BAR (22) *bêl ṣi-bu-u bêl* . . . (23) *li-iš-pu-ru* . . (24) . . . (25) . . . (26) *ša* ^m*Kal-ba-a* (27) *bêl saṭ-ru* . . . (Left-hand edge) (28) *bêl liš-ši-ma* '*-i-ti ši-ma* . . . (29) *a-na muḫ-ḫi saluppi* . . . (30) *ina ḳatâ* ^{II pl} ^{m ilu}*Bêl-eriba in-na-ru-uk na-ad-ni.*

[No. 41,612.]

NO. 201.—OBV.: (1) *Duppi* ^m*Ri* (?) *-* [*mut* (?) . . .] (2) *a-na* ^m. . . (3) *aḫi-šu* ^{ilu}*Nabû* [^{ilu}*Marduk*] (4) *a na aḫi-ia* [*liḳ-ru-bu*] (5) *ša bêl iš-pu-ru* . . . (6) *um-ma I-šu II-šu a-na* (7) [*eli bêli*]*-ia al-tap-ra* (8) [*u gab*]*-ri ša bêli-ia* (9) [*ul a*]*-mur en-na* (10) [*a-me*]*-lu-ut-ti at-tu-u-a* (11) *u*

No. **199**.—Letter from Ri[mut to] the Priest of [Sippar], my lord. Daily I pray unto Bêl and Nabû for [the life], happiness, health, and long days of my lord.

May my lord be aware that . . .

. . . With regard to the fields . . . let them be ploughed and let my lord send whether they will give the fields instead of the fields. We have hitherto kept watch, but if there should be none, then we will gather the oxen into my lord's house, and all the seed corn we will sow . . .

No. **200**.—Letter from Ri[mut- . . .] unto the lady . . . , my sister. May [Bêl and Nabû] grant peace [unto my sister].

. . . , the father of . . . the King's son . . . hath commanded for the sixth day . . . Behold, he is coming into Babylon with him. Let my sister send unto Kalbâ that he may receive my letter on the sixth day when he cometh in. Let my sister send Buršû that I may discuss with him here.

According as my sister wisheth let my sister send . . .

No. **201**.—Letter from Ri[mut(?) . . .] unto . . . , his brother. May Nabû [and Marduk bless] my brother.

Of that which my lord sent, saying, "Once, nay twice, have I sent unto my [lord]," I have not seen my

at-tu-ka ešten(en) pir-ku (12) *ina pani-ia la šak-kın* (13) *a-na nu-up-tu ana bêli-ia* (14) *at-ta-din-ni-ma* (15) *a-me-lu-ut-ti kur-ba-ni-tu* (16) *ši-i* (17) *a-mur a-na* REV.. (18) *a-ḫat-ti-ka* (19) *al-tap-ra a-dı la* (20) *šarru ir-ru-bu* (21) [*at*]-*ta u aḫati-ka* (22) [*al*]-*ka-nim-ma* (23) . . . *ša-nım-ma* (24) . . . *nı* . . . (25) *a-me-lu-ut-ti* . . . (26) *ši-ı ina eli* . . . (27) BAR *ma-na kaspi la* . . . (28) *ummi iš-par-ti eli* . . . (29) *mu-tal-li* . . . (30) *a-na im-ma-ḳa* (?) . . . (31) *kaspı a-nam*-[*dın*] (32) *ı-* . . .

[No. 29,261 + 29,335.]

NO. **202**.—OBV.: (1) *Duppi* ^{m}*Rı-mut-*^{ilu}*Nabû* (2) *a-na* $^{m\,ilu}$*Bêl-ib-ni* (3) *u* ^{m}*Šuma-iddina aḫı*^{pl}*-šu* (4) ^{ilu}*Nabû u* ^{ilu}*Marduk ana aḫi*^{pl}*-ia* (5) *lik-ru-bu III IV šanâti*^{pl} (6) *a-ḫat-ku-nu ul a-mur* (7) *ûmu(mu) ša a-mu-ru-šu a-na* (8) *šub-ti-ıa ta-at-ta-šab* (9) *II šanâti*^{pl} *a-ga-a* $^{m\,ilu}$*Nabû-ki-ṣır* (10) *i-kab-ba-šu um-ma* (11) *a-me-lu-ut-ti at-tu-u-a* (12) *šı-i* ^{sal}*Ḫi-ip-ta-a* (13) *uz-na-a ına lıb-bi* (14) *ul tap-ti at-tu-nu* (15) . . . *panı* (?)$^{am(?)}$ ŠA-KU (16) *pal-ḫa-tu-nu* (17) *a-na šarri* (18) *ul ta-ḳab-ba-'* REV.: (19) *u šu-u ša ana muḫ-ḫi-ia ša* (20) *i-dib-bu-ub la katâ*^{II}*-ıa* (21) *tu-še-la-a-šu ḫi-ṭu* (22) *ia-a-nu pa-ni-ku-nu* (23) *ına eli la i-ba-'-iš* (24) *ul i-šal-lim* (25) $^{m\,ilu}$*Nabû-ki-ṣır ıt-te-šib* (26) *ki-i un-dış-šir* (27) *u en-na-a a-na-ku* ^{m}*Pir-ku* (28) *ta-na-šuḳ-an-na-in-nu* (29) *ak-ka-i ki-i* (30) *ša ram-nı-ku-nu ana muḫ-ḫi-ia* (31) *ta-nam-di-nu I-šu* (?) (32) *a-ga-a ḫa-pı-i ša bîti-ia* (33) *la tu-u-ma-lı* (?) (34) *ana-ku ıštenit(it) gal-lat* (Left-hand edge) (35) *kur-ba-ni-tum ana* ^{sal}*Ka-bit-tı a-šap-par-ru.*

[No 29,470]

lord's [letter]. Now, my slaves are thine—there is no (question of a) single disagreement with me. I will give as the tax unto my lord even the slaves—it is a gift. Lo, I send unto thy sister. Before the King cometh in, do thou and thy sister come . . .

No. **202.**—Letter from Rimut-Nabû unto Bêl-ibni and Šuma-iddina, his brothers. May Nabû and Marduk bless my brothers.

For three or four years I have not seen your sister. The day that I last saw her, she sat herself down in my chair. But for the last two years Nabû-kiṣir hath said of her "She is my slave," but the woman Ḫiptâ never let me know of this. Ye are afraid of the *šaku*-official—ye will not speak to the King; or else as for that fellow who is mine adversary, ye will not take up my cause (*lit.* raise up my hands) against him. There is no doubt that ye are not unconsenting to this, and it is not good. Nabû-kisir is (still) dwelling (here), (but) if he were to leave, then would she kiss me and Pirku. How (would it be) if of your own accord you were to give her to me? Will ye not . . . this—the ruin of my home?

I would send a slave as a present to the lady Kabitti.

NO. **203.**—OBV.: (1) *Duppi* ^{m}*Šu-lum*-E-KI *a-na* (2) ${}^{m\,ilu}$*Marduk-uballiṭ-su bêli-ia* (3) *ûmu(mu)-us-su* ^{ilu}*Bêl u* ^{ilu}*Nabû* (4) *a-na balat napšâti*^{pl} *ša bêli-ia* (5) *u-ṣal-la a-mu-ur* (6) *XXX gur* ŠE-BAR *mid-gul* (7) *ina ḳatâ*^{II} ${}^{m\,ilu}$*Nabû-id-dan-nu* (8) *apil* ${}^{m\,ilu}$*Nabû-itti-ia* . . . *-ka* (9) *ina lib-bi ša mar-ṣi* (10) *ki-i a-na pani bêli-ia* (11) *la aš-pur-ru-šu.*

[No. 25,924.]

NO. **204.**—OBV.: (1) *Duppi* ^{m}*Šu-ma-a* (2) *u* ${}^{m\,ilu}$*Nabû-na-din-aḫi* (3) *a-na* ${}^{m\,ilu}$*Nabû-aḫi-* . . . (4) *aḫi-i-ni* ^{ilu}*Nabû* [*u* ^{ilu}*Marduk*] (5) *a-na aḫi-i-ni* [*lik-ru-bu*] (6) ŠE-KUL *ša* ^{m}*Ša-du-*[*nu*] (7) *apli-šu ša* ${}^{m\,ilu}$*Bêl-na-* . . . (8) [^{am}E]-BAR UD-KIB-NUN-KI (9) . . . ^{isu}LI-ḪU-SI-UM *labiru* (10) . . . ^{isu}LI-ḪU-SI-UM (11) *eš-šu ana muḫ-ḫi-šu* (12) *ša-ṭi-ir ana eli* (13) . . . *a* . . .

[No. 60,672.]

NO. **205.**—OBV.: (1) *Duppi* ^{m}*Ša-lam-ma-nu* (2) *a-na* ^{m}*Ki-na-apli* (3) *u* ${}^{m\,ilu}$*Šamšu-aḫi-iddin* (4) *aḫi*^{pl}*-šu* ^{ilu}*Bêl u* ^{ilu}*Nabû* (5) *šu-lum ša aḫi*^{pl} (6) *lik-bu-u a-na eli* (7) *alpi ša ina pani* ^{m}*Za-za-a* (8) *ša bêl iš-pu-ra* (9) *am-mi-ni-i* (10) . . . *-ṣa-ti* (11) . . . (12) . . . *ub* (Remainder of obv. and top of rev. broken off.) REV.: (13) . . . *lu* . . . (14) . . . *i-man-gur* (15) . . . *u*(?)*-šim-man-an-ni* (16) [*iḳ*]*-ta-bak-ka* (17) *um-ma ina Sip-par*^{ki} (18) *alpi a-na* ^{m}*Ša-lam-ma-nu* (19) *u-kal-lam en-na* (20) *ul i-man-gur* (21) *ki-ma aš-šim-ma* (22) *a-na Sip-par*^{ki} (23) *li-bu-kam-ma* (24) ^{am}*ṣabi*^{pl} *it-ti-ia* (25) *li-mu-ru-uš* (Left-hand edge) (26) . . . *nu ešten(en) ki-i il-li-ku* (27) [*iḳ-bu-u*] *um-ma V immeri a-na* ${}^{m\,ilu}$*Šamšu-*[*aḫi-iddin*] (28) . . . *at-ta-din.*

[No. 49,417.]

No. **203.**—Letter from Šulum-Babili unto Marduk-uballiṭsu, my lord. Daily I pray unto Bêl and Nabû for the life of my lord.

Behold, thirty *gur* of corn entrusted into the hand of Nabû-iddannu, the son of Nabû-ittiya [I send] thee. It was because he was sick that I did not send it unto my lord.

No. **204.**—Letter from Šumâ and Nabû-nadin-ahi unto Nabû-aḫi- . . . , our brother. May Nabû [and Marduk bless] our brother.

The seed corn for Šadu[nu], the son of Bêl-na . . . the Priest of Sippar, [instead of] the old account a new account hath been written against him . . .

No. **205.**—Letter from Šalammanu unto Kina-apli and Šamaš-aḫi-iddin, his brothers. May Bêl and Nabû grant peace unto (my) brothers.

Concerning the ox which Zazâ hath, of which my lord sent, why . . . ?

. . . he was [not] willing, according as he told me. He said to thee, "I will shew the ox to Šalammanu in Sippar." Now he is not willing, according to what I have heard. Let him send it to Sippar that the men may see it with me . . . After one had gone, [he spake] saying, "I will give five sheep to Šamaš-[aḫi-iddin] . "

No. **206**.—Obv.: (1) [*A*]-*na* ^{am}TIL-LA-GID-[DA] (2) . . . *ardi-ka* (3) [^{m}]*Šul-ma-nu ûmu*(*mu*)-*us-su* (4) [^{ilu}]*Šamšu u* ^{ilu}*Bu-ne-ne* (5) [*a*]-*na balaṭ napšâti*^{pl} *arak ûmu*(*mu*) (6) *ṭu-ub u ṭu-ub šeri* (7) [*ša bêli-ia*] *u-ṣal-la* (8) . . . (Remainder of obv. and top of rev. broken off.)

[No 52,150]

No. **207**.—Obv.: (1) *Duppi* $^{m\,ilu}$*Šamšu-eriba a-na* (2) $^{m\,ilu}$*Bunene-ibni aḫi-ia* (3) *a-mur* $^{m\,ilu}$*Šamšu-uballiṭ*(*iṭ*) *a-na pani-ka* (4) *al-tap-par* 90 *ḳa ḳi-me* (5) *ina ḳatâ*^{II}-*šu šu-bi-lu* (6) *lu-u-ti-i-di* Rev: (7) *a-mur* 12 *ḳa ḳi-me* (8) *maḫru*(*u*) *ina pa-ni-ka* (9) ^{arḫu}*Addaru ûmu XIII*^{kam}.

(Seal)

[No. 74,730]

No. **208**.—Obv.: (1) *Duppi* $^{m\,ilu}$*Šamšu-eriba a-na* (2) ^{am}*šangi Sip-par*^{ki} *bêli-ia* (3) *ûmu*(*mu*)-*us-su* (4) ^{ilu}*Bêl u* ^{ilu}*Nabû a-na* (5) *balaṭ napšâti*^{pl} *ša bêli-ia* (6) *u-sal-la* (7) *šu-lum a-na ekurra*(*ra*) (8) *ali u bîti ša bêli-ia* (9) *ša-ki-in* (10) *a-na eli* (11) *na-as-ba* (?)-[*ti*] (12) *ša* ^{am}*rab-*[*ka-ṣir*] (13) *a-na* . . . Rev: (14) *iḳ-bu-*[*u*] (15) *um-ma* ^{am}*rab-*[*ka-ṣir*] (16) *it-ti ia* (17) *lil-lik* (18) *mi-nu-u ki-i* (19) *bêl si-bu-u* (20) *a-na bêli-ia lu-še-bi-la* (21) *a-na eli ta-bar-ri* (22) *u ta-kil-tum* (23) *ša* ^{ilu}*A-nu-ni-tum* (24) *bêl la i-sil-li* (25) *a-mur* ^{m}*Ki-i-*^{ilu}*Bêl* (26) *u* ^{m}*Mu-še-zib-*^{ilu}*Marduk* (27) *a-na pani bêli-ia* (28) *it-tal-ku-u-ni* (29) *it* (?)-*ti-i* (Left-hand edge) (30) *bêli-ia a-na* ^{am}*rab-ka-ṣir liḳ-bu-u*.

[No. 79,350]

No. **209**.—Obv.: (1) [*Duppi*] $^{m\,ilu}$*Šamšu-inamir*(*ir*) (2) [*a-na*] $^{m\,ilu}$*Mu-še-zib-*^{ilu}*Marduk* (3) [*bêli-ia*] ^{ilu}*Šamšu u* ^{ilu}*Bu-ne-nè* (4) [*šu*]-*lum u balati ša bêli-ia* (5) [*liḳ*]-*bu-u a-na* (6) . . . ŠE-BAR *II C* (?) (7) . . *saluppi* . . . (8) . . . -*di*^{pl}

No. **206.** — Unto the Warden, thy slave . . . Šulmanu. Daily I pray unto Šamaš and Bunene for the life, long days, happiness, and health [of my lord] . . .

No. **207.**—Letter from Šamaš-erîba unto Bunene-ibni, my brother.

Behold, I am sending Šamaš-uballiṭ into thy presence; send ninety *ḳa* of flour by his hand. Take note; see, there is twelve *ḳa* of the former flour in thy keeping.

Month Adar, thirteenth day.

No. **208.**—Letter from Šamaš-eriba unto the Priest of Sippar, my lord. Daily I pray unto Bêl and Nabû for the life of my lord. Peace be upon the temple, city, and house of my lord.

Concerning the taking of the captain (?) about [which my lord] spake unto [me], saying, "Let the captain (?) come with me"; whatever my lord desireth, that will I send unto my lord. Concerning the *tabarri*-cloth and the purple cloth for Anunitum, let not my lord be neglectful. Behold, Kî-Bêl and Mušezib-Marduk are coming into my lord's presence; with my lord let them speak unto the captain . . .

No. **209.** — [Letter from] Šamaš-inamir [unto] Mušezib-Marduk [my lord] May Šamaš and Bunene grant peace and life unto my lord . . .

ša [isu] *elippi* (9) . . . -'- (Remainder of obv and top of rev. lost.) REV. (10) . . . (11) . . *ṣu* (?)-*pi-ti ša a-* . . . (12) *a-na-ku man-ma ul u-maš-*[*šir*] (13) *it-ti-šu-nu ul aḫ-tu* (14) *man-ma ina it-ti-ia* (15) *ia-a-nu*[1] *dul-lu ša ip-pu-uš* (16) *ina* [am] *limnu-u-tu* (17) *ip-pu-uš* (18) *ṭe-e-mu u šu-lum* (19) [*ša*] *bêli-ia lu-uš-me.* [No 67,855]

No. **210**.—OBV. (1) *Duppi* [m ilu] *Šamšu-šarri-uṣur* (2) *a-na* [am] *šangi* UD-KIB-NUN-KI (3) *aḫi-ia* [ilu] *Nabû u* [ilu] *Marduk* (4) *a-na aḫi-ia lik-ru-bu* (5) *mi-na-a aš-me-e pir-ku* (6) *it-ti* [m] *Mu-ra-nu* (7) *i-na pa-ni bêli-ia* (8) *id-dib-bu-ub* (9) *man-ma pir-ku i-na* (10) *pa-ni bêli-ia* (11) *it-ti-šu la i-dib-bu-ub* (12) *ša dîni-šu it-ti* (13) [m] *Mu-ra-nu* REV.: (14) *i-ba-aš-šu-u* (15) *it-ti* (16) [m] *Mu-ra-nu* (17) *bêl li-iš-pur-im-ma* (18) *i-na pa-ni* (19) [am] *daîani* [pl] (20) *a-gan-na dib-bi-šu-nu* (21) *li-ik-tu-'.* [No 60,354]

No **211**—OBV.: (1) [*Duppi*] [m ilu] *Šamšu-šuma-u-kin a-*[*na*] (2) . . . *-ziri aḫi-ia* [ilu] *Bêl u* [ilu] (*Nabû*) (3) [*šulum u balati*] *ša aḫi-ia lik-bu-u* (4) *a-na-ku i-di ša mimmu*(*mu*) *ma-*[*la*] (5) *it-ti-ia ta-dib-bu-*[*ub*] (6) *pi-ir-ṣa-at u ša a-* . . . (7) *mi-na-a ul-tu eli* (8) *iš-ka-ri u* [isu] *dalti* . . . (9) *ma-la in-ni-ip-šu* . . . (10) *ul taš-pu-ru en-na* (11) *al-tap-rak-ka iš-ka-*[*ri*] (12) [*u* [isu]]*dalti ša* [alu] *U-pi* (?)-[*e*] (13) . . . (Remainder of obv. and top of rev. broken off) REV.: (14) . . . (15) *te-en-ka lu-uš-*[*me*] (16) [m ilu] *Bêl-mušallim a-na eli-*[*ka*] (17) *al-tap-ru sabi* [pl] . . . (18) *a-mu-ur u iš-kar* . . . (19) *ka-la-mu la tu-*[*še-ti-iḳ*] (20) . . . *-di mimmu*(*mu*) *ma-la* [*i-ba-aš-šu-u*] (21) *la ta-sil-li a-na* . . . (22) . . *ta gab-ri ši-pir-*[*tum*] (23) [*lu-u mu*]*-kin-nu* [ilu] *Bêl* . . . (24) . . . *iṣ-sa-bat.* [No. 67,902.]

---

[1] This word has been inserted on the extreme left-hand edge after the tablet was written.

. . . I have left no one; against them I have not sinned. There is no one with me, (so that) the work, which I am doing, I am doing badly. Let me hear the news and welfare [of] my lord.

No. **210**.—Letter from Šamaš-šarri-usur unto the Priest of Sippar, my brother. May Nabû and Marduk bless my brother.

What have I heard? Hath abuse against Muranu been spoken before my lord? No one can have spoken abuse before my lord against him. Whoever hath a case against Muranu—let my lord send him with Muranu, that they may settle their matter here before the judges.

No. **211**.—Letter from Šamaš-šuma-ukin unto . . . -ziri, my brother. May Bêl and (Nabû) grant peace unto my brother.

I know that all that thou hast laid to my charge is false; . . . Why, ever since the *iškaru* and door were all made, hast thou not sent? Now I send unto thee . . .

. . . Let me hear news of thee. Bêl-mušallim unto [thee] I send; see the workmen, and do not omit any of the *iškar*, . . . as many as there are, be not neglectful . . . let my letter be my witness . . .

No. **212**.—Obv.: (1) *Ardi-ka ki-nu* ^m ^ilu^ *Šamšu-* . . . (2) *a-na* ^am^ *ki-*[*i-pi*] (3) *u* ^am^ *šangi* UD-[KIB-NUN-KI] (4) *bêlı-e-a* [^ilu^ *Šamšu u* ^ilu^ *Bu*]*-ne-ne* (5) *šu-lum u balati ṭu* (sic) *lıbbi tu* (sic) *šeri* (6) *a-ra-ku ûmu*(*mu*) *ša bêli-e-a* (7) *liḳ-bu-u a na* [*eli*] ŠE-BAR (8) *ûmu* (?) *XXVIII*^kam^ *ša bêlı-*[*e*]*-a iš-pu-ru-nu* (9) . . . ^m^ *Mu-ra-nu* (10) . . . [*ıt*]*-ta-din* (Remainder of obv. and top of rev. broken off.) Rev.: (11) . . . (12) *ia-a-nu al-la ešten*(*en*) *alpi* (13) *u ešten*(*en*) ^am^ *irrıši a-mur I gur* ŠE-KUL (14) *az-za-kap te-mu u šu-lum* (15) *ša bêlı-e-a lu-uš-mu.*

[No. 75,446.]

No. **213**.—Obv.: (1) *Duppi* ^m ^ilu^ *Šamšu-* . . . (2) ^m ^ilu^ *Sin-aḫi-* . . . [*a-na*] (3) ^m ^ilu^ *Bêl-ibni bêli-*[*ia*] . . . (4) *a-mur ûmu*(*mu*)*-us-su* (5) ^ilu^ *Bêlit ša Uruk*^ki^ *u* ^ilu^ *Na-na-a* (6) *a-na balaṭ napšâti*^pl^ *ša bêli-ı*[*a*] (7) [*nu-ṣal-la*] . . . (8) *ša* . . . (9) ŠE-BAR *a-na XX gur uš* (?) . . . (10) *ul tu-še-bi-la-*[*an*]*-nu* (11) ŠE-BAR *ina ba-* . . . *-aš* (?)*-tum* (12) *a-ga-a ul at-ra-at* (13) ŠE-BAR *a-na dul-lu ul-tu* (14) *lıb-bi ni-te-pu-uš* (15) . . . *sa-ḫa-ru-tum* Rev.: (16) . . . *-al u* (17) *ri-iḫ-tum XX gur* ŠE-[BAR] (18) *a-na bêli-ıa nu-*[*še-bi-la*] . . . (19) *ri-iḫ-tum* ŠE-BAR . . . (20) ^arbu^ *Âbu u* ^arbu^ . . . (21) *bêli-ia nu-še-*[*bi-la*] (22) *a-na muḫ-ḫi* ^am^ *la-mu-ta-*[*ni*] (23) *ša bêl iš-pu-ru man-ma* (24) *ina lıb* ^m ^ilu^ *Daîanu-re'u*(*u*) (25) *ul ik-šu-du gab-bı* . . . (26) *a-na e-bu-ru it-*[*tal-ku*] (27) *man-ma al-la* ^m ^ilu^ *Šamšu-* . . . (28) ^m^ *Ka-ṣir u* ^m^ *Tim-kak* . . . (29) *it-ti-i-nı ia-a-*[*nu*] (30) *mâr ša* ^sal ilu^ . . . (31) *ul-tu eli* . . . (32) . . . (Left-hand edge) (33) *it-ti-i-ni ul i-pu-uš.*

[No. 40,527.]

No. **212**.—Thy faithful servant Šamaš- . . . to the Warden and Priest of Sippar, my lords. May [Šamaš and Bu]nene grant peace and life, happiness, health, long days unto my lords.

Concerning the corn for the twenty-eighth day (?) of which my lords sent me . . . Muranu . . .

. . . There is none except one ox and one gardener. Lo, I have planted one *gur* of seed corn. Let me hear the news and welfare of my lords.

No. **213**.—Letter from Šamaš . . . and Sin-aḫi- . . . (unto) Bêl-ibni, my lords. Lo, daily [we pray] unto Bêltis of Erech and Nanâ for the life of my lords . . .

. . . Thou hast not sent us the corn, up to twenty *gur* . . . The corn for . . . , this is not luxuriant. We will arrange the corn for the work thereto . . . The rest of the twenty *gur* of corn unto my lord we will send; the rest of the corn . . . in the months of Ab and . . . unto my lord we will forward.

Concerning the slave, about whom my lord sent, not one hath reached Daîan-re'u-ụ- . . . They have all gone to harvest (and) there is no one beside Šamaš- . . . , Kasir, or Timkak with us; the son of the lady . . . ever since the . . . . , hath not worked with us.

No. **214**.—Obv.: (1) *Duppi* [m]*Ši-rik-tum* (2) *a-na* [m]*U-bal-liṭ-su-*[ilu]*Bêl* (3) *bêli-ia* [ilu]*Bêl* [ilu]*Nabû šu-lum u balati* (4) *ša bêli-ia liḳ-bu a-mur* (5) *ûmu(mu)-šam a-gan-nu* [ilu]*Bêl* [ilu]*Nabû* (6) *a* (sic) *bu-luṭ napšâti*[pl] *ša bêli-*[*ia*] (7) *u-ṣal-la a-mur ul taš-*[*pu-ra*] (8) . . . *IV immeri* . . . *bi IV immeri* (9) *ta-* . . . *eš-ru-u ša* [m]*Šuma-ukin* (10) [am]*gal* (?) . . . *a-gan* (?)-*na-a* (11) [m]. . . *-eriba u* [m]*Arad-*[ilu]*Šamši* (12) *a-* . . . (13) . . . (14) . . . Rev.: (15) [m ilu]*Bêl-* . . . [*u*] (16) [m ilu]*Marduk-ri-man-ni* . . . (17) *i-ta-mar-ru-šu-nu-tu* (18) *ša ba-ḳa-nu-' u ga-zu-* . . . (19) *a-mur ûmu XIV*[kam] *immeri* (20) *a-na bêli-ia al-tap-par* (21) *kap-du ḫarrana*[II] *a-na šepi* (22) *ša* [am]*la-mu-ta-nu* (23) *šu-kun man-ma it-ti-ia* (24) [*ia-a*]*-nu*.

[No. 61,106]

No. **215**—Obv.: (1) *Duppi* [m]*Ši-ir-ki* (2) *a-na* [m ilu]*Nabû-šar-an-ni* (3) *aḫi-ia* [ilu]*Bêl u* [ilu]*Nabû* (4) *šu-lum u balati ša aḫi-ia* (5) *liḳ-bu-u II-šu III-šu* (6) *ki-i aš-pur-rak-ka* (7) ŠE-BAR *ul tu-še-bi-lu* (8) *eburu na-a-di* (9) [m ilu]*Daîan-iddin* (10) [*ana*] *pa-ni-ka* Rev: (11) *al-tap-rak* (12) ŠE-BAR *ma-la* (13) *i-riš-šu-u-ka* (14) *in-na-aš-šu* (15) *kap-du ḫarrana*[II] (16) *a-na šepâ*[II]*-šu šu-kun* (17) *la tu-še-ti-iḳ-šu*.

[No. 31,236.]

No. **216**.—Obv. (1) *Duppi* [m]*Šil-kul* (2) *a-na* [m ilu]*Nergal-uballit(iṭ)* (3) *abi-ia* [ilu]*Bêl u* [ilu]*Nabû* (4) *šu-lum u balaṭi ša abi-ia* (5) *liḳ-ru-bu a-mur* [isu]. . . (6) [*a-na eli* (?)] *pa-ni* (7) . . . *-ḫa-ti ši-i-* . . . (8) . . . *rabu(u) u-ḫu* (?) *a* . . . (9) . . . *I šiḳlu kaspi* (10) . . . *te ša* . . . (11) . . . (Remainder of obv. and top of rev. broken off.) Rev.: (12) . . . (13) [am]*banûti*[pl] *i-* . . . (14) *ṭe-en-ku-*[*nu*] (15) *ina ḳatâ*[II] *man-ma al-*[*la-ku*] (16) *šu-*[*bi-la*]. [No. 36,501]

No. **214.**—Letter from Širiktum unto Uballiṭsu-Bêl, my lord. May Bêl (and) Nabû grant peace and life unto my lord. Lo, daily here I pray unto Bêl (and) Nabû for the life of my lord . . .

. . . Bêl- . . . . (and) Marduk-rimanni have seen them . . .

Lo, the fourteenth day I sent a sheep unto my lord. Speedily set a servant on his way, (for) there is no one with me.

No. **215.**—Letter from Širki unto Nabû-šar-anni, my brother. May Bêl and Nabû grant peace and life unto my brother.

Although I have written to thee two or three times, thou hast not sent the corn. The harvest is ready; I am (now) sending Daîan-iddin unto thee; deliver to him all the corn that he desireth of thee. Speedily set him on his way (back); do not omit it.

No. **216.**—Letter from Šitḳul unto Nergal-uballiṭ, my father. May Bêl and Nabû bless my father . . .

NO. **217**.—OBV.: (1) *Duppi* ^{m}*Šit-ḳul* (2) *a-na* ^{m}*Ba-la-ṭu* (3) *abi-ia* ^{ilu}*Nabû u* ^{ilu}*Marduk* (4) *a-na abi-ia* (5) *lik-ru-bu* (6) *ša bêl iš-pu-ra* (7) *um-ma a-sa-ar me-e* (8) *lu-uṣ-ba-tu* (9) ^{ilu}*Nabû lu-u-i-di* (10) *ki-i i-nim u-* . . . (11) *dul-la in-ni-pu-uš* (12) *a-na-ku* (13) . . . [*ana*] *pa-ni* REV.: (14) ^{am}*šak-nu* (15) *ki-i bêl i-dag-gal-lu* (16) *um-ma a-di eli* (17) *ša* ^{am}*šaḳû ip-ḳi-du* (18) *ina lib-bi ki-i* (19) *la al-li-ku* (20) *en-na a-mur* (21) *ûmu XXII*^{kam} *uṣ-ṣa-a* (22) *ši-na na-da-bak-ku* (23) *ina eli bîti a-nam-da* (24) *u gi-sal-lu-u* (25) *a-nam-da* (26) *ḳi-i-bi-ma* (27) *ḳanî*^{pl} *li-ḳi-lu-pu-'*. [No. 64,385.]

NO. **218**.—OBV.: (1) *Duppi* ^{m}*Šit-ḳul a-na* (2) $^{m\,ilu}$*Bunene-ibni aḫi-ia* (3) 90 *ḳi-me a-na* (4) [^{am}]*sabi*^{pl} *ša nâri i-ḫi-ru-u* (5) *i-din* ^{arhu}*Nisannu* REV.: (6) *ûmu IX*^{kam} *šattu V*^{kam} (7) ^{m}*Ku-ra-aš šar* NUN-KI (8) *šar mâtâti*. [No 60,080]

NO. **219**.—OBV.: (1) *Duppi* ^{m}*Šit-kul a-na* (2) $^{m\,ilu}$*Bunene-ibni aḫi-ia* (3) *ilâni*^{pl} *šu-lum-ka* (4) *liḳ-bu-u* 94 (?) *ḳi-*[*me*] (5) *a-na* ^{am}*ṣabi*^{pl} REV.: (6) *ša ḫi-ru-tu nâri* (7) *i-din* ^{arhu}*Kisilimu ûmu X* . . . [^{kam}] (8) *šattu V*^{kam} ^{m}*Ku-raš šar* E-KI (9) *šar mâtâti*^{pl}. [No. 74,445.]

NO. **220**.—OBV.: (1) *Duppi* ^{m}*Tab-ni-e-a* (2) *a-na* ^{m}*Da-an-ki-du* (?) (3) *aḫi-ia* ^{ilu}*Bêl u* ^{ilu}[*Nabû*] (4) *šu-lum u balaṭi* [*ša aḫi-ia*] (5) *liḳ-bu-u* . . . (6) ^{m}*Ši-ṣi* . . . (7) *muš-* . . . (8) *ešten*(*en*) *na-* . . . (9) TIN-TIR-[KI] . . . (10) *ni-* . . . (Remainder of obv. and top of rev. broken off.) REV.: (11) . . . (12) *id-di* . . . (13) *i-ba-aš-ši* . . . (14) *ki-i ta-ad* (?)- . . . (15) *al-ku u-* . . . (16) ^{m}*Iddina-*^{ilu}*Bêl* . . . (17) *it-te-ki-*[*ir* ?] . . . (18) *ku-um-mi* . . . (19) [*kap*]-*du ešten*(*en*) . . . (20) . . . (21) . . . *i-ku* . . . [No. 84,995]

No. **217**.—Letter from Šitkul unto Balaṭu, my father. May Nabû and Marduk bless my father.

Concerning that which my lord sent, saying, "Let me take away the . . . of water." I call Nabû to witness whether I have set (?) eye (?) (on it); the work hath been completed. I [will come], if my lord will trust to a deputy, otherwise I shall not have left until he hath appointed a headman over the work. Behold, now, I am going forth on the twenty-second day to put a double ridge (?) on the house, and lay down the flooring. Do thou order that they cut the reeds.

No. **218**.—Letter from Šitḳul to Bunene-ibni, my brother. Give ninety *ḳa* of flour to the workmen who are digging out the river. Dated the ninth of Nisan, the fifth year of Cyrus, the king of Sippar, the king of countries.

No. **219**.—Letter from Šitkul unto Bunene-ibni, my brother. May the gods grant peace unto my brother.

Give ninety-four (?) *ḳa* of flour to the workmen on the digging-works on the river.

Dated the . . . day of Kislew, the fifth year of Cyrus, the king of Babylon, the king of countries.

No. **220**.—Letter from Tabnêa unto Dankidu (?), my brother. May Bêl and Nabû grant peace and life [unto my brother].

. . . .

No. **221**.—Obv. (1) *Duppi* ^sal^*Amti-ia* (2) *a-na* ^m ilu^*Bêl-eṭir* (3) *en-na ki-i ḳatâ*^II^*-ka* (4) *kal* (?)*-da-ti* (5) *šeri-' ša ina pani-ka* (6) *šu-bal-li-ka* (7) *ina ṭâbti* (8) *šu kun-ku-uš* (9) *u ki-i ḳatâ*^II^*-ka* (10) *la kal*(?)*-da-ti* Rev. (11) *ultu ûmi IX*^kam^ (12) *šeri a-na* (13) ^m^*Na-sir i-din* (14) *šu-u ti-lu šu-bal-li-ka* (15) *a-mur ina ḳatâ*^II^ (16) ^m^*Itti-*^ilu^*Nabû-gu-zu* (17) *al-tap-par-rak-ka*. [No. 29,255.]

No. **222**.—Obv.: (1) *Duppi* ^sal^*Ga-ga-a a-na* (2) ^m^*Ša-pî-*^ilu^*Bêl abi-šu lu-u* (3) *šu-lum a-na abi-ia* (4) ^ilu^*Bêl u* ^ilu^*Nabû šu-lum* (5) *ša abi-ia lik-bu-u* (6) *am-me-ni ina pa-ni-ka* (7) *a-na-ku u mârâti*^pl^*-ia* (8) *ina ṣu-um-me-e* (9) *ša ši-pir-tu a-ba-a-ta* (10) *ri-ši-ka di-ki-e-ma* (11) ^ilu^*Šamši a-mur am-me-ni* (12) ^m ilu^*Bêl-uballit*(*it*) *ina pani-ka* (13) *saluppi-ia* (14) *gab-bi iš-ši* (15) *a-na* ^m ilu^*Bêl-upaḫḫir*(*ir*) (16) [*ki*]*-i ak-bu-u* (17) *i-ḳab-ba-a* Rev.: (18) *um-ma a-mur* (19) *saluppi-i-ka* (20) *ana pa-ni* ^m ilu^*Bêl-uballiṭ*(*iṭ*) (21) *u* ^m ilu^*Bêl-uballiṭ*(*iṭ*) (22) *saluppi ka-la-ma* (23) *ul id-din-nu* (24) *ki-i aḳ-ba-aš-šu-nu-ti* (25) *um-ma saluppi* (26) *i-bi-na-nu* (27) *i-ḳab-bu-nu* (28) *um-ma al-ki-ma* (29) *a-na apil* ^m^*Da-ku-ru* (30) *a-na muḫ-ḫi ki-bi-i* (31) *ša-ni-ia-a-na* (32) *ki-i aḳ-ba-aš-šu-nu-ti* (33) *um-ma* (34) *al-ki-ma* (Left-hand edge) (35) *ilâni*^pl^ *ši-si-i a-na-ku pa-ni* (36) *bêli-ia ad-da-gal mi-nu-u* (37) *ši-pir-ti a-mat ša bêli-ia lu-uš-mu* [No. 64,380.]

No. **223**.—Obv.: (1) *Duppi* ^sal^*Ḫa-ba-šu-ša-a* (2) *a-na* ^m^*Šad-din-nu* (3) *aḫi-ia* ^ilu^IM-SU-AN-NA (4) *u* ^ilu^ŠU-ZI-AN-NA (5) *šu-lum u balaṭi ša aḫi-ia* (6) *lik-ba-' a-* . . . (7) *kaspi a-na* ^m ilu^*Bêl-* . . . (8) . . . *nu u* . . . (9) . . . (Remainder of obv. and top of rev broken off) Rev.: (10) *ul* .

[No 67,911]

No. **221**. — Letter from the lady Amtia unto Bêl-eṭir.

Now if thy hand is set (ready), put the meat which hath been brought thee into salt; but if thy hand is not set (ready), give the meat to Nasir from the ninth day, (for) he is dependent(?) on what is sent thee.

See, I have sent unto thee by the hands of Itti-Nabû-guzu.

No. **222**.—Letter from the lady Gagâ unto Ša-pî-Bêl, her father. Peace be upon my father: may Bêl and Nabû grant peace unto my father.

Why, an 't please thee, have I and my daughters passed the time in thirst for a letter from thee? Rack thy brains (for an excuse, and then) by Šamaš, see why Bêl-uballit, an 't please thee, hath taken away all my dates. After I had spoken to Bêl-upaḫḫir, he said, "Lo, thy dates belong to Bêl-uballiṭ," and Bêl-uballit hath not given (back) a single date. When I spoke to them, saying, "The dates are our fruit(?)," they said to me, "Go away and tell the son of Dakuru about it," (and) when I spoke to them a second time about it, (they said) "Go away and call on the gods." Now do I put my trust in my lord; whatever the letter, let me hear word from my lord.

No. **223**.—Letter from the lady Ḫabašušâ unto Šaddinnu, my brother May Imsuanna and Šuzianna grant peace and life unto my brother.

. silver unto Bêl- . .

NO. **224**. — OBV.: (1) *Duppi* ^{sal}*Mu-še-zib-tum* (2) *a-na* ^{m}*Ba-lat-su* (3) *mâr-šu* ^{ilu}*Bêlit Uruk*^{ki} (4) *u* ^{ilu}*Na-na-a* (5) *šu-lum ša mâri-ia* (6) *lik-ba-a* . . . (7) *pa-ni-ka ma-ḫi-ri* (8) *ša ina ṣilli-ka* (9) *a-na ka-a-te šaknu*(*nu*) (10) *a-na-ku me-* . . . (11) *u-kal-la-*[*mu*] REV.: (12) $^{sal\ ilu}$*Na-na-a-ḫu-si* (?) . . . (13) *a-gan-na-ka* (14) *aš-ba-at* (15) *a-na bêlit gal-la-ti-ia* (16) *ul at-tu-ka-a* (17) *ul ta-ḳab-ba-'* (18) *um-ma ina a-la-ki-ia* (19) *a-ga-a a-šap-par-ki-iš* (20) *en-na am-me-ni* (21) *ina ḳatâ*^{II} *man-ma* (22) *al-la-ku* (23) *la ta-aš-pu-raš* (Left-hand edge) (24) ^{sal}*Mu-še-zib-tum šu-lum* (25) *ša* ^{sal}*Ṣi-ra-a mârti-šu ta-ša-lu.*

[NO. 40,525.]

NO. **225**.—OBV.: (1) *Duppi* ^{sal}*Pu-ḳa-a a-na* (2) ^{m}*Iddina-*^{ilu}*Nabû aḫi-ia* (3) *ûmu*(*mu*)*-us-šu* ^{ilu}*Dam-ki-na* (4) ^{ilu}*Bêlit* TIN-TIR-KI *a-na eli-ka* (5) *u-ṣal-la* ^{sal}*Pu-ḳa-a* (6) *šu-lum ša* ^{sal}*Ṣabitum*(*tum*)*-ri-mat* (7) *aḫati*(*ti*)*-šu ta-ša-lu* (8) *te-ki-tum ša* . . . (9) *a-na ênâ*^{II}*-ka ta-ad-*[*da-gal*] (10) *ki-i aš-mu-u* (11) *um-ma* ^{m}*Iddina-*^{ilu}*Nabû* (12) *i-ru-bu* (13) *aḫ-ta-mi* REV.: (14) *u en-na* (15) *lu-ma-a-du* (16) *da-al-ḫa-ak* (17) *lu-ma-a-du* (18) *sa-ba-ka* (19) ^{am}*apil-šipri-ka* (20) *la i-ba-aṭ-ṭi-il.*

[NO. 84,943.]

NO. **226**.—OBV.: (1) *Duppi* ^{sal}*Ḳud-na-nu* (2) *a-na* ^{sal}*In-ṣab-tum* (3) *aḫati-ia* ^{ilu}*Bêl u* ^{ilu}*Nabû* (4) *sulum u balati ša aḫi-ia* (5) *lik-bu-u* (6) *a-mur IV ma-na šipâti* (7) *bêl lu-ka-* . . . *-mu* (8) *ul-te-bi-la-ka* (9) . . . *-da-da* REV.: (10) *u* . . . (11) . . . *-ka* (12) . . . (13) . . . ^{ilu}*Šamši* (?).

[NO. 36,518]

No. **224**.—Letter from the lady Mušezibtum unto Balatsu, her son. May Bêltis of Erech and Nanâ grant peace unto my son.

If thou art willing that it should be brought under thine own care, I will shew thee a matter (?).

The woman Nanâ-ḫusi . . . is dwelling yonder with thee; yet didst thou not say to the head-woman of my slaves (not thine), "When I go, I will send thee this one"? Now why hast thou not sent her with some traveller?

Mušezibtum sendeth greeting to her daughter Ṣirâ.

No. **225**.—Letter from the lady Puḳâ unto Iddina-Nabû, my brother. Daily I pray unto Damkina (and) Bêltis of Babylon on thy behalf.

Puḳâ sendeth greeting to the lady Ṣabitum-rimat, her sister.

The end to . . . thou shalt see with thine own eyes. After I heard thus, "Iddina-Nabû hath arrived," I hasted, and now greatly am I troubled, greatly am I distressed (?).

Let not thy messenger be wanting.

No. **226**.—Letter from the lady Ḳudnanu unto the lady Inṣabtum, my sister. May Bêl and Nabû grant peace and life unto my brother (*sic*).

Behold, I am sending thee four manas of wool . . .

No **227**—Obv. (1) *Duppi* ^{am} *daiani* [^{pl}] (2) *a-na* ^{am} E-BAR UD-[KIB-NUN-KI] (3) *abi-i-ni* ^{ilu}*Nabû u* ^{ilu}[*Marduk*] (4) *a-na abi-i-ni lik-ru-*[*bu*] (5) $^{m\,ilu}$*Šamšu-šuma-ešir* (6) *u* ^{m}*Šit-ḳul a-na pa-*[*ni-nu*] (7) *ki-i i-ru-bu-'* (8) *duppi*^{pl} *ša I C ḳanê*^{pl} (9) *ša* $^{m\,ilu}$*Šamšu-šuma-ešir* (10) *a-di XX ḳanê*^{pl} *ina ḳatâ*^{II} (11) ^{m}*Ri-mut mâr* ^{m}*Amel-*^{ilu}*Sin* (?) (12) . . *mar* . . . (13) . . . (Remainder of obv and top of rev. broken off) Rev.: (14) *I C X* (?) . . . (15) *a-di XX* [*ḳanê*^{pl}] . . . (16) *ša a-na* ^{ilu}*Šamši* . . . (17) *duppi ša XX kanê* [^{pl}] . . . (18) *ul ni-mur* ^{m}*Šit-ḳul* (19) *i-kab-bi um-ma* (20) *al-la I C ḳanê*^{pl} (21) *a-di ša a-na* ^{ilu}*Samši* (22) *na-ad-nu ia-a-nu* (23) *niši*^{pl} *a-gan-na-*[*ka*] (24) *te-en-šu-nu ki-*[*i iš-mu-u*] (25) *u ḳanê*^{pl} . . . (26) *ina* UD-KIB-[NUN-KI] (27) *X ḳanê*^{pl} . . . (28) *iš-* . . . (Left-hand edge) (29) [*ḳanê*]^{pl} *a-na* ^{ilu}*Šamši bêl lid-din u mi-ṣa-ri-šu-nu* (30) . . . *-ba-'-i-ma man-nu ina mi-iṣ-ri-šu* (31) . . . *bêl lu-ša-aṣ-bat.* [No 63,229]

No. **228**—Obv: (1) *Duppi* ^{am}*daiani*^{pl} (2) *a-na* ^{am} E-BAR UD-KIB-NUN-KI (3) *abi-i-ni* ^{ilu}*Nabû u* ^{ilu}*Marduk* (4) *a-na abi-i-ni lik-ru-bu* (5) $^{m\,ilu}$*Šamšu-šuma-ešir* (6) *a-na muḫ-ḫi* (7) $^{m\,ilu}$*Šamšu-uballit(it)* (8) *ki-i iḳ-ba-an-na-šu* (9) *ki-i niš-pur-ra-aš-ši* (10) *li-il-li-ka* (11) *u* (?) $^{m\,ilu}$*Samšu-šuma-ešir* Rev: (12) *a-gan-na* (13) $^{m\,ilu}$*Šamšu-uballit(iṭ)* (14) *bêl liš-pur-ra-am-ma* (15) *purussi-šu-nu* (16) *niš-kun*

[No. 67,357]

No. **229**—Obv.: (1) *Duppi* ^{am}*daiani*^{pl} *a-na* (2) ^{am}*šangi* UD-KIB-NUN-KI (3) *aḫi-i-ni* ^{ilu}*Bêl u* ^{ilu}*Nabû* (4) *šu-lum u balati ša aḫi-*[*i-ni*] (5) *liḳ-bu-u* ^{sal}*Ka-la-tu* (?) (6) *taḳ-ta-ba-an-na-*[*šu*] (7) *um-ma di-na-a id-*[*din*] (8) $^{m\,ilu}$*Bêl-uballit(iṭ) u* $^{m\,ilu}$*Nabû-balaṭ-su-iḳ-bi* (9) *i-ba-aš-ši-u* (10, 11, and 12 erased) (13) $^{m\,ilu}$*Bêl-uballit(it)* (14) [*u* ^{m}]^{ilu}*Nabû-balaṭ-su-ik-bi* Rev.: (15) . . . *šu šup-ra* (16) *purussi-šu-nu* (17) *niš-kun.* [No. 38,171]

No. **227**.—Letter from the Judges unto the Priest of Sippar, our father. May Nabû and [Marduk] bless our father.

When Šamaš-šuma-ešir and Šitkul had come into [our] presence, [they laid up] contracts for one hundred reed-canes belonging to Šamaš-šuma-ešir, besides twenty reeds in the hands of Rimut, the son of Amel-Sin (?) . . .

. . . We did not see the contract-tablet for the twenty reed-canes. Šitkul spake thus, "Except the hundred reed-canes (besides those given to Šamaš), there are none." The people yonder, when [they had heard] their instructions, and [had brought] the reeds, . . .

No. **228**.—Letter from the Judges unto the Priest of Sippar, our father. May Nabû and Marduk bless our father.

After Šamaš-šuma-ešir had spoken to us about Šamaš-uballit, we sent to him that he might (?) come. Now Šamaš-šuma-ešir is here; let our lord send Šamaš-uballiṭ that we may settle their judgment.

No. **229**.—Letter from the Judges unto the Priest of Sippar, our brother. May Bêl and Nabû grant peace and life unto [our] brother.

The lady Kalatu (?) hath spoken unto us, saying, "Give (?) me my judgment." Bêl-uballiṭ and Nabû-balaṭsu-iḳbi are concerned in the case. Send Bêl-uballiṭ [and] Nabû-balaṭsu-ikbi that we may settle their judgment.

No **230**.—Obv.: (1) *Dup-pi* ^{am}*daiâni*^{pl} (2) *a-na* ^{am}*šangi* *Sip-par*^{ki} (3) *abi-i-ni* ^{ilu}*Nabû* *u* ^{ilu}*Marduk* (4) [*a*]-*na* *abi-i-ni-ni* (5) [*lik*]-*ru-bu* ${}^{m\ ilu}$*Nabû-u-bul-liṭ* (6) [*iš-pur*]-*an-na-a-ši* (7) *um-ma* ${}^{m\ ilu}$*Nabû-bulliṭ-su* *a-lik* (8) . . . *mu-ṣi-pi-e-ti-ia* (9) *u* *u-di-e-a* *it*-[*ta-šu-u*] (10) *u* *iḫ-ti-li-ku* (11) *u* ^{am}*rab* *bît-kil-li* . . (12) *ša* ^{am}*šangi* *Sip*-[*par*^{ki}] (13) *ina* *Sip* - *par* [^{ki}] . . Rev.: (14) *ki* - [*i* *iš-mu-u*] (15) *ina* *bît-kil-li* (16) *it-ta-az-* . . . (17) *u* *mu-ṣi-e-pi-ti*-[*šu*] (18) *u* *u-di-e-šu* *it-ta*-[*ši*] (19) *a-mur* *ši-pir-tum* *a-na* (20) *bêli-ia* *ni* *il-tap-par* (21) *mu-ṣip-ti-šu* *u* *u-di-e-šu* (22) *u* ^{am}*gal-la* *u* *mimma* *ša* (23) *ma-la* *ina* *Sip-par*^{ki} (24) *a-na* *kaspi* *id-din-nu* . . (25) *gab-bi* *bêl* *liš-ša-'* (26) . . . *mâr-šip-ri* (27) . . . *Nabû* (?)-*ubulliṭ*(*iṭ*) (28) . . .

[No. 75,610]

No **231**.—Obv.: (1) [*Duppi* ^{am}*daiâni*]^{pl} *a-na* (2) [^{am}*šangi*] UD-KIB-NUN-KI (3) [*abi-i*]-*ni* ^{ilu}*Nabû* *u* ^{ilu}*Marduk* (4) [*ana*] *abi-i-ni* *lik-ru-bu* (5) [*a-mat*] *šarri* *ši-i* *man-ma* (6) [*ša* *a*]-*na* *eli* *bêl* *di-i-ni-šu* (7) [*i*]-*kab-ba-an-na-a-šu* (8) [*a*]-*na* ^{am}E-[BAR] *ša* *ali* (9) . . . *di-i-ni* (Remainder of obv. and top of rev. broken off.) Rev.: (10) . . . (11) *a-na* *bîti* (?) . . .

[No. 84,958.]

No. **232**.—Obv.: (1) *A-na* ^{am}*ki-i-pi* *bêli-ia* (2) *ardi-ka* ^{m}*Ilu-iš-tu-* . . . *-ia* (3) *ûmu*(*mu*)-*us-su* ^{ilu}*Šamši* (4) *u* ^{ilu}*Bu-ne-ne* (5) [*a*]-*na* *balat* *napšâti*^{pl} (6) *arak* *ûmu*(*mu*) *tu-ub* *libbi* (7) [*tu*]-*ub* *šeri* *ša* *be-ili-ia* (8) [*u-sal-la*] *šad-da-giš* (9) . . . (Remainder of obv. and top of rev. broken off.) Rev.: (10) . . . (11) . . . *-du-u* (12) . . [*pu*]-*ḳud-du-ti* (13) . . . *ṣi-e-nu* (14) *ik-tal-du* (15) *VI* *immeri* *bu-ḫal* (16) *be-ili* *lu-še-bi-lam* (17) *u* *ši-pir-tum* (18) *ša* *bêli-ia* *a-na* (19) ^{am}*ša-ka-a-du* (20) *ina* *bâbi* *nâr* ^{ilu}*Šamši* (Left-hand edge) (21) [*li*]-*tal-li-ka*

[No. 50,959]

No. **230**.—Letter from the Judges unto the Priest of Sippar, our father. May Nabû and Marduk bless our father.

Nabû-ubulliṭ [hath sent] unto us, saying, "Nabû-bulliṭsu, having come [hither], took away my clothes [1] and furniture, and ran away, and the Chief of the Prison, whom the Priest of Sippar in Sippar [had appointed (?)] when [he heard of it] put him in prison, and took back his clothes and furniture." Now behold, we are sending a letter to my lord; his clothes, furniture, slaves, and whatever can be sold for money in Sippar, let my lord take it all . . .

No. **231**.—[Letter from the Judges] unto [the Priest] of Sippar, our [father]. May Nabû and Marduk bless our father.

This is the King's [decree]: Anyone who speaketh to us concerning his adversary at law . . .

No. **232**.—Unto the Warden, my lord, thy slave Ilu-ištu . . . -ia. Daily [I pray] unto Šamaš and Bunene for the life, long days, happiness, and health of my lord.

. . . The flock of sheep hath arrived; let my lord send six rams, and let my lord's letter go to the shepherd (?) on the Gate of the Šamaš-canal.

---

[1] Exact meaning doubtful; *cf.* No. 56, 8.

No. **233**.—Obv.: (1) *Duppi* ^{am}*šangi*^{pl} *a-na* (2) $^{m\,ilu}$*Bunene-ibni aḫi-i-ni* (3) *ilâni*^{pl} *šu-lum-ka liḳ-bu-u* (4) *I pi ḳi-me a-na* ^{m}*Arad-*^{ilu}*Bunene* (5) *a-na* ^{am}*ṣabi*^{pl} *ša ma-la-ku* (6) *ša nâri i-ḫi-ru-'* (7) *i-din* Rev.: (8) ^{arḫu}*Kisilimu ûmu XXIV*^{kam} *šattu V*^{kam} (9) *Ku-ra-aš šar* E-KI *šar mâtâti*.

[No 74,378.]

No **234**—Obv.: (1) *Duppi* ^{am}*šar-tin-na* (2) ^{am}*rabûti*^{pl} *u* ^{am}*daîani*^{pl} (3) *a-na* ^{am}E-[BAR UD]-KIB-NUN-KI (4) *aḫi-ni* ^{ilu}[*Nabû u* ^{ilu}]*Marduk* (5) *a-na* [*aḫi*]-*ni* (6) *lik*-[*ru-bu*] *a-na* (7) . . . *bît* (8) [^{m}]*Gi-mil-lu* (9) [*ni*]-*iš-pu-rak-ka* (10) *um-ma* . . . -*ma* (11) *u* . . . (12) *mi-nam-ma* . . . (13) *ul taš-pu* (?) - [*ru*] . . . (14) ^{m}*Gi-mil*-[*lu*] (15) *iḫ-ḫi-sa*-[*as*] Rev.: (16) *iḳ-ba-an*-[*na-ši*] (17) *um-ma ina eli* . . . (18) *ša* . . . (19) ^{am}*šangu* . . . (20) *ad-bu-ku-ma* . . . (21) ^{am}*šangi* UD-KIB-NUN-KI (22) *iš-ta-ka-aṣ* (23) . . -*ḫa-ak* (24) *um-ma la-tum ter-tum-šu-nu* (25) *en-na ri-ka-su* (26) *ša* ^{m}*Gi-mil-lu* (27) *ša tak-nu-ku u bêl-di-ni-šu* (28) *ša u-il-tim*^{pl}-*šu* (29) *a-na la-tum ter-tum* (30) *u-te-e-ri* (31) *u a-na eli di-ni-šu* (32) *šup-ra-am-ma* (33) *dib-bi-šu-nu* (Left-hand edge) (34) *ni-iš-me* . . .

[No 65,046]

No. **235**—Obv.: (1) *Duppi* [^{am}]*šar-te-nu* ^{am}*rabûti*^{pl} (2) *u* [^{am}]*daîani*^{pl} *a-na* (3) ^{am}E-BAR UD-KIB-NUN-KI (4) *aḫi-i-ni* ^{ilu}*Nabû u* ^{ilu}*Marduk* (5) *a-na aḫi-i-ni lik-ru-bu* (6) $^{m\,ilu}$*Nabû-apli-iddin ša* $^{m\,ilu}$*Marduk eriba* (7) *abu ša* ^{m}*Ḫar-si a-na ṣabi* (8) *i-du-ku ša ina pa-ni-ka* (9) *ni-ip*-[*ḳi-du*] . . . (Remainder of obv. and top of rev. broken off) Rev: (10) . . . (11) . . . *da a-a i-* . . . (12) . . . *ki-i niš-pu-rak*-[*ka*] (13) *ul taš-pu-ra-aš* (14) *lu-u-ti-i-di* (15) *ki-i iḫ-te-el-ḳu* (16) *mâr šarri a-na muḫ-ḫi* (17) *i-šim-mi*-[*šu*].

[No. 61,355]

No. **233.**—Letter from the Priests unto Bunene-ibni, our brother; may the gods grant peace unto thee.

Give one *pi* of flour to Arad-Bunene for the workmen who are digging out the bed of the canal.

(Dated) Kislew, the twenty-fourth day, the fifth year of Cyrus, the King of Babylon, the King of countries.

No. **234.**—Letter from the Šartennu, the Officers, and Judges unto the Priest of Sippar, our brother. May [Nabû and] Marduk bless our [brother].

[Concerning the] . . . of the house of Gimillu we sent thee thus: " . . . "; why hast thou not sent [an answer]? Gimillu hath pondered on it [and] hath spoken to us, saying, " . . . [Unto] the Priest [of Sippar] I sent, and the Priest of Sippar issued [an order and spake] thus ' . . . is their law.' " Now the bond of Gimillu, which thou and his adversary have sealed, that he should pay back his debts according to the . . . of the law; and do thou send concerning his judgment and we will hear their plaint.

No. **235.**—Letter from the Šartennu, the Officers, and Judges unto the Priest of Sippar, our brother. May Nabû and Marduk bless our brother.

Nabû-apli-iddin, the son of Marduk-eriba, the father of Ḫarṣi, had slain a workman whom we had appointed in thy presence . . .

. . . after we had sent to thee, thou didst not send him. Now be thou made cognizant that he hath fled; the son of the King shall hear of this.

No. **236**. — Obv.: (1) *Duppi* ^{am}[*ša*] - *tam*^{pl} *a* - [*na*] (2) $^{m\,ilu}$*Bunene - ibni I pi* . . . (3) *a - na* $^{m\,ilu}$*Šamšu-mâri-* . . . (4) *u* $^{m\,ilu}$*Šamšu-iķiša*(*ša*) *ša* . . . (5) *a-na šamaššammi* . . . (6) *i-din* ^{arḫu}*Šabaṭu ûmu III* (?)^{kam} (7) *šattu II*^{kam} ^{m}*Kam-bu-zi-*[*ia*] (8) *šar* TIN-TIR-[KI] *šar mâtâti.* [No. 60,732.]

No. **237**.—Obv.: (1) *Duppi* [^{m} *Kal*]-*du a-na* (2) ^{m}*Ri-mut aḫi-ia* (3) ^{ilu}*Nabû u* ^{ilu}*Marduk a-na* (4) *aḫi-ia lik-ru-bu* (5) *ma-ak-ka-su* (6) . . . (7) . . . (8) *saluppi a-na* (9) *ma-ak-ka-su* (10) *ķi-bi-ma* (11) *lu-ul-li-lu-ma* (12) *a-na* ^{ilu}*Nabû* (13) *li-iķ-ķi-su-'* Rev.: (14) *a-mur V* ^{am}*ardâni*^{pl} (15) *a-na pa-ni-ka* (16) *al-tap-par* (17) *it-ti ḫa-ṣa-ra-nu* (18) *ša eķli*^{pl} *ša* ^{ilu}*Nabû* (19) *šu-lu-ma-aš-šu-nu-tim-ma* (20) *a-na* ^{am} . . . (21) *li-ip-ķi-du-ma* (22) *lu-ul-li-lu-ul-ma* (23) *li-iķ-su-'* (24) *ki-i na-kut-tu* (25) *al-tap-rak-ka* (Nothing more is visible) [No 26,397.]

No **238**—Obv: (1) *E-gir ša minut-su ša tak-ka-su-u* (2) *u gu-ku-ni-e*^{pl} *a-di ûmi XXVII*^{kam} (3) *ša* ^{arḫu}*Simâni šattu XXXIV*^{kam} (4) *ša* $^{m\,ilu}$*Nabû-id-dan-nu* ^{m}*Lib-lut* (5) ^{m}*Arad-* ^{ilu}*Taš-me-tu u* $^{m\,ilu}$*Nabû-bulliṭ-su* (6) *apil* ^{m}*Šelibi itti a-ḫa-miš ķa-bu-*[*u*] (7) ^{arḫu}*Simânu ûmu XXVII*^{kam} *ša* . . . (8) *e-lat XIV pa-tu*(?) *kaspi ina pani* (9) $^{m\,ilu}$*Nabû-bulliṭ-su ultu ûmi I*^{kam} (10) *ša* ^{arḫu}*Du'uzi karanu ka-su-*[*u*] (11) *ina pani-šu ana gu-ķu-u* . . . (12) ^{arḫu}*Ululi ûmu XXII*^{kam} Rev.: (13) [*ana*] *gu-ķu-u* ^{arḫu}*Du'uzi ûmu* [*VIII*^{kam}] (14) *ana gu-ķu-u* ^{arḫu}*Nisanni* (15) *ûmu IX*^{kam} *šattu XX* (16) *ana gu-ķu-u ûmu XI*^{kam}.

[No. 25,851.]

No. **236.**—Letter from the *šatam*-officials unto Bunene-ibni.

Give one *pi* [of corn] to Šamaš-mâri- . . . , (and) Šamaš-ikiša . . . for sesame . . .

(Dated) month of Sebat, the third (?) day, the second year of Cambyses, King of Babylon, King of countries.

No. **237.**—Letter from [Kal]du to Rimut, my brother. May Nabû and Marduk bless my brother.

The *makkasu* dates . . . dates for the *makkasu*. Command that they cleanse (them) and present them to Nabû.

Behold, I am sending into thy presence five slaves; send them up (?) to the store-places for dates of the fields of Nabû, and let them direct the . . . -men that they cleanse and present them, although I am sending what is a trouble to thee.

No. **238.**—Tablet of accounts of the dues (?) and payments (?) up to the twenty-seventh of Siwan of the thirty-fourth year which Nabû-iddannu, Liblut̩, Arad-Tašmetu, and Nabû-bulliṭsu, the son of Šelibi, have agreed upon amongst themselves.

Twenty-seventh of Siwan, besides the fourteen and . . . shekels (?) of silver with Nabû-bulliṭsu, from the first day of Tammuz the *kasu*-wine is with him as a payment; on the twenty-second of Elul as a payment; on the [eighth] of Tammuz as a payment; the ninth of Nisan, twentieth year as a payment: (Nisan), the eleventh day.

No. **239**. — Obv: (Top wanting.) (1) . . (2) *ša* $^{m\ ilu}$*Nabû-id-dan-nu u* . . . (3) *ša a-di ûmi XXVII*^{kam} *ša* ^{arḫu}*Simâni* (4) *šattu XXXIV*^{kam} *itti a-ḫa-miš ḳa-bu-u* (5) *e-lat XIV pa-ṭu*(?) *kaspi* [*ina pani*] $^{m\ ilu}$*Nabû-bullit-su* (6) ^{arḫu}*Simânu ûmu XXVII*^{kam} *šattu XXXIV*^{kam} (7) *ša* . . . $^{m\ ilu}$*Nabû* . . . (8) *ultu ûmi I*^{kam} *ša* ^{arḫu}*Du'uzi karanu ka-su-u* (9) *ina pani* $^{m\ ilu}$*Nabû-bullit-su apil* ^{m}*Šelibi* (10) *ana gu-ḳu-u* ^{arḫu}*Ululi ûmu XXII*^{kam} (11) *ana* [*gu*]-*ku-u* ^{arḫu}*Du'uzi ûmu VIII*^{kam} (12) [*ana gu*]-*ḳu-u* ^{arḫu}*Nisanni* (13) *ûmu IX*^{kam} *šattu XXXV*^{kam} Rev.. (14) *ana gu-ḳu-u* ^{arḫu}*Nisanni* (15) *ûmu IX*^{kam} *ana gu-ku-u* (16) ^{arḫu}*Nisanni ûmu XI*^{kam}.

[No. 25,847]

No **240** — Obv: (1) [*Duppi* ^{m}]^{ilu}*Bêl-aḫi*^{pl}-*iddin a-na* (2) [$^{m\ ilu}$ . .]-*aḫi-id-dan-nu aḫi-ia* (3) ^{ilu}*Bêl u* [^{ilu}*Nabû*] *šu-lum balati ša aḫi-ia* (4) *liḳ-bu-u a-di ma-a-ti* (5) *ki-i kaspi la tu-še-bi-li* (6) *en-na kaspi ša eburi tuk-ta ḳatâ*$^{II\ pl}$-[*ka*] (7) *ša ûmu*(*mu*) *ša ultu eli na-pa-a-ṣu* (8) *a-di eli en-na ina ḳatâ*^{II} (9) *ana* (?) *ina ḳatâ*^{II} ^{m}*A-na-eli-*^{ilu}*Bêl-tag-gil* Rev.: (10) *šu-bi-lu u ki-ma taḳ-ḳa-bu-u* (11) *um-ma a-na* ^{m}*Kaš-*[*ba-nu*] *kaspi* (12) *at-ta-di-in* [*ti* ?]-*ba-am-ma* (13) *it-ti* ^{m}*Kaš-ba-nu kaspi ḳi-*[*bu-u*] (14) *i-bi-in* ^{ilu}*Bêl šu-u* . . . *a-di* (15) [*ki*]-*i kaspi ul tu-še-*[*bi*]-*il* (16) . . . ^{am}*mâr-šip-ri ša* ^{am}*daîani*^{pl} (17) . . . (18) . . . *kaspi innadin* . . . (19) . . . *ša* . . . *da u ešten*(*en*) (20) . . . *lu-nu-uḫ-su ina ḳatâ*^{II} (Left-hand edge) (21) *u a-na eli* . . . (22) *šu-bi-*[*lu*].

[No. 25,688]

(No. **239** *is very similar.)*

No. **240**.—[Letter from] Bêl-aḫi-iddin unto . . . -aḫi-iddannu, my brother. May Bêl and [Nabû] grant peace and life unto my brother.

How long will it be until thou sendest the money? Now thy hand hath ceased the payment for the crops from the day ever since the winnowing up to now. Send (it) by the hand of Ana-eli-Bêl-taggil, or if thou sayest, "I will pay the money to Kaš[banu]," go and speak about the money with Kašbanu.

. . . .

No. 241.—OBV.: (Top broken.) (1) ᵐŠa-ⁱˡᵘNabû-ıttı-šu-balaṭu ... (2) ᵐPanı-ⁱˡᵘNabû-a-dag-gal ... -ki i-ḳab-ba-' (3) um-ma a-na-ku a-[gan]-na al-lak-ku at-ta (4) kunukki ša bîtı it-tı ᵐŠa-ⁱˡᵘNabû-ıtti-šu-balatu ku-nu-uk (5) u it-ti-ka i-ša-' a-na-ku (6) kunukki ša bîti it-ti ᵐŠa-ⁱˡᵘNabû-ıttı-šu-balatu (7) ak-ta-nak u XX ma-na kaspi ᵃᵐ apil-šıpri (8) ša ᵐPani-ⁱˡᵘNabû-a-dag-gal ına Bar-sib ᵏⁱ (9) a-na ᵐŠa-ⁱˡᵘNabû-itti-šu-balaṭu ıt-ta- ... -tı (10) X ma-na kaspi ba-ab-tu BAR bıltı ᵐPanı-ⁱˡᵘNabû-a-dag-gal (11) ... ᵐŠa-ⁱˡᵘNabû-ittı-šu-balaṭu ina pani ᵐⁱˡᵘBêl-etir (12) ... a-mur a-di muḫ-ḫı en-na (13) ... (Remainder of obv. and top of rev. broken off) REV. (14) ... (15) ıl-tap-par um-ma ... ᵏᵃᵐ (16) al-lak-ku u mımma ša ... -na (17) a-na-aš-ša-am-ına u-kal-lam-ka-ma (18) ᵐⁱˡᵘNabû-bullit-su a-di muḫ-ḫi en-na (19) a-na ᵃˡᵘLum(?)-šu(?)-nu ul ıl-lık-ku (20) a-mur ᵐⁱˡᵘNabû-bul-lıṭ-su ıl-lak-ku (21) u šu-u u ᵐŠa-ⁱˡᵘNabû-ıttı-šu-balatu (22) e-gır ša mınuti ıt-ti a-ḫa-mıš ıp-pu-šu-' (23) u kı-ba-nu-u u-pa-ar-ra-su (24) [a-na] bêlı-ıa a-šap-par ana muḫ-ḫı ⁱˢᵘelıppi (25) [ša ıš]-pur-ru a-mur ⁱˢᵘelıppı ša ᵐⁱˡᵘSamšu-zira-ıddın (26) ... -tı ᵃᵐ gal-la ša ᵐⁱˡᵘNabû-na-ṣır(?) (27) ... u ... (Left-hand edge) (28) ... lı-bu-ku ṭe-e-me u šu-lum ša bêlı [lu-uš-me]. [No 25,736.]

No 242 —OBV.· (1) Duppi ᵐⁱˡᵘBu-[ne]-ne-uṣur(?) (2) a-na ᵐⁱˡᵘMarduk-šuma-iddın abı-ıa (3) ⁱˡᵘBêl u ⁱˡᵘNabû šu-lum u balaṭı ša abı-ıa (4) lık-bu-u a-(na) muḫ-ḫı a-mır-tum (5) ᵃᵐṣabıᵖˡ ša ḳatâ ⁱⁱ ᵃᵐkı-ı-pi (6) bêl ıš-pur-ru a-mur a-kı-ı (7) a-mir ša ᵐⁱˡᵘDaîan-šarrı-uṣur (8) ᵃᵐšangı ekallı ı-mur-ru (9) ... [No. 84,970]

No. **241**. — . . . Pani-Nabû-adaggal hath spoken thus: "I am coming here; do thou seal the seal of the house with Ša-Nabû-ittišu-balaṭu, and bring (him) with thee." I have sealed the seal of the house with Ša-Nabû-ittišu-balaṭu, and the messenger of Pani-Nabû-adaggal hath given twenty mana of silver in Borsippa to Ša-Nabû-ittišu-balatu. Ten manà of silver is wanting; half a talent Pani-Nabû-adaggal [unto] Ša-Nabû-ittišu-balatu before Bêl-etir [hath paid ?]. Behold, up to now . . . . . . he sent thus: "I will come on the . . . -th day and bring everything that . . . , and will shew (it) thee." Nabû-bulliṭsu up to this present time hath not come to the city of Lumšunu (?). Behold, Nabû-bulliṭsu is coming, and he and Ša-Nabû-ittišu-balaṭu shall make a statement of accounts between themselves [1] and shall settle the discussion (?).

Unto my lord I send; concerning the boat, of which he sent, behold, the boat of Šamaš-zira-iddin, . . . the servant of Nabû-naṣir (?) . . . [Let me hear] the news and welfare of my lord.

No. **242**. — Letter from Bunene - uṣur (?) unto Marduk-šuma-iddin, my father. May Bêl and Nabû grant peace and life unto my father.

Concerning the produce of the workmen under the hands of the Warden (about which) my lord sent, behold, when the Priest of the Palace saw the produce of Daîan-šarri-usur . . .

[1] Cf. Nos. 238 and 239.

No. **243**—Obv.: (1) *Duppı* ^{m}*Ba* (?)-*nı* (?)-*a-nı* . . . (2) *a-na* $^{m\,ilu}$*Marduk-šuma-uṣur* (3) *aḫi-ia* ^{ilu}*Nabû u* ^{ilu}*Marduk* (4) *a-na aḫi-ıa lık-ru-ub-bu* (5) *a-na muḫ-ḫi saluppi* (6) *ša* ^{m}*Arad-*^{ilu}*Marduk ša aš-pur-rak-ka* (7) *III C saluppı* (8) *ul-tu bır-ri nâri*^{pl} (9) *ın-na-aš-šu saluppı* (10) *ša ı-ma-at-tu-u* (11) *ul-tu* ^{alu}*Bîtı-ṭâbi-*^{ilu}*Bêl* (12) *ın-na-aš-šu* (13) *u-il-tim*^{pl} (14) *ša ırrıši*^{pl} Rev.: (15) *ša bır-ri nâri*^{pl} (16) *a-na* $^{m\,ilu}$*Daîan-bêl-uṣur* (17) *i-dın saluppi* (18) *ma-la ul-tu* (19) ^{alu}*Bîti-tâbi-*^{ilu}*Bêl* (20) *ın-na-aš-šu-u* (21) *lib-bi tu-* . . . (22) *man-ga-ga* . . . *-bı* (23) *in-na-aš-šu* (24) *lu-u-ma-du* (25) *ul tam* (?)-*ḫar-an-ni* (26) *kap-du ḫarrana*^{II} (27) *a-na šepâ*^{II}*-šu šu-kun.* [No. 30,738]

No **244**—Obv: (1) . . . *-bar a-na* (2) [$^{m\,ilu}$*Nabû* (?)-*bul*]*-lıt-su* ^{am}*bêl-pı-ḳı-tum* (3) ^{m}*E-zi-du* ^{m}*Aḫi-šu-nu apil-šu ša* (4) ^{m}*Ri-mut u* $^{m\,ilu}$*Nabû-bul-lit-su apıl-šu ša* (5) ^{m}*Rı-mut u Bar-sıb*$^{ki\,pl}$ (6) *aḫi*^{pl}*-ıa* ^{ilu}*Bêl u* ^{ilu}*Nabû šu-lum u balati* (7) *ša aḫı*^{pl}*-ıa lık-bu-u en-na* (8) *I M VI C XL gur* ŠE-BAR *a-di-ı* (9) *ḫi-iṣ-ṣu u ı-pı-ri* (10) *a-na X* ^{isu}*elıppi ul-te-li* (11) . . . *-ın-nı-ga* (?)*-'* . . . (12) . . . Rev.: (13) . . *u* . . . (14) *a-na* ^{m}*Ilu-ma-ga* . . (15) *a-na muḫ-ḫı-ku-nu a-šap-par* (16) *ba-ga-* . . ^{m}*Da-a-rı-muš* (17) *šarru ına muḫ-ḫi-ku-nu kı-ı dul-lu* (18) *ša šarrı ıp-te ḳid* (19) *kap-du kap-du ṭe-e-mu-ku-nu* (20) *ına ḳatâ*^{II} $^{m\,ilu}$*Bêl-ıd-dan-nu* (21) [*lu*]*-uš-mu.*

[No. 77,094]

No. **243**.—Letter from Baniani (?) . . . unto Marduk-šuma-uṣur, my brother. May Nabû and Marduk bless my brother.

Concerning the dates of Arad-Marduk, about which I sent thee, three hundred (measures) of dates from the *birri* of the canals have been received. Dates (which are too few) have been received from the town of Bîti-ṭâbi-Bêl. Give promissory notes for the gardeners of the *birri* of the canals to Daîan-bêl-usur. All the dates that have been received from the town of Bîti-ṭâbi-Bêl thou wilt . . . therein. The *mangagu* (of the dates) and the . . . have been received. Especially do thou not . . . me; speedily set (them) on their way.

No. **244**.—[Letter from . . .] -bar to [Nabû (?)-bul]liṭsu, the overseer, Ezidu, Aḫišunu, the son of Rimut, and Nabû-bulliṭsu, the son of Rimut, and the people of Borsippa, my brothers. May Bêl and Nabû grant peace and life unto my brothers.

Now I am sending up in ten boats one thousand six hundred and forty *gur* of corn, including the sand[1] and dust (mixed with it) . . .

. . . unto you I send . . . Darius the King, if he commissioneth you with the royal works. Speedily, speedily let me hear news of you by the hand of Bêl-iddannu.

---

[1] *Ḫiṣṣu*: cf. the late Hebrew חֲצָצָא "sand" or "gravel."

No. **245**.—Obv. (1) *Duppi* [m]. . . (2) [am] E-BAR UD-KIB-[NUN-KI] (3) *aḫi-ia* [ilu]*Nabû u* [ilu]*Marduk* (4) *a-na aḫi-ia lik-ru-bu* (5) *a-ki-i ḫurasa-' a-na* (6) TIN-TIR-KI *tu-* . . . (7) . . . *-la-* . . . (8) . . . *ma-ḫar-* . . . (9) *ki-i aš-me-u a-na* . . . (10) [isu]*maîali ša-na-'-a* (11) *a-na mâr šarri ki-i* (12) *aḳ-bu-u* (13) *ik-ta-ba-a* (14) *um-ma kaspi* Rev.: (15) . . . *-ta Sip-par* [ki] (16) . . . *-li-e* . . . (17) *e-li šumi* (?) [m]*Šuma-uṣur* (18) *li-ik-ba-a* (19) *la ta-sil-li* (20) *a-ki-i ša i-kaš-ša-di* (21) *it-ta-ši-iz* (22) *ma* (?)*-ḫar* . . . *-ut-su* (23) *II III-šu iḳ-ta-ba-a* (24) *um-ma a-mur* [am]*šangi* [pl] *Sip-par* [ki] (25) *ûmu I* [kam] . . . *-aš-ki* (?) *Sip-par* [ki] (26) *bit-li* . . . (27) . . .

[No 75,765]

No **246**—Obv: (1) *Duppi* [m ilu]. . . (2) *a-na apil* [am] . (3) *bêli-šu* [ilu]*Šamšu u* [ilu]. . . (4) [ilu]*Bu-ne-ne* . . . (5) *a-na bêli-ia* . . . (6) *ûmu(mu)-us-su* . . . (7) . . . *-ut-* . . . (8) . . . Rev.: (9) . . . (10) . . . *-pu-uš-* . . .

[No. 52,291]

No. **247**—Obv · (Top broken) (1) . . . (2) . . . *-tim* . . . (3) *u šarru be-ili* . . . (4) *um-ma-na-a-ti ša* (5) . . . *-ma-tim ki-* . . . (6) [mâtu]*Aš-šur* [ki] . . . (7) *ûmu(mu) šarru be-ili mât-su la id-di-ku* . . . (8) [[am]*ṣabi*] [pl] *ša* [mâtu]*Ka-ra-an-du-ni-ia-[aš]* . . . (9) . . . *-i-la-lu-u i-na-aš-ši-ma* . . . (10) *buša ša ma-a-ti ki-i pi-i-ka ip-pu-[šu]* . . . (11) *buša ša ma-a-ti ki-i pi-i-ka la ip-pu-šu* . . . (12) *i-na ba-li-ka* [alu]*U-ri-zu ul aṣ-[ba-at-ma]* (13) *kaniki-ka u ku-nu-uk-[ki-ka]* (14) *i-na ba-li-ka* [alu]*Ri-mi-iz* (?)*-ḫu-u ul aṣ-ba-at kaniki-[ka u kunukki]-ka* (15) *i-na ba-li-ka* [alu]*Šad-* . *-u-* . . *man-da-ru ul aṣ-ba-at*

No **245**.—Letter from . . [unto] the Priest of Sippar, my brother. May Nabû and Marduk bless my brother.

As thou didst [send?] the gold to Babylon . . when I heard (of it) and ordered another couch for the King's son, he spake thus, "Let [my lord send?] the money [from] Sippar, on the . . . of Šuma-usur let him speak. Be not neglectful; when it arriveth, it shall be set in hand . . ." He spake thus two or three times, "Behold, the Priest of Sippar the first day . Sippar . .".

No. **246**.—Letter from . . unto the son of the . . , his lord. May Šamaš . . . [and] Bunene bless my lord . . .

No **247**.—(*Large letter to the King.*)

. . . The King my lord . . . the troops of . . . Assyria . . . the day the King my lord did not assemble his people . . . the [troops] of Karanduniaš . . -ilalû will take and . . . the possessions which the land according to thy command had gotten . . . the possessions which the land according to thy command had not gotten . . . Without thee I had not taken the city Urizu, by thy seal and signet! Without thee I had not taken the city Rimizḫû (?), by thy seal and signet! Without thee I had not taken the city of Šad . . u . . mandaru, by thy seal and signet!

kanıkı-[*ka u*] *kunukkı-ka* (16) *mâr* [m]*Zı-ık-rı a-ši-ıb U-rı kı-na-at*-[*tum*] (17) *ıḫ-te-bı-la-an-nı* (18) *šarru be-ılı kı-ı u-še-e-ı-du dı-ı-na ul ı-pu-uš* (19) *a-na-ku u* [m] *U-zu-ub-šı-ı-ḫu* [am] *rabûtı* [pl] *ša šarrı bêlı-ıa nı-ı-nu* (20) *ıa-a-šı ıt-ta-ta aṣ-ṣa-ra-an-nı* (21) *u aḫı*[pl]*-e-a i-na ka-nı-e um-taḫ-ḫı-ıs* (22) *šarru be-ılı kı-ı am-taḫ-ḫa-ru dı-ı-na ul ı-pu-uš* (23) *kı-i ša-šu-u ı-pu-ša-an-nı a-na-ku ma-la e-pu-uš* . REV. (24) *ša šarru be-ılı iš-pu*-[*ra*] (25) *um-ma* [m]*Ka-mu-u* [m] *Pa-kı-rı* [m] *Še-e-nı u* [m]*Ba-ar-* . (26) *a-ra-du-u*-[*ma*] (27) *šarru ıd-dı-na šarru-um-ma ıt-ta-ba*-[*al*] (28) *be-el šarrı-i i-ba-aš-šı* (29) *ša šarru iš-pu-ra* (30) *um-ma ša-kı-ka-a-tım ša ka-na-ak-tı* (31) *ša i-na ḳa-tı* [m]*Ardi-ıa mâr* [m]*Zı-ık-rı a*-[*šıb*] *U-rı ta-am-ḫu-ru šu-bı-la* (32) *a-na-ku ma-la aḫ-šı-ıḫ* . . . *-šam-ma la u-še-bı-la* (33) *kı-ı pa-ni šarrı be*-[*ıli*]*-ıa maḫ-ru lu-uš-pu-ur-ma* (34) *ul-tu* [matu]*Ku-mı-na lı-bu-ku-nım-ma* (35) *a-na šarrı be-ılı-ıa lı-ıd-dı-nu* (36) *ûmu*(*mu*) *šarru be-ılı a-na* [m ilu] *Bêl-mal-kı-dı-e-nu u-bı* (?)- . . (37) *i-na II-ı ûmu*(*mu*) *ı-sı-lı-ıḳ-ku* . (38) *šu-ḫa-at-tı šarrı u-la-* . (39) *a-ka-lu ı-na pa-nı šarrı ık-ka-al šı-ka*-[*ru*] . (40) *ka-ra-nu a-na* *-tap-šu* . . . (41) *u ša-am-ni ka-* . *-tım a-na* (42) *ûmu*(*mu*) *šarru be-ılı a-na* [m ilu] *Sın-* . (43) *kı-ı ša* . . (44) *ûmu*(*mu*) *šarru be-ılı a-* . (45) . .

[No 38,493 + 38,852.]

NO. **248** — OBV: (1) *šu a* (2) *a-lu* . . *na* (?) . *ına* . . (3) *a-na alânı* [pl] *-šu ı-ša-a-tum a-na alânı*[pl]*-šu ı-ša*-[*a-tum šu-kun*] (4) *ı-na alı u ṣeri šuk-nam-ma bı-ḳı*-[*ti*] (5) *kı-ı ša šarru bêli-a ık-ba-a e-te-pu-uš a-na*-[*ku*] (6) *a-na alânı*[pl]*-šu i-ša-a-tum a-na*

The son of Zikri, who dwelleth in the city of Ur (a servant!), grossly insulted me; the King, my lord, although I informed him of it, hath not done justice to me. I and Uzubšiḫu are officers of the King, my lord; yet me he put in ward, and had my brothers beaten with rods. Though I besought the King, my lord, he did not do justice for me. Although he hath done this thing to me, yet I will forget (?) everything that he hath done.

Of that which the King, my lord, sent, thus:—"Shall I pursue (?) Kamû, Pakiri, Šêni, and Bar . . ." The King hath given and the King hath taken away—he is lord of kings.

Of that which the King sent, thus:—"Send specimens (?) of the signet which thou hast received from the hands of Ardia, the son of Zikri, who dwelleth in Ur"; I would desire greatly to [send] it, but he hath not sent it, if it be pleasing to the King, my lord, I will send that they bring it from the land of Kumina and give it to the King, my lord.

The day that the King, my lord, . . . to Bêl-malki-dînu . . . in two days . . .

No. **248**.—[*Large letter to the King.*] . . . [The King commanded] "Set his cities on fire, set his cities on fire, bring woe on city and field." According as the King, my lord, commanded, so did I; I set his cities on fire, I set his cities on fire, and after I had brought woe on city and field, I scattered the spoil of

alâni^{pl}*-šu aškuna(na)* [1] [*i-ša-a-tum*] (7) *i-na ali u ṣeri ki-i aš-kun-nam-ma bi-ki-*[*ti*] (8) *ḫu-ub-tum ša Aššur*^{ki}*-a-a a-na ṣeri*^{pl} *a-šad-da-*[*ad*] (9) *ul-tu ul-lu-u ki-i ir-da-a* . *šak-nu-ma* (10) *mâti-ka mi-na-a la tap-ṭir* . . (11) *rîš ka-ra-šu mi-na-*[*a*] (12) [*a-ra*]*-a-tum ša* ^{am}*rabûti*^{pl} *a* (13) . *šarru be-ili-ia* . (14) . *nu la kir* . REV: (15) . . *a-na ša-*[*kin* (?)] *ḫa* (?)*-ma-tum a-ra-a-tum* . (16) [*šu*]*-la-a* [*i-maḫ*]*-ḫaṣ-an-ni ḫu-um-*[*mi-šu-nu*] (17) [*a-gan-na*] *ia-a-nu* [*šu*]*-la-a a-ra-a-tum* . (18) *ki-i aṣ-*[*ba-tu im*]*-ma* (?)*-ḫa-ṣu bîti-šu-nu* . . (19) *ḳaḳkad mal-ki* [*ak*]*-ki-su a-na šarri be-ili-ia* [*ul-te-bi-la*] (20) *pa-ni-ia ki-i aš-ku-nu a-na bi-ra-na-a-tum ša* (21) ^{am}*rabûti*^{pl} *sa bi-ra-na-a-tum šarru e-ka-a ḳi-ba-nu* (22) *šarru e-ka-a ḳi-ba-nu ḫarrana*^{II} *a-na šepâ*^{II}*-ia šu-*[*kun*] (23) *šarru ina* ^{alu}*Bag-da-du*^{ki} *rîš ka-ra-ši-šu* [*iš-kun*] (24) ^{am}*rabûti*^{pl}*-šu te-e-mu i-šak-kan a-na Aššur*^{ki}*-a-a* (25) *pa-ni-ia ki-i aš-ku-nu-ma a-na* (26) *a-na ru-u-ḳu i-na-ab* (?)*-*[*bit* (?)*-ma*] . (27) . ^{am}*rîšu* . . (28) *ni-nu-u li-zib-šu* (?)*-nu* (?) *u* . (29) . *as-ba-ta-šu-nu* .

[No. 51,082]

[1] This interpretation of the last two characters legible in this line is doubtful. The lacunæ in the middle of the tablet are so large as to make any restoration doubtful, and the translation of ll. 12–17 is, consequently, uncertain.

the Assyrians over the land. Then, when he retreated, [a clamour] arose, "Why hast thou not delivered thy land? . . . Why dost thou [not bring up thy advance] camp?" The spears[2] of the officers . . . to [afford] assistance, "Send up the spears, (for) he is attacking me; hasten (?) [them], (for) there are none [here]; send up the spears!" When I had captured . . . they were defeated, their house [I destroyed (?), and] I cut off the head of the prince; unto the King, my lord, [I send it]. Then, when I had turned my attention to the fortresses, the commanders of the fortresses [cried], "Tell us where is the King, tell us where is the King! Set us on our way (back)!" Now the King had pitched his advance camp at Baghdad, and issued orders [thence] to his officers. After I had turned my attention to the Assyrians and [marched] against [him], he fled (?) away, afar . . . [and his] officers [said] . . . "Let us (?) leave him" . . . I captured them.

[2] Perhaps here "spearmen."

Index and Vocabulary.

A.

^{ilu}**Aa**: 35, 6; 36, 4; 64, 7, 22; 67, 21; 136, 5.
$^{sal\ ilu}$**Aa-enḳit**: 40, 17
^{m}**Abdu'**: 86, 6.
^{m}**Abu-ila'**: 185, 12
$^{m\ ilu}$**Adad-riṣû**: 104, 2.
$^{m\ ilu}$**Adda-iddina**: 44, 5.
^{m}**Adgal-ana-mâr-Esaggil**: 74, 23.
^{m}**Adnalu**: 185, 4, 11, 22.
^{m}**Adrâ**: 64, 18.
^{m}**Aggiya**: 105, 12, 13, 16
^{am}**agiru**: 133, 13, 74, 17.
^{m}**Aḫi**^{pl}**-â**: 39, 40.
^{m}**Aḫi-iddin-**^{ilu}**Marduk**: 11, 1, 2, 12, 1.
^{m}**Aḫišunu**: 244, 3.
aḫu—aḫu, "some—others": 78, 9, 10. Cf 112, 21.
^{m}**Aḫu-** . . : 10, 1.
^{m}**Akar-apli**: 155, 2.
^{m}**Akar-**^{ilu}**Nabû**: 174, 44.
alla: 11, 26; 44, 13, 57, 7; 79, 23; 87, 49; 159, 8 (*alla'*), 23 (?); 182, 11; 191, 29; 196, 12; 212, 12; 213, 27; 227, 20.
allanu: 92, 5, 8.
allanukku: 43, 6
^{sal}**Amat-**^{ilu}**Ba'u**: 129, 19.

^{m}**Ambulu**: 66, 29.
^{m}**Amel-**^{ilu}**Sin (?)**: 227, 11
^{sal}**Amtia**: 194, 28, 221, 1
^{sal}**Amti-inadanni**: 82, 20.
^{m}**Ana (?)** . 40, 16
^{m}**Ana-amat-**^{ilu}**Bêl-adgal**: 30, 1; 51, 2, 164, 18 (?); 173, 3.
^{m}**Ana-eli-**^{ilu}**Bêl-taggil**: 240, 9
ana'tu: 172, 4
^{ilu}**Anunitum**: 15, 13, 27, 8, 88, 13, 208, 23
^{am}**apil-šipri**: 4, 9; 9, 8, 35, 11, 36, 25, 56, 17, 101, 7; 225, 19; 241, 7
^{m}**Aplâ**: 1, 5, 32, 1, 174, 40
appitti: 11,, 19, 20
apu: 139, 23
^{m}**Arad-**^{ilu}**Anu[niti]**: 178, 9
^{m}**Arad-**^{ilu}**Bêl**: 37, 1, 38, 1; 39, 1, 41, 40, 1, 15, 41; 72, 2; 70, 2, 77, 2; 88, 11, 120, 6, 161, 4, 168, 6
^{m}**Arad-**^{ilu}**Bunene** · 42, 1, 233, 4
^{m}**Arad-**^{ilu}**Gula** · 60, 5 (?), 64, 11 (?), 99, 2.
^{m}**Arad-**^{ilu}**Marduk**: 103, 2, 109, 2, 116, 5, 243, 6
^{m}**Arad-**^{ilu}MEME 41, 1.
^{m}**Arad-**^{ilu}**Šamši**: 214, 11
^{m}**Arad-**^{ilu}**Tašmetu**: 238, 5
aratum (?): 69, 18, *arâtum*, 248, 12, 15, 17
^{am}**arbâ**: 86, 7
^{m}**Ardia**: 2, 19, 33, 11; 45, 14, 72, 18, 21; 141, 2, 23, 176, 6; 247, 31.
^{am}**ardu**: 53, 21; 237, 14: ^{am}*arad-ekalli*, 126, 7.
^{m}**Arkat-ilâni**: 1, 5.
^{m}**Arrabi**: 193, 2, 195, 23.
asar mê: 217, 7
asni (of dates): 41, 9
asseveration, forms of · 4, 8; 7, 13; 21, 5; 36, 10, 29; 40, 4 (?); 43, 11 (?), 46, 24; 62, 16; 78, 11, 101, 9, 105, 23, 32; 112, 23, 174, 6, 47; 176, 19, 194, 12, 196, 22, 217, 9; cf 222, 11.

Assyria: 1, 30: 247, 6; 248, 8, 24.
ataru: I, 1; *atrat*, 213, 12.
atru: 49, 3

B.

ba'âtu (cf. Arabic بات): I, 1, spend time; *abâta*, 18, 15; 222, 9; *ibatâ*, 83, 18, *ibâta*, 126, 20; *ibâtu*, 176, 8, *ibatum*, 149, 34; *tabataia*, 83, 11; *tabat*, 89, 14.
babtu: 72, 16; 76, 14; 241, 10
Babylon: 30, 6, 8; 35, 22, 28; 36, 17; 43, 12; 51, 11; 59, 8; 66, 11; 74, 3, 30; 81, 8; 88, 15, 93, 8; 97, 16; 98, 17; 104, 19; 105, 27, 34; 114, 7; 142, 9, 18; 143, 9; 165, 12; 166, 10; 173, 9; 179, 9; 182, 16; 200, 10; cf. 218, 7; 219, 8; 220, 9, 225, 4, 233, 9; 236, 8; 245, 6.
bagani': 74, 25; 244, 16. Cf. *baḳanu'*.
^{alu}**Bagdadu**^{ki}: 248, 23
bakanu': 214, 18. Cf. *bagani'*.
^{m}**Bakû**· 133, 21.
^{m}**Balaṭsu**: 63, 1; 64, 1, 224, 2
^{m}**Balaṭu**: 14, 3, 16, 3; 70, 4, 7, 155, 3; 217, 2.
^{m}**Bania**: 72, 1; 105, 38
^{m}**Baniani (?)**: 243, 1.
banû (?): I, 1; *ibinni*, 113, 25.
^{m}**Banunu**: 183, 8.
^{am}**banûti**: 216, 13.
^{m}**Bar**: 247, 25
Barsib^{ki}: 1, 6; 29, 9 (?); 241, 8, 244, 5.
^{m}**Barzenna**: 73, 20.
^{m}**Basia**: 44, 1.
$^{m\ ilu}$**Ba'u-na'id**: 160, 15.
^{sal}**Bazitu**: 39, 42; 40, 15, 19.
$^{m\ ilu}$**Bêl-** . . . : 16, 9; 49, 4; 214, 15; 223, 7.
^{ilu}**Bêl** (in greetings *passim*): 4, 8; 6, 10; 7, 13; 29, 8; 46, 24; 59, 29; 66, 19; 78, 11, 101, 9; 105, 23, 32; 149, 8; 174, 4, 6; 176, 11; 188, 21; 191, 12; 193, 23; 194, 12; 196, 22; 211, 23; 214, 5; 240, 14.

m ilu **Bêl-aḫi-eriba**: 39, 35 (?); 64, 14
m ilu **Bêl-aḫi-ibašši**: 45, 1
m ilu **Bêl-aḫi-iddin**: 46, 1; 47, 1; 48, 1; 49, 1; 79, 7, 174, 26; 240, 1.
m ilu **Bêl-aḫi-ikiša**: 50, 1; 140, 1
m ilu **Bêl-apli-iddin**: 14, 2; 15, 3, 16, 2, 18, 2; 20, 15; 21, 1; 22, 1, 51, 1; 69, 3; 115, 3, 116, 3, 117, 3, 118, 3, 119, 3; 120, 2, 121, 3, 124, 2, 134, 8, [12], 143, 1; 163, 2.
m ilu **Bêl-asûa**: 44, 4
m ilu **Bêl-balatsu-iḳbi**: 114, 7, 229, 14
m ilu **Bêl-bullitsu**: 59, 1
bêl-dababi: 105, 36; 144, 6
m ilu **Bêl-dânu**: 62, 6
bêl-dini: 234, 27
m ilu **Bêl-epuš**: 155, 7
m ilu **Bêl-eriba**: 200, 30.
m ilu **Bêl-etir**: 1, 4; 70, 2; 82, 6, 221, 2; 241, 11.
bêl-ḫarrani //: 185, 23.
m **Bêlia** (?): 45, 18.
m ilu **Bêl-ibni**: 45, 12, 15; 69, 1, 144, 2, 149, 9; 202, 2; 213, 3
m ilu **Bêl-iddannu**: 162, 6, 244, 20.
m ilu **Bêl-iddin**: 2, 18; 5, 5, 11, 3; 31, 2; 56, 1; 57, 1; 58, 1; 100, 3; 132, 12; 151, 7; 157, 11; 192, 3 (?).
m ilu **Bêl-imkut**: 164, 15.
m **Bêlišunu**: 30, 12, 64, 13, 68, 4; 80, 11, 88, 6, 9; 112, 3, 114, 2; 191, 14, 15.
ilu **Bêlit**: 6, 10, 59, 29; 123, 3; 129, 24; 213, 5, 224, 3; 225, 4.
sal **Bêlit**: 129, 21, 149, 2
m ilu **Bêl-kiṣir**: 65, 1; 66, 1.
m ilu **Bêl-iû-aḫûa**: 39, 22, 28
m ilu **Bêl-malki-dînu**: 247, 36.
m ilu **Bêl-mušallim** 85, 6; 185, 2, 211, 16
m ilu **Bêl-na . . .**: 204, 7.
am **bêl-piḫati**: 142, 11.
am **bêl-piki(t)ti**: 148, 8; 244, 2.
am **bêl-pitki**: 191, 33.

$^{m\ ilu}$**Bêl-rimanni**: 67, 1; 88, 12; 148, 7, 12.
$^{m\ ilu}$**Bêl-riṣûa**: 98, 2
$^{m\ ilu}$**Bêl-šarri-uṣur**: 68, 1.
$^{m\ ilu}$**Bêl-šulimanni**: 9, 10
$^{m\ ilu}$**Bêl-šuma-ešir**: 27, 3.
$^{m\ ilu}$**Bêl (?)-šuma (?)-iddin**: 46, 2.
$^{m\ ilu}$**Bêl-šuma-ukin**: 45, 20
$^{m\ ilu}$**Bêl-supî-muḫur**: 6, 40.
$^{m\ sal}$**Bêlti-šu**: 129, 2.
$^{m\ ilu}$**Bêl-uballiṭ**: 20, 16; 21, 2; 23, 3; 49, 1; 52, 1; 53, 1; 54, 1; 55, 1; 70, 1, 89, 2; 116, 3; 119, 3; 149, 32; 164, 2; 165, 2; 222, 12, 20, 21; 229, 8, 13.
$^{m\ ilu}$**Bêl-upaḫḫir**: 222, 15.
$^{m\ ilu}$**Bêl-uṣur**: 48, 13; 84, 5; 165, 7.
$^{m\ ilu}$**Bêl-zira-ibni**: 60, 1, 61, 1; 62, 1.
$^{m\ ilu}$**Bêl-ziri** · 1, 20.
birru: 80, 19, 243, 8, 15
^{m}**Biru** . . . : 125, 3.
^{sal}**Biššâ**: 90, 3
bitannu: 61, 14.
Bît-Dakuru: 74, 30.
bitlî: 2, 17; 105. 39, 41; 130, 28; 193, 14; 245, 26.
^{alu}**Bît-ṭâbi-** ^{ilu}**Bêl**: 243, 11, 19.
bud: 21, 21.
budu: 105, 10, 148, 18.
^{m}**Bulluṭu**: 171, 5.
bultu (?): 118, 10.
^{ilu}**Bunene**: 13, 9, 20; 63, 3; 68, 8; 192, 18; 206, 4; 209, 3; 212, 4; 232, 4; 246, 4.
$^{m\ ilu}$**Bunene-ibni**: 2, 21; 64, 17; 93, 2; 126, 5, 18; 207, 2; 218, 2; 219, 2; 233, 2; 236, 2.
$^{m\ ilu}$**Bunene-šarri-uṣur**: 51, 7.
$^{m\ ilu}$ **Bunene-usur (?)**: 242, 1.
^{kanu} **buranî**: 152, 7, 13, 19
^{am} **burla**: 87, 31.
^{m}**Buršû**: 73, 1, 11, 14; 98, 6; 200, 15.

D.

m ilu **Daîan-bêli-uṣur**: 8, 2; 78, 1, 79, 1, 80, 1; 81, 1; 82, 1; 83, 1, 148, 20; 230, 1, 231, 1, 234, 2, 235, 2; 243, 16

m ilu **Daîan-iddin**: 73, 6, 30; 215, 9

m ilu **Daîan-ri'u**: 213, 24

m ilu **Daîan-šarri-uṣur**: 85, 1; [86, 1]; 242, 7.

m ilu **Daîan-šuma-usur**: 84, 1.

(am) **daîanu**: 66, 28, 85, 11, 113, 31; 210, 19; 227, 1; 228, 1; 229, 1; 230, 1, [231, 1]; 234, 2; 235, 2; 240, 16.

m **Dakuru**: 222, 29.

sal **Damkâ**: 6, 15

am **damḳaru**: 3, 7.

ilu **Damkina**: 90, 5, 225, 3

alu **Danipinu**: 74, 17.

m **Dankidu (?)**: 220, 2.

Darius: 74, 25, 108, 7; 244, 16.

Dilbat ki: 43, 18

am **dînu**: 82, 21.

dirâta: 65, 10

m **Dumuk**: 6, 17; 87, 1; 105, 39; 158, 5

isu **duppa** MA-GAN-NA: 158, 8

am **dupšarru**: 5, 6; 12, 12; 126, 2; 150, 5.

alu **Dur-gazzâ**: 186, 8.

Dur-ili ki: 159, 21.

E.

ilu **Ea**: 1, 16; 90, 5.

m ilu **Ea-mudammik**: 42, 6.

m ilu **Ea-šuma(?)-epuš**: 42, 7

Ebabbara: 5, 4, 6; 19, 16; 139, 32.

m **Ebabbara-šadunu**: 2, 1; 3, 1; 4, 1; 186, 2.

am E-BAR, 34, 2; 106, 3; 150, 2, 154, 2, 168, 2; 184, 2, 6; 204, 8; 227, 2, 228, 2; 231, 8; 234, 3; 235, 3; 245, 2

eburanu: 36, 9.

edêdu: III, 1, *šudidaš*, 9, 21.

edêru: II, 1, *uduraš*, 9, 22.

[am]ekalli: 150, 1.
ekašši: 52, 7.
ekêpu: II, 1, *ukkupat*, 107, 6.
Ekurru: 35, 9; 36, 8; 78, 23, 150, 14; 164, 15, 208, 7.
[sal]Epirtum: 40, 2.
[m]Eriba- . . .: 34, 1.
[m]Eriba-apli: 139, 4
[m]Eriba-[ilu]Marduk: 35, 1, 36, 1, 10.
eritu: 46, 9.
Esagila: 46, 4, 59, 7; 174, 39.
eširtu: 46, 28.
[am]ešritu: 64, 7.
etêḳu I, 1, *etak*, 105, 14; I, 2, *etetaḳ*, 105, 7; III, 1, *lušetaḳ*, 37, 20; *ušetiḳšu*, 75, 13; *ušitiḳunu*, 44, 8; *tušetiḳšu*, 98, 15, 104, 10, 16; 215, 17; *tu[šetiḳ]*, 211, 19; *šitiḳetu*, 19, 23.
eteru: 31, 11; 113, 9, 24, 126, 16; 194, 24
[m]Etir-[ilu]Marduk: 13, 1; 14, 1; 15, 1; 16, 1; 17, 1; 18, 1; 19, 1; [20, 1], 22, 2, 23, 1 (?); 24, 2, 25, 2; 73, 16; 178, 2.
Ezida 1, 9, 58, 5, 161, 17.
[m]Ezidu. 244, 3

G.

gabaru: 141, 13.
gadida': 195, 25
[sal]Gagâ: 222, 1.
[m]Galala 174, 29
[am]gallabu · 186, 11
[(am)]gallatu: 183, 5, 192, 7, 9; 202, 34; 224, 15.
[(am)]gallu: 54, 8, 14, 96, 16; 138, 16; 139, 11; 159, 18; 214, 10 (?); 225, 8 (?); 230, 22; 241, 26
gašrû: 160, 26.
gidmu: 80, 6.
[m]Gimillu: 76, 1; 77, 1, 5, 7, 11; 234, 8, 14, 26.
gînu: 40, 11.
GIŠ-DA · see *li'u*.
GIŠ-MA: 139, 23.
[m]Gubbâ: 73, 7

guku 238, 2, 11, 13, 14, 16; 239, 10, 11, 12, 14, 15.
m ilu **Gula-balatsu-ikbi** 75, 1.
gumutanu: 10, 18
m **Guzanu**: 14, 26; 73, 22, 74, 1, 174, 33

H.

m **Ḫabasiru** 6, 23; 27, 4; 78, 29; 88, 1.
sal **Ḫabašušâ**· 223, 1
ḫabburu: 193, 10
ḫaburru. 120, 12.
m **Ḫaddâ** 183, 8.
ḫadiranu: 19, 21.
m **Ḫaḫḫu** . . . 174, 24
ḫaltikku 37, 17
sal **Ḫamaranatu** 194, 27
m **Ḫambaḳu** 195, 6
ḫamû, to hasten: I, 2, *aḫtami*, 225, 13, II, 1, *uḫammuka*, 194, 17, *ḫum*[*mišunu*] (?), 248, 16.
ḫanâḳu, to be angry I, 1, *ḫannaḳata*, 4, 20, IV, 1, *iḫḫannaḳ*, 46, 13.
sal **Ḫaninâ**· 40, 16
ḫarâṣu IV, 1, *liḫḫarsannima*, 199, 12.
ḫarrabitu (?). 154, 8
am [**ḫar**]**raku**: 160, 25
alu **Ḫarranu**. 97, 7
m **Ḫarṣi**· 235, 7
ḫašâlu (?) I, 2, *iḫtašal* (or *iḫtarak*), 114, 10.
haṣaranu 237, 17.
m **Ḫašdâ**: 59, 2.
m **Ḫaššadâ**. 76, 24.
ḫibbu: 138, 7.
ḫindi . . : 122, 11
sal **Ḫiptâ**: 202, 12
m **Ḫiritum**. 174, 27.
hiṣṣu 244, 9
ḫišûtu: 188, 16.
ḫusi. 145, 7.

I.

ilu IB 57, 3
m **Ibgi-** ilu **Bêl** 92, 2.
ibinu · 222, 26, 240, 14 (?).
idatum: 98, 18
m **Iddina-apli**: 6, 1, 12, 14, 16, 23, 25, 34, 9, 12, 19, 43, 2, 95, 2; 96, 2, 97, 2; 127, 6; 183, 2; 194, 2, 195, 11.
m **Iddina-** ilu **Bêl**: 7, 1, 111, 7, 220, 16.
m **Iddina-** ilu **Marduk** 6, 12, 8, 1, 9, 1; 48, 2, 55, 2; 78, 2; 79, 2, 24, 80, 2; 81, 2, 110, 2; 148, 2, 151, 8; 157, 2; 182, 2; 195, 2.
m **Iddina-** ilu **Nabû** · 192, 2; 225, 2, 11.
m **Iddina-** ilu **Nergal**. 73, 23.
i-i-lu. I, 1, *li'il*, 75, 9, *li'ilšu*, 48, 16, *i'lû*, 186, 9
m **Ikiša-apli** 113, 28, 137, 15, 151, 8, 186, 7.
am **ikkaru** (see am **irrišu**) · 8, 8, 243, 14
ikkibu 40, 4
illanuššu, "besides it" 144, 23
m **Iltalâ** 64, 6, 16.
iltatu: 63, 7.
m **Ilu-ištu-** . . . : 232, 2
m **Ilu-maga-** . . . : 244, 14.
sal **Imat**: 6, 24
immaka. 159, 16.
ilu IM-ŠU-AN-NA. 223, 3
sal **Ina-ašar-šî-** . . . 172, 8
sal **Ina-E-Sagila-bêlit**: 6, 36.
m **Ina-E-Sagila-lilbur**: 31, 1.
sal **Ina-E-Sagila-ramat**: 6, 13.
m **Ina-silli-** ilu **Bêl**: 9, 4
innitu: 114, 5.
sal **Insabtum**: 226, 2.
inû I, 1, *inna'*, 5, 16, 14, 11; 16, 12; 31, 8, 33, 12, 40, 11; 73, 14; 131, 29; 192, 20; *inna*, 20, 12; *innî*, 40, 10.
am **irrišu** (see am **ikkaru**): 38, 21: 65, 17; 116, 8, 14, 16, 121, 8, [19]; 212, 13.

am **išparu** · 51, 7; 133, 6; am *išparu birmu*, 57, 5; am *išpar isi*, 45, 10; 57, 6; *ummi išparti*, 201, 28.
iššênu 193, 11
m **Issur**: 33, 1.
m ilu **Ištu** . ia 232, 2.
ittahu · 73, 5, 11
m **Itti-** ilu **Bêl-limhir** (*v* **limhur**): 100, 6, 12, 17.
m **Itti-** ilu **Marduk-balatu**: 110, 1.
m **Itti-** ilu **Nabû-balatu** 6, 25; 43, 1.
m **Itti-** ilu **Nabû-guzu** (?): 33, 4; 221, 16
m **Itti-** il **Nabû-pania**: 38, 23, 28
m **Itti-** ilu **Nabû-** . . . : 130, 29.
m **Itti-** ilu **Šamši-balatu** 137, 16.

K

m **Ka** . 173, 6
kabâsu I, 1, *kabas*, 69, 7
sal **Kabitti** 202, 35
kakkib: 83, 8
kalakku. 21, 9, 164, 29, 33.
kalâlu · III, 1, *šuklulu*, 46, 7; 153, 6.
sal **Kalatu** (?): 229, 5
m **Kalbâ**: 39, 36 (?), 52, 21; 56, 16; 76, 23; 95, 1, 16, 96, 1; 131, 3; 200, 11, 26
m **Kaldu** (?): 237, 1.
kallanu (?): 103, 6.
Kambyses. 88, 15; 236, 7.
m **Kamû**: 247, 25
kanâtu (?) I, 1, *kunta'*, 17, 16
kandaku. 44, 12.
m **Kannanu**: 185, 16.
kânu: II, 1, *kunnu*, 167, 7
kapdu 13, 24; 17, 21; 24, 16, 27, 17; 31, 12; 33, 13; 37, 19; 44, 23; 54, 18; 59, 26; 60, 11; 61, 15; 62, 10; 72, 23 (*kapda*); 73, 27; 76, 28; 78, 24, 30; 81, 25; 82, 30; 83, 9, 10, 16, 87, 30; 105, 21, 24, 40; 117, 8; 119, 14,

129, 26 (*kapad*); 130, 26; 134, 6; 141, 11; 148, 16; 151, 16; 156, 7; 157, 13; 158, 16; 161, 21; 167, 9; 171, 10, 20; 174, 49; 182, 9; 191, 36; 196, 34; 214, 21; 215, 15; 220, 19; 243, 26; 244, 19; *kapadaia* (?), 129, 13; *kapâdi*, 52, 8; *ana kapadu*, 38, 17; 39, 7.

kapsanu: 109, 11.

m **Kar** . . . . 130, 24.

sa **Karanati**: 172, 8.

matu **Karanduni[aš]**: 247, 8.

kâru: 14, 24.

karû, in *bît karî*: 115, 8, 143, 6

m **Karuhiya**: 10, 12, 19, 21.

kaš: 5, 14.

m **Kašbanna (?)**: 174, 9.

m **Kašbanu**: 76, 23; 240, 11 (?), 13

m **Kašbibanu**: 147, 5, 16.

kasia: 40, 24, 26; 123, 7.

am **kaṣir**: 63, 14, 22, 32.

m **Kaṣir**: 33, 3; 98, 1; 213, 28.

kasû: 238, 10, 239, 8.

m **Kasusu**: 87, 5, 41.

ḳâtu: II, 1, *uḳat*, 138, 15, 18.

m (?) **Ki (?)** . . : 84, 13.

m **Ki-** 173, 2

kibanû: 241, 23.

m **Kî-** *ilu* **Bêl**: 13, 3; 14, 3; 16, 4, 27, 3; 92, 1; 118, 4 (?), 163, 2; 164, 2; 165, 2; 208, 25.

kidinnî: 35, 40.

m **Kidin-** *ilu* **Sin**: 174, 44.

m **Kidiu (?)**: 10, 9.

m **Kikisia**: 174, 22.

ḳilu: 44, 6

m **Kinâ**: 36, 22; 144, 19; 156, 2; 205, 2.

m **Kî-** *ilu* **Nabû**: 18, 4; 20, 1; 21, 3; 23, 4; 50, 3; [51, 1]; [69, 3]; 93, 1, 94, 1 (?); 115, 3; 116, 4; 117, 4; 118, 4; 119, 4; 120, 3; 121, 4; 143, 2; 166, 2; 179, 1; 192, 2.

Kinaltum: 76, 17.

^{am}**kinat** . . . : 125, 2

King mentioned: I, 1, 10, 14; 3, 15, 20; 7, 12; 34, 6; 35, 34; 37, 5; 40, 10; 46, 9, 12; 51, 11, 53, 7, 17; 60, 17, 62, 19 (king's son); 63, 5 (king's son); 74, 25; 88, 15; 93, 8, 9; 101, 14; 105, 27; 108, 8, [143, 9]; 150, 20 (king's son), 21; 160, 7, 9, 10, 22; 165, 12; 166, 10, 11; 173, 9; 174, 46; 176, 5; 179, '9, 10; [198, 9]; 200, 7 (king's son); 202, 17; 218, 7, 8; 219, 8, 9; 231, 5; 233, 9; 235, 16 (king's son); 236, 8; 244, 17, 18; 245, 11 (king's son); 247, 3, 7, 18, 19, 22, 24, 27, 28, 33, 35, 36, 38, 39, 42, 44, 248, 5, 19, 21, 22, 23.

^{am}**kîpu**: 2, 2; 3, 2; 4, 2; 15, 14; 35, 2; 36, 2; 39, 19; 40, 33; 47, 2; 50, 9, 11; 67, 2; 175, 12; 212, 2; 232, 1; 242, 5.

^{m}**Kiramma**: 64, 15.

^{m}**Kiribtum-**^{ilu}**Marduk**: 99, 1; 100, 1.

kirubutu: 2, 27.

Kiš^{ki}: 95, 19.

^{m}**Kî-**^{ilu}**Šamši**: 139, 11.

kisati: 60, 9.

kitu: 155, 17.

^{m}**Kubanna-**^{ilu}**Marduk**: 142, 16.

^{sal}**Ḳudašu**: 6, 1.

^{m}**Ḳuddâ** (= ^{m}**Suḳâ** ?): 44, 19; 48, 13, 16.

^{sal}**Ḳudnanu**: 226, 1.

^{m}**Kudur-** . . . : 91, 1.

^{m}**Kukurra**: 174, 26.

^{am}**kulû**: 183, 9.

^{am} KU-MAL-MAL: 196, 31.

^{matu}**Kumina**: 247, 34.

^{am}**kummu**: 76, 25.

$^{m\ ilu}$**Ḳumurputu**: 79, 6.

^{m}**Kunâ**: 91, 2.

kunta': 17, 16.

$^{(işu)}$**ḳuppu**: 165, 9; 196, 20.

^{m}**Kuraš**: 93, 8; 166, 10; 179, 9; 218, 7; 219, 8; 233, 9.

^{m}**Kurbanni-**^{ilu}**Marduk**: 75, 2; 100, 9; 101, 1.

ḳurubîtu: 82, 25.
m**Kusurûa**: 80, 14.
kutulâ: 200, 19.
ḳutulukanu: 191, 26.

L.

m**Lâbaši**: 103, 1.
m**Labâši**: 66, 2; 102, 1; 104, 1.
m**Labaši**: 145, 2; 174, 21.
laḫâmu: I, 1, *ilḫim*, 14, 29.
m**Lakipi**: 39, 17.
am**lamutanu**: 16, 10, 139, 21; 213, 22; 214, 22.
m**Lamutanu**: (cf. 16, 10); 110, 6.
latum: 234, 24, 29.
ilu**Laz**: 184, 5.
libbatu: 114, 21.
m**Liblut**: 6, 37, 106, 1; 139, 13, 238, 4.
m**Liblutu**: 74, 5, 9, 15; 105, 1.
m**Liburu**: 194, 19.
m**Liši-** . . . : 107, 1.
m**Lišir**: 20, 4.
litamu (?): 127, 11.
li'u: 12, 14; 23, 13, 15; 161, 11 (?); GIŠ-DA, 11, 23; 14, 22; 21, 13; 42, 8; 128, 8, 10, 14; 170, 11; 178, 6, 7, 8, 10; 189, 10, 14.
m**Lû-aḫûa**: 9, 15.
m**Luddu-ana-ṣabi**: 131, 23, 29
m ilu LUGAL-MARADA-**ibni**: 87, 42.
alu**Lumšunu** (?): 241, 19.

M.

madaktum: 157, 16
magâru: I, 1, *imangur*, 12, 22; 160, 8, 164, 31; 205, 14, 20; *imgur*, 185, 18.
makâru: I, 2, *mitkur*, 114, 12.

makkasu: 192, 15; 237, 5, 9.
malâku: I, 2, *mitlaka*, 121, 13.
am **mâr-banitu**: 5, 12; 28, 6; 38, 22; 74, 19; 114, 6, 9 (?).
ilu **Marduk** (in greetings *passim*): 1, 16; 29, 4; 35, 31; 36, 11, 29; [62, 16].
m **Marduk**: 127, 1.
m ilu **Marduk-** . . . : 125, 1; 126, 1; 128, 1; 173, 2; 174, 31
m ilu **Marduk-bêlišu-uṣur**: 108, 2.
m ilu **Marduk-bullitsu**: 203, 2.
m ilu **Marduk-epuš**: 111, 1.
m ilu **Marduk-eriba**: 109, 1; 235, 6.
m ilu **Marduk-eṭir**: 112, 3.
m ilu **Marduk-mâri-** . . . : 188, 17.
m ilu **Marduk-mušallim**: 45, 25.
m ilu **Marduk (?)-na'id**: 126, 6.
m ilu **Marduk-naṣir**: 42, 2; 114, 1.
m ilu **Marduk-naṣir-apli**: 82, 2; 83, 2.
m ilu **Marduk-rimanni**: 9, 2; 214, 16.
m ilu **Marduk-šuma-iddin**: 10, 2; 37, 1; 115, 1; 116, 1; 117, 1, 118, 1; 119, 1; 120, 1; 121, 1; 122, 1; 123, 1; 124, 1; 242, 2.
m ilu **Marduk-šuma-usur**: 243, 2.
m ilu **Marduk-uballiṭsu**: 203, 2.
m ilu **Marduk-ukin-apli**: 108, 1.
m ilu **Marduk-zira-ibni**: 113, 1; 137, 29.
m ilu **Marduk-zira-ukin**: 112, 1.
marru: 117, 8; 159, 23.
am **mâr-šipri**: 41, 7, 15; 43, 16; 73, 20, 26; 78, 27; 94, 18; 183, 11; 195, 22; 230, 26; 240, 16.
am **mašmašu**: 68, 5.
maššarâta: 31, 10.
am **maṣṣarti abulli***pl*: 74, 28
mašširtu: 115, 6.
maṣû: I, 1, *maṣû*, 36, 16; *maṣu*, 36, 21.
maṭû: I, 1, *maṭû*, 46, 28 (cf. 5); 141, 31; *maṭu*, 96, 9; *imaṭṭû*, 243, 10.

midıtu: 112, 17; 144, 24.
m **Minû**: 123, 2.
mirsu: 38, 27.
miṭku: 1, 29 (?); 2, 24; 116, 14; 174, 5 (?)
mitkuru: 114, 12.
am MU: 17, 8.
m **Mugallu**: 174, 17.
(am) **mukinnu**: 104, 18; 119, 13; 176, 18; 211, 23.
m **Mukkîa**: 174, 38.
m **Muranu**: 19, 5, 20, 28; 105, 6; 116, 17; 129, 1; 130, 1, [31]; 142, 2 (and envelope), 174, 22; 209, 6, 13, 16; 210, 6, 13, 16; 212, 9.
m **Murašû**: 174, 30, 35; 197, 17.
muruḳu · 40, 12.
m **Mušallim**: 49, 3, 11.
m **Mušallim-Marduk**: 24, 1; 25, 1; 26, 1; 28, 1; 51, 4; 131, 1.
mušanitum · 65, 16.
m **Mušer-** . . . : 128, 7.
m **Mušezib** . 87, 37.
m **Mušezib-** . . . : 132, 13.
m **Mušezib-**ilu **Bêl** . 45, 26; 56, 6; 66, 6, 11; 132, 1.
m **Mušezib-**ilu **Marduk** . 26, 2, 28, 2, 56, 2; 68, 2; 85, 2; 86, 2; 106, 2; 133, 1; 134, 1 (?), 135, 1, 2; 136, 1 (?); 159, 2; 161, 2; 208, 26; 209, 2.
sal **Mušezibtum**: 224, 1, 24.
subatu **musıptu** (pl. **musi(p)pêti**) · 56, 8, 14; 230, 8, 17, 21.
am **mûtu**: 94, 11; 115, 7.
muzibtum: 53, 22.

N.

m **Nabâ**: 95, 17.
m **Nabannu**: 174, 18.
m **Nabaṣu** . 174, 21.
ilu **Nabû** (ın greetings *passım*) 4, 8; 7, 13; 21, 5; 43, 11 (?); 46, 24; 62, 16; 66, 19, 78, 11; 101, 9; 105, 22, 32; 112, 23; 174, 6, 47; 176, 19; 180, 6; 189, 13; 194, 12; 196, 22; 217, 9; 237, 12, 18.

m ilu **Nabû-** . . . : 69, 2; 83, 16 (?); 166, 6; 172, 1; 173, 1; 174, 1; 214, 5.
m ilu **Nabûa**: 110, 17.
m ilu **Nabû-aḫi (?)-** . . . : 149, 1.
m ilu **Nabû-aḫi-** . . . : 138, 1; 139, 1; 204, 3.
m ilu **Nabû-aḫi-iddannu**: 189, 6; 240, 2 (?).
m ilu **Nabû-aḫi-iddin**: 113, 29; 137, 1.
m ilu **Nabû-aḫi**pl**-ukin**: 5, 5; 11, 3; 31, 3; 161, 5; 181, 4.
m ilu **Nabû-aḫišu**: 73, 15; 181, 4.
m ilu **Nabû-apli-iddin**: 115, 9; 137, 6; 141, 1 (?); 142, 1 (and envelope); 194, 21; 235, 6.
m ilu **Nabû-bâdi**: 24, 11.
m ilu **Nabû-balaṭsû-alik**: 230, 7.
m ilu **Nabû-balatsu-iḳbi**: 229, 8, 14.
m ilu **Nabû-bani-aḫi**: 146, 1.
m ilu **Nabû-bâni-ipšari**: 26, 3.
m ilu **Nabû-battûa**: 182, 14.
m ilu **Nabû-bêl (?)-ibašši**: 45, 9.
m ilu **Nabû-bêl-uṣur**: 177, 2.
m ilu **Nabû-bêl-zikri**pl: 155, 3
m ilu **Nabû-bulliṭsu**: 230, 7; 238, 5, 9; 239, 5, 9; 241, 18, 20; 244, 2, 4.
m ilu **Nabû-dânu**: 147, 1.
m ilu **Nabû-dîni-epuš**: 110, 20; 139, 28 (?).
m ilu **Nabû-dini-šarri**: 148, 1.
m ilu **Nabû-eṭir**: 176, 4.
m ilu **Nabû-etir-napšâti**pl: 144, 1; 188, 2.
m ilu **Nabû-gamil**: 101, 2.
m ilu **Nabû-ḫili-ilâni**pl: 156, 1.
m ilu **Nabû-iddannu**: 57, 2; 66, 14, 24; 203, 7; 238, 4; 239, 2.
m ilu **Nabû-iddin**: 160, 19.
m ilu **Nabû-it** . . . : 130, 20.
m ilu **Nabû-ittia**: 203, 8.
m ilu **Nabû-kaṣir**: 186, 10, 13, 17 (?).
m ilu **Nabû-kisir**: 45, 19; 202, 9, 25.
m ilu **Nabû-kuṣur-anni**: 157, 1.

m ilu **Nabû-li (?)-** . . . : 62, 13.
m ilu **Nabû-ludda**. 158, 1.
m ilu **Nabû-mulidi-imbi (?)**: 183, 19.
m ilu **Nabû-mušezib**: 174, 11.
m i u **Nabû-nadin-aḫi**: 84, 2; 204, 2.
m ilu **Nabû-na'id**: 51, 11; 53, 17 (?); 143, 8; 160, 19; 165, 12; 173, 9; 185, 6.
m ilu **Nabû-naṣir**: 39, 39; 241, 26 (?).
m ilu **Nabû-nipšu-uṣur**: 161, 1.
m ilu **Nabû-nûru**: 159, 1.
m ilu **Nabû-rimanni**: 64, 19
m ilu **Nabû-šar-anni**. 215, 2.
m ilu **Nabû-šarri-usur** 160, 6.
m ilu **Nabû-silim**: 19, 25; 61, 6; 160, 1.
m ilu **Nabû-šuma-ešir**: 13, 2; 14, 1; 15, 2, 16, 2; 18, 2; 23, 2; 32, 9, 69, 2 (?); 115, 2; 116, 2; 117, 2; 118, 2; 119, 2; 121, 2, 122, 2, 124, 2; 163, 1; 164, 1; 165, 1; 166, 1.
m ilu **Nabû-šuma-** . . . : 92, 10.
m ilu **Nabû-šuma-ibni**: 153, 1; 154, 1.
m ilu **Nabû-šuma-iddin**: 145, 6, 10; 172, 2 (?).
m ilu **Nabû-šuma-ikiša (?)**: 11, 17.
m ilu **Nabû-šuma-iškun** 167, 1; 168, 1; 169, 1 (?); 170, 1, 171, 1 (?); 176, 2.
m ilu **Nabû-šuma-ukin**: 81, 7.
m ilu **Nabû-šuma-uṣur**: 13, 2; 88, 6, 92, 10 (?), 118, 7; 162, 1; 174, 23.
m ilu **Nabû-tukkinannu**: 186, 6.
m ilu **Nabû-uballiṭ**: 38, 21, 24.
m ilu **Nabû-ubulliṭ**: 230, 5 (cf. 27).
m ilu **Nabû-ukin-ziri**: 45, 4.
m ilu **Nabû-zira-ešir**: 13, 3; 14, 2; 16, 2; 45, 3; 102, 2; 105, 18, 30.
m ilu **Nabû-zira-ibašši**: 151, 1.
m ilu **Nabû-zira-ibni**: 64, 20; 152, 1; 155, 1; 190, 1.
m ilu **Nabû-zira-iddin**: 129, 7.
m ilu **Nabû-zira-ukin**: 150, 1; 171, 6, 19.
nadabakku: 217, 22.

nadâdu: I, 1, *inadıd*, 66, 10.
ᵐNadin: 10, 2; 50, 7; 78, 8.
ᵐNadinu: 175, 1; 176, 1.
nadu: 112, 21.
ᵃᵐnaggaru: 57, 8.
naḫâsu: I, 1, *inıḫısı*, 182, 18.
ᵐNa'id-ⁱˡᵘMarduk: 24, 3; 25, 3; 26, 4; 51, 11; 161, 3; 187, 2 (?).
ˢᵃˡNakiatum: 141, 20.
nakuttu: 1, 27; 3, 18; 6, 7; 75, 10; 101, 23; 130, 9; 142, 19; 147, 18; 155, 19; 184, 21; 237, 24.
ⁱˡᵘNanâ: 213, 5; 224, 4.
ᵐⁱˡᵘNanâ- . . . : 6, 38; 155, 5.
ˢᵃˡⁱˡᵘNanâ-ḫusi (?) . . . : 224, 12.
ˢᵃˡⁱˡᵘNanâ-ittia: 139, 9.
napâsu: 240, 7.
napata: 73, 23.
narâku: IV, 1, *innaruk*, 200, 30.
narbû: 118, 9; 144, 5, 7.
Nargia: 174, 42.
nartu (?): 113, 8.
⁽ˢᵘᵇᵃᵗᵘ⁾nasbatu: 105, 9; 208, 11.
ᵐNaṣir: 22, 2; 23, 3; 49, 17; 50, 2; 51, 1; 118, 3; 119, 4; 120, 2; 121, 3; 143, 1; 179, 1; 192, 3; 221, 13.
nazâku: I, 2, *inamzık* (?), 150, 17; III, 1, *uśanzaḳannı*, 105, 20.
ⁱˡᵘNergal: 8, 6; 37, 3; 38, 4; 66, 30; 78, 17, 22; 184, 3, 5; 198, 4.
ᵐⁱˡᵘNergal- . . . : 186, 1.
ᵐⁱˡᵘNergal-aḫi-iddin: 182, 1.
ᵐⁱˡᵘNergal-edu (?)-usur: 9, 11.
ᵐⁱˡᵘNergal-gimilli: 185, 1; 187, 1 (?).
ᵐⁱˡᵘNergal-iddin: 45, 17; 109, 16, 18; 111, 11; 184, 1.
ᵐⁱˡᵘNergal-muśallim: 183, 1.
ᵐⁱˡᵘNergal-riṣûa: 9, 3.
ᵐⁱˡᵘNergal-śuma-epuś: 150, 5.
ᵐⁱˡᵘNergal-uballiṭ: 216, 2.
ᵐⁱˡᵘNergal-uṣur: 137, 13; 148, 6.

m Nidinittum: 88, 2.
m Nidintum. 53, 20; 108, 3.
m Nidintum-ilu Bêl: 44, 3; 177, 1, 178, 1 (?).
niḫû: 193, 11.
m Niḳudu (cf 8, 12): 78, 32; 180, 1.
ilu Ninib 42, 8; 191, 12.
am niše 77, 16
nisiḫtum: 87, 7
nubattum (√ba'âtu?): 83, 10, 17, 89, 12, 126, 19, 149, 33; 176, 7
sal Nubtâ 89, 8; 110, 5, 11, 13.
nukusu: 78, 10, 13.
nuptu· 201, 13.
m Nur· 181, 1, 9.
m Nur-ilu Šamši. 82, 8.

P.

m Pa- . . . 236, 2
am PA: 31, 7
m Pakiri: 247, 25.
am paḳudu: 73, 22.
palâtu· I, 1, *ipallaṭu*, 114, 15.
m Pani-ilu Nabû-adaggal 241, 2, 8, 10
mâtu Paniragana (?): 6, 9
pappasu: 51, 3; 52, 12, 115, 6, 17
pasî. 63, 25.
piḫatu: 78, 18, 31
am piḫatu. 29, 15; 76, 30.
m Piki . . . : 172, 13
šeru pinû. 172, 9
pînu: 172, 10.
m Pirku: 112, 13; 202, 27
pirku: 66, 7; 74, 20; 201, 11; 210, 5, 9
m Pir'u: 192, 1.
piški: 29, 7; 73, 17 (?).
pîsûtu: 21, 10.

sal **Puḳâ** : 225, 1, 5.
m **Purkû** : 6, 33, 37.
purku : 6, 33.
m **Puṣâ** : 22, 6.

R.

am **rab-** . . . : 112, 10.
am **rab-** *isu* . . . : 166, 7.
am **rab-banûti** *pl* : 134, 10.
am **rab-bît-killi (?)** : 230, 11.
am **rab-dûri** : 74, 7, 21.
am **rab-ešriti** : 64, 6, 21 ; 76, 7.
am **rab-kasir** : 208, 12, 15, 30.
am **rab-ṣipti** : 80, 17, 27.
am **rabû** : 234, 2 ; 235, 1 ; 247, 19 ; 248, 12, 21, 24.
šipâtu **rammu** : 69, 8, 10.
am **riḳḳu** : 50, 6 ; 144, 18.
alu **Rimizḫû (?)** . 247, 14.
m **Rimut** : 73, 15 ; 105, 2 ; 112, 2 ; 137, 2, 27 ; 152, 2 ; 160, 17, 18 ; 164, 23, 174, 41 ; 193, 1 ; 194, 1 ; 195, 1, 196, 1 ; 197, 1, 198, 1 ; 199, 1 ; 200, 1 (?) ; 201, 1 (?) ; 227, 11 ; 237, 2 ; 244, 4, 5.
m **Rimut-** *ilu* **Ba'u** (cf. *m* **Rimut-** *ilu* KA) · 95, 8, 12 ; 96, 7.
m **Rimut-** *ilu* **Bêl** : 100, 8, 16.
m **Rimut-ili** : 55, 4, 13.
m **Rimut-** *ilu* KA (cf. *m* **Rimut-** *ilu* **Ba'u**, and see 37, 8) : 38, 18.
m **Rimut-** *ilu* **Nabû** : 202, 1.
am **ri'u** : 3, 5 (*ša ṣêni*), 22 ; 71, 2 ; 168, 5 ; 181, 1.
am **ri'u atudi** : 69, 26.
am **ri'i iṣṣuri** *pl* : 12, 8.
am **ri'i-** *imeru* **sisi** *pl* : 100, 10.
ruḫ[tu] : 149, 16.

S.

alu **Ša** . . . **ri** : 101, 8.
m **Ša-** *ilu* **Bêl-atta** : 73, 25.

šabašu: I, 1, *nišbuš*, 199, 17.

sabâtum. 77, 12.

am **sabbizu**: 76, 20.

sal **Ṣabitum-rimat**: 225, 6

sâbu: I, 1, *sabaka*, 225, 18.

sabû: I, 1, *isibbu*, 174, 49.

(am) **sabû**· 7, 10, 17; 19, 6 (?); 34, 7; 45, 28; 50, 9; 53, 10; 56, 7; 57, 14, 59, 21; 72, 20, 74, 19, 21, 24, 29, 31; 79, 20; 87, 8, 114, 23; 120, 5; 121, 25, 152, 8, 16, 160, 7, 8, 164, 17, 174, 4, 17, 45, 185, 8, 19; 193, 16, 196, 25, 27; 198, 20; 205, 24; 211, 17; 218, 4, 219, 5; 233, 5; 242, 5.

alu **Šad . . . mandaru**: 247, 15

šaddagiš: 37, 14; 69, 12, 24, 78, 20; 116, 23, 232, 8.

m **Šaddinnu**: 6, 24, 43, 26; 66, 23, 75, 6; 97, 6; 139, 2, 6; 223, 2.

m **Šadunu**: 1, 1; 32, 2; 204, 6.

šagallu: 157, 10.

saḫâdu: I, 1, *saḫid*, 38, 9; *-saḫad*, 38, 28; I, 2, *issaḫaid*, 38, 30.

am **šakâdu**: 232, 19.

šakâtu: II, 1, *lušakkilu*, 155, 15

am **šaknu**: 63, 16, 19; 217, 14.

am ŠA-KU: I, 32, 21, 20, 21, 28, 42, 12; 101, 21, 29; 202, 15 (?)

am **šakû**: 87, 42, 164, 22, 25; 217, 17, 248, 27 (?)

m **Šalammanu**: 205, 1, 18.

salkuttu: 46, 31.

m **Sallum**: 144, 18.

salû: I, 1, *tasilli*, 40, 25, 29; 151, 12; 187, 15 (?), 211, 21; 245, 19; *tasilla'*, 69, 9, 21, 114, 18, 131, 7, 133, 20, 161, 10, 19; *tasilla*, 193, 8; *tasillân*, 172, 6; *tasillu*, 6, 21, *isilli*, 24, 22; 32, 16; 78, 24, 80, 23, 141, 16, 176, 15, 208, 24; II, 1, *usil*[*la*], 159, 10.

ilu **Šamaš**, in greetings frequently: 11, 9, 24; 12, 15, 13, 8, 20; 19, 22, [26]; 21, 16 (?); 34, 15, 35, 5, 31, 36, 3, 10, 29, 38, 3; 42, 9; 46, 19, 63, 3, 8; 69, 11, 15, 19, 26, [71, 3], 72, 14; 102, 7, 121, 9, 10, 22; 125, 4; 126, 9, 136, 5; 152, 6; 168, 6; 178, 6, 7 (?), 8 (?), 10 (?), 184, 11, 188, 4, 11; 196, 8, 34; 197, 16; 198, 4; 206, 4; 209, 3; [212, 4]; 222, 11, 227, 16, 21, 29; 232, 3, 20; 246, 3.

m ilu Šamšu- . . . 108, 3; 125, 7; 212, 1; 213, 1, 27.

m ilu Šamšu-aḫia: 62, 7.

m ilu Šamšu-aḫi-eriba: 197, 20

m ilu Šamšu-aḫi-iddin: 13, 6; 39, 2; 40, 21; 51, 5; 134, 9, 26; 205, 3, 27.

m ilu Šamšu-aḫi-ukin: 12, 7; 13, 6, 39, 2; 40, 21.

m ilu Šamšu-apli- . . . : 236, 3.

m ilu Šamšu-bani: 62, 2.

m ilu Šamšu-bêl-ilâni: 88, 3.

m ilu Šamšu-epuš: 166, 3

m ilu Šamšu-eriba: 69, 4, 164, 22; 207, 1; 208, 1

m ilu Šamšu-eṭir: 162, 7; 190, 8

m ilu Šamšu-ibni: 17, 11, 13.

m ilu Šamšu-id . . . (cf. m ilu Šamšu-ittia): 134, 26.

m ilu Šamšu-iddin: 45, 12; 131, 9; 160, 16; 179, 2.

m ilu Šamšu-iḳiša: 236, 4.

m ilu Šamšu-inamir: 209, 1.

m ilu Šamšu-ittadû: 37, 13.

m ilu Šamšu-ittia (cf m ilu Šamšu-id . . .): 140, 5

m ilu Šamšu-mâri- . . . 236, 3

m ilu Šamšu-pir'-uṣur: 165, 8.

m ilu Šamšu-rabû-šarri-uṣur: 90, 2

m ilu Šamšu-ri'išunu: 44, 2

m ilu Šamšu-ri'ûa: 22, 5

m ilu Šamšu-šarri-uṣur: 107, 11; 143, 5; 210, 1

m ilu Šamšu-šuma- . . . : 125, 8.

m ilu Šamšu-šuma-epuš: 45, 13.

m ilu Šamšu-šuma-ešir: 227, 5, 9; 228, 5, 11.

m ilu Šamšu-šuma-ukin: 211, 1.

m ilu Šamšu-uballiṭ: 89, 6; 187, 14; 207, 3.

m ilu Šamšu-udammiḳ: 155, 4.

m ilu Šamšu-udannin (?): 38, 18.

m ilu Šamšu-upaḫḫir: 20, 11, 37, 7, 18; 38, 8, 25; 196, 19; 198, 16.

m ilu Šamšu-zira-ibašši: 184, 8, 16.

m ilu Šamšu-zira-iddin: 241, 25.

samû: I, 1, *samaku*.

^{m}**Sa-^{ilu}Nabû-ittišu-balatu**: 241, 1, 4, 6, 11, 21.

^{am}**šangu**: 10, 3, 12, 2; 17, 2; 30, 2; 36, 12; 38, 2; 39, 19, 20; 40, 35; 41, 2; [42, 3], 47, 3; 52, 2; 53, 2, 54, 2; 58, 2; 60, 2; 61, 2; 64, 2; 65, 2; 72, 10; 76, 5, 27, 107, 2; 108, 2; 133, 2; [134, 2]; 136, 2; 140, 2; 153, 2; 158, 2; 163, 3; 164, 3; 167, 2; 169, 2; 170, 2; 171, 2; 175, 2; 180, 2, 196, 2; 197, 2; 198, 2; 199, 2; 208, 2; 210, 2; 212, 3; 230, 2, 12; 233, 1; 234, 19, 21; 245, 24.

^{am}**šangu ekalli**: 242, 8.

šapânu: I, 1, *šupni*, 17, 15.

^{m}**Ša-pî-^{ilu}Bêl**: 160, 18; 222, 2.

^{m}**Ša-pî-ilia**: 174, 29.

$^{(subatu)}$**sapitum** (article of cloth): 53, 10, 79, 8.

^{ilu}ŠAR-ḪU. 192, 17

^{ilu}**Ṣarpanitum**: 29, 4, 59, 4; 111, 4, 162, 3.

^{m}**Šarru-di** . . : 43, 9.

^{m}**Šarru-ludari**: 5, 3

^{am}**Šartinnu**. 234, 1; 235, 1

^{am}ŠA-TAM · 1, 32; 35, 24; 42, 11, 58, 5, 132, 2, 160, 2, 11; 182, 16; 236, 1.

šatiku (cf. the modern *mastich*?): 84, 20.

^{m}**Šebarranu**: 121, 12.

^{m}**Šellibi**: 78, 26; cf. 238, 6, and 239, 9.

^{m}**Šênu**: 247, 25.

šiba: 78, 19.

šikirtum: 78, 30.

^{sal}**Sikkû**: 151, 2

^{m}**Sillâ**: 127, 2, 12.

sillatu: 133, 7.

šillu: 43, 9.

^{ilu}**Sin**: 71, 3; 188, 3, 11.

$^{m\,ilu}$**Sin-** . . . : 49, 9; 247, 42

$^{m\,ilu}$**Sin-aḫi-** . · 213, 2.

šindu: 63, 28.

sinḳa: 14, 23.

*m ilu*Sin-nadin-aḫi: 71, 9; 188, 1.

Sippar: 10, 3; 12, 2; 30, 2; 34, 2; 36, 12; 38, 2; 39, 19; 40, 35; 41, 2; 42, 3; 47, 3; 52, 2, 53, 2; 54, 2; 58, 2; 60, 2; 61, 2; 64, 2; 65, 2; 76, 6, 27, 30; 106, 3; 107, 2; 136, 2; 140, 2; 150, 2; 153, 2; 154, 2; 158, 2; 163, 3; 164, 3; 167, 2; 168, 2, 169, 2; 170, 2; 171, 2; 175, 2; 179, 6; 180, 2; 184, 2, 6; 192, 17; 196, 2; 197, 2; 198, 2; [199, 2]; 204, 8; 205, 17, 22; 208, 2; 210, 2; 212, 3; 218, 7 (?); 227, 2, 26; 228, 2; 229, 2; 230, 2, 12, 13, 23; 231, 2; 234, 3, 21; 235, 3; 245, 2, 15, 24, 25.

*sal*Ṣirâ: 224, 25.

*subatu*sirameti (cf. 40, 13 ?): 172, 7.

*m*Širik: 162, 2.

*m*Širikki: 189, 2.

*m*Širiktum: 5, 2; 214, 1.

*m*Širiša-*ilu*Bêl: 181, 3.

*m*Širku: 6, 21, 37; 74, 1; 215, 1.

*m*Šišdi: 111, 2.

*am*sisi: 74, 6, 9, 18

*m*Šiṣi . . . : 220, 6.

*m*Šiški: 127, 5, 19.

šîti: 183, 5.

*m*Šitḳul: 13, 6; 51, 5, 6, 9; 216, 1; 217, 1; 218, 1; 219, 1; 227, 6, 18.

šiṭu: 32, 13 (?)

*m*Su . . . : 133, 9.

šugarrû: 9, 17; 142, 5.

*am*ŠU-ḪA: 56, 5.

*m*Suḫâ: 139, 14.

*m*Suḳâ (see *m*Ḳudda): 14, 27; 31, 7; 58, 19; 61, 7; 79, 18; 87, 2; 92, 6; 100, 2; 189, 1; 190, 1; 191, 1.

*am*sukkallu: 73, 21.

*m*Šulâ: 45, 2; 66, 15 (?), 113, 2; 143, 3.

*m*Šullûa: 66, 18.

*m*Šullumâ: 52, 5; 76, 26.

*m*Šullumu: 6, 15.

^{m}Šulmanu: 206, 3.
šulû: 24, 8.
^{m}Šulum-Babili: 203, 1.
^{m}Šumâ: 1, 3; 204, 1.
^{m}Šuma-iddin: 114, 2, 202, 3
^{m}Šuma-iddina: 135, 5.
^{m}Šuma-ukina: 1, 4; 116, 21; 214, 9.
^{m}Šuma-usur: 131, 2; 132, 5; 160, 6, 245, 17.
^{m}Šumu (?): 14, 14.
^{urudu}sunî: 85, 15.
^{alu}Šûnu: 111, 8.
šunu'i: 24, 7
Šušan^{ki}: 59, 22.
^{m}Šutnu (?): 110, 10.
^{ilu}ŠU-ZI-AN-NA: 223, 4.

T.

tabarru: 208, 21.
^{m}Ṭâbia: 89, 1; 90, 1.
^{m}Tabnîa: 45, 16; 174, 27; 220, 1.
^{m}Ṭâbti-^{ilu}IB: 33, 2.
ṭabû: II, 1, "to impress," [*lu*]*tubbu'*.
^{m}Takiš: 14, 10; 24, 18; 38, 15.
takkasû: 238, 1.
^{m}Talimu: 168, 5.
^{m}Tallâ: 17, 12, 14.
tappudu: 146, 7
^{m}Tarḫuru: 48, 10.
târu: II, 1, *turru*, 167, 8.
^{ilu}Tašmetum: 6, 33; 174, 34
^{sal} ^{ilu}Tašmetum-tabni: 6, 35.
tedutum: 77, 10.
tektu: 29, 18; 43, 20; 60, 13; 118, 10; 121, 23; 133, 21, 225, 8 (*tekitum*).
telittum: 5, 18.
Temple: 36, 8; 45, 28; of Nergal, 66, 30.

am TIL-LA-GID-DA : 5, 4 ; 63, 2 ; 206, 1
m **Timkak** . : 213, 28.
tipû : 65, 15, 17.
sal **Ṭunâ** : 147, 2.
am TU-**u** : 66, 30.

U.

m **Uballitsu-** ilu **Bêl** : 214, 2.
m **Uballitsu-** ilu **Marduk** : 5, 1.
m **Ubar** : 7, 1 ; (cf. 244, 1).
m **Udanu** : 123, 2.
uddu : 139, 23.
uiltim : 48, 16 ; 66, 31 , 75, 8 ; 98, 8 ; 100, 11 ; 186, 5, 15 ; 234, 28 ; 243, 13.
m **Ukin-ziri** : 45, 27.
am **umma(n)nu** : 1, 6 ; 93, 4
ilu **Ûmu** (= ilu **Šamaš**) : 37, 3.
alu **Upîa** : 3, 9 ; 211, 12 (?)
am **upisu** : 73, 23.
am **urašu** : 99, 5 ; 141, 19, 30
alu **Urizu** : 247, 12.
am **urlišu** : 74, 6, 11, 19.
Uru : 247, 16, 31.
Uruk ki : 213, 5 ; 224, 3
m **Uruk** ki**-a** : 185, 15.
usâ : 107, 7.
ušmarra : 21, 8, 29.
m **Uzubšîḫu** : 247, 19.

Z.

m ilu **Zamama-iddin** : 73, 6, 29
alu **Zamat** : 7, 7.
z(ṣ)abbi(l)lu : 45, 8 ; 117, 9 ; 140, 10
m **Zazâ** : 205, 7
m **Zikri** : 247, 16, 31

zirmû: 157, 9
^{m}**Zirtu**: 164, 14.
^{m}**Zirutu**: 174, 33.

[^{m} . .]-**a**: 29, 2.
^{m} . **â**: 191, 1.
^{m} . . . -^{ilu}**Âa**: 64, 21.
[$^{m\,ilu}$ . . .]-**aḫi-iddannu** 240, 2.
^{m} . . -**apli**: 19, 2; 138, 2.
[^{m} . .]-**bar**· 244, 1
^{m} . . -**budia**: 39, 29
[^{m} . -**bul**]**liṭsu**: 244, 2.
[^{m}] . **du**: 237, 1
^{m} . -**eriba**: 214, 11
^{m} . . . -**eṭir**: 146, 2; 160, 17, 181, 2.
^{m} . . **gilibu**: 132, 7.
^{m} . . . **ia**: 128, 3.
[^{m} . .]-**iddina**: 49, 10.
[^{m} .]-^{ilu}**Nabû**: 64, 12.
[^{m} . .]-^{ilu}**Šamši (?)**: 226, 13
^{m} . . . **su**: 128, 2.
^{m} . . -**šuma-** . . . : 29, 1.
[^{m} . . .] **sur-iddinnu**: 82, 18
[^{m} . . -**uballit**](**it**): 45, 21
[^{m} . . .]-**ziri**: 211, 2

EMENDATIONS AND CORRECTIONS

P. 9, No. 6, l. 2, delete the second 'daily'

P. 28, No. 30, l. 1, read ^{m}*Ana-amat-*^{ilu}*Bêl-adgal*, and also in translation

P. 43, No. 44, l. 1, read *Šamaš-ri'i-šunu*.

P. 44, No. 46, l. 5, read [*ma*]-*tu-u*.

P. 48, No. 49, l. 17, *te-te-ša-in-ni* may be a scribal error for *te-ri(š)-ša-in-ni*.

P. 55, No. 57, l. 8, a better translation is 'If there be none, the work will cease.'

P. 62, No. 66, l. 24, read *$^{m\ ilu}$Nabû-id-dan-nu*.

P. 63, No. 66, l. 10, for 'Nabû' read 'Nergal.'

P. 67, No. 73, l. 22, for 'stopped' read 'spoken of.'

P. 70, No. 77, l. 15, perhaps read *ma-la al-la*, 'all except'

P. 73, No. 79, l. 6, perhaps translate 'except what he had heard.'

P. 137, No. 174, l. 5, in place of 'thy dead man' perhaps read 'thy course.'

P. 152, No. 194, l. 28, read *^{sal}Amti-ia*, a proper name, and translate accordingly.

P. 162, No. 205, l. 2, read *^{m}Ki-na-a*, and also in translation.

P. 188, No. 242, l. 1, read *$^{m\ ilu}$Bunene-usur* (?), and also in translation.

www.ingramcontent.com/pod-product-compliance
Lightning Source LLC
Chambersburg PA
CBHW062011220426
43662CB00010B/1288
9781666749113